BEATING CANCER
WITH NUTRITION

"A goldmine of meticulously documented information that is bound to serve as a guidepost for colleagues and cancer patients alike." Keith Block, MD, Vice President Chicago chapter American Cancer Society, Clinical Instructor University of Illinois College of Medicine, Chicago

"A cancer patient's battle plan. Shows that nutrition is a powerful tool that is readily available to help everyone prevent and conquer this dreaded illness. Should be required reading for all cancer patients and their families." Melvyn Werbach, MD, author of *Healing Through Nutrition*

"In this landmark book, Dr. Quillin takes a giant step in clarifying the role nutrition and other alternative approaches play in whipping cancer–and most commendable, does so without diminishing the contributions of traditional medicine." Arline & Harold Brecher, authors of *Forty-Something Forever*

"All therapists advising and treating patients with cancer, whether traditional or non-traditional, will help their patients more when they have mastered the vast amount of information presented." Abram Hoffer, MD, PhD, physician, author, researcher and pioneer in orthomolecular nutrition

"Cancer signifies the ultimate loss of control over one's body. Dr. Quillin puts us back in control. Through the use of cutting edge research and his vast clinical experience, he supports the point that we can beat cancer. ...A must for everyone." Shari Lieberman, PhD, RD, author *The Real Vitamin and Mineral Book*

"Anyone who wants to know the latest breakthroughs in preventing or treating cancer with nutrition ought to put this on their 'must read' list... This may be the landmark cancer information book of 1994." Russell Jaffe, MD, PhD, researcher, author, holistic physician

BEATING CANCER
WITH NUTRITION

CLINICALLY PROVEN AND EASY-TO-FOLLOW STRATEGIES
TO DRAMATICALLY IMPROVE YOUR QUALITY AND QUANTITY
OF LIFE AND INCREASE CHANCES FOR A COMPLETE REMISSION

PATRICK QUILLIN, PhD, RD
WITH NOREEN QUILLIN

N T P

The Nutrition Times Press, Inc.
Tulsa

Other books by Patrick Quillin, PhD, RD

Safe Eating, M. Evans, NY, 1990
The La Costa Book of Nutrition, Pharos, NY, 1988
Healing Nutrients, Random House, 1987
The La Costa Prescription for Longer Life, Ballantine, NY, 1985

Copyright © 1994 Patrick Quillin, Ph.D., R.D.
ISBN 0-9638372-0-6

Design & Production by: Kilburn, ink, Tulsa, OK 918-438-4719
Cover photography: Over 180 patients have been honored at Celebrate Life Reunions at Cancer Treatment Centers of America. Left to right are former cancer patients (cp) who went from advanced cancer to 5 years disease-free as of August 1993; also included are family members (fm): Gunter Pillar (fm), Anneliese M. Pillar (cp), Audrey R. Ward (cp), Ann E. Smith (cp), Donald E. Smith (fm), Jeanette Elaine Holland (cp), Stena Ree Payne (fm), Phyllis Colclough (cp), Ida Bobrick (fm).
Illustrations by: Noreen Quillin

Printed in the United States of America

How to order:

Quantity discounts are available from:
The Nutrition Times Press, Inc., Box 700512, Tulsa, OK 74170-0512
Telephone 918-495-1137.
On your letterhead include information concerning the intended use of the books and the number of books you wish to purchase

CONTENTS

DEDICATION

To my many patients. Your courage, determination, tolerance, and commitment in the face of severe adversity taught me much more than I could have ever taught you.

ACKNOWLEDGEMENTS

My heartfelt appreciation to the thousands of scientists worldwide who pursued this area of nutrition and cancer with only their courage and intellectual curiosity to counter the scorn and rejection of others. Very special thanks to my wife, Noreen, for her artwork and essential chapter on foods, recipes and menus; and even more importantly, for the safety net of love that she brings to my life. My sincere admiration goes to Richard J Stephenson and Doc Pennington, whose verve, vision and vivacity have propelled this field. To Robert W. Mayo, for your encouragement, guidance, and autonomy. And a salute to my dedicated research associate, John P. Quinn.

PREFACE

C ancer is the best thing that ever happened to me." The words almost knocked me over. I was listening to the testimonials from several cancer survivors who had gathered in a class reunion to celebrate life. These people later went on to explain this strange statement. "My life wasn't working. I didn't take care of my body. I didn't eat right. I didn't allow enough rest. I didn't like my job, or myself or those around me. I didn't appreciate life. My life was a mess. Cancer was a great big red light flashing on the dashboard of my car saying 'pull this vehicle over and fix it now'."

These cancer victors had shown the ultimate courage by turning adversity into a major victory. In Oriental language, "crisis" is written by two characters, one meaing "danger" and the other meaning "opportunity". Cancer is a crisis of unparalleled proportions, both for the individual and humanity. For a minority of cancer patients, cancer has become an extraordinary opportunity to convert their life into a masterpiece.

Over 2.5 million Americans are currently being treated for cancer. Each year over 1.3 million more Americans are newly diagnosed with cancer. Half of all cancer patients in general are alive after five years. Europe has an even higher incidence of cancer. For the past four decades, both the incidence and age-adjusted death rate from cancer in America has been steadily climbing. Ironically, amidst the high tech wizardry of modern medicine, at least 40% of cancer patients will die from malnutrition, not the cancer itself. This book highlights proven scientific methods using nutrition to:

- reduce the toxicity of chemo and radiation therapies while enhancing the tumor-killing capacity
- dramatically lower the mouth sores, fatigue, vomiting, hair loss and organ toxicity that the average poorly nourished cancer patient experiences
- bolster the cancer patient's immune system to provide a microscopic army of warriors to fight the cancer throughout the body
- eliminate or dramatically reduce the common side effects of cachexia (lean tissue wasting)
- help to selectively starve the tumor cells through dietary changes
- introduce Nature's own cancer fighters from plants to help check the spread of cancer
- slow down cancer with high doses of nutrients that are selectively toxic to tumor cells
- protect against the chance that the chemo or radiation therapy may cause cancer

- lower the risk for recurrent tumors in people who have demonstrated a genetic vulnerability toward cancer
- significantly elevate the chances for complete or partial remission–by changing the underlying conditions that brought about the cancer

Essentially, there is an abundance of scientific evidence showing that a clinically guided nutrition program for the cancer patient who is concurrently working with his or her oncologist can improve quantity of life by 12 to 21 fold with substantial improvements in quality of life and a greater likelihood of complete remission.

Because no cancer patient is suffering from a deficiency of adriamycin, a common chemotherapy drug. Cancer is an abnormal growth, not just a regionalized lump or bump. Chemo, radiation and surgery will reduce tumor burden, but they willdo nothing to change the underlying conditions that allowed this abnormal growth to thrive. In a nutshell, this book is designed to change the conditions in the body that favor tumor growth and return the cancer victor to a healthier status.

Fungus grows on a tree because of warmth, moisture and darkness. You can cut, burn and poison fungus off the tree, but the fungus will return as long as the

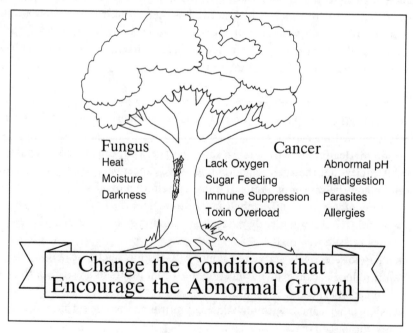

Fungus
Heat
Moisture
Darkness

Cancer
Lack Oxygen
Sugar Feeding
Immune Suppression
Toxin Overload

Abnormal pH
Maldigestion
Parasites
Allergies

Change the Conditions that Encourage the Abnormal Growth

conditions are favorable. Similarly, there are conditions that favor the growth of cancer. My extensive work with cancer patients shows that the cancer patient will thrive or wither, live or die based upon being able to change the conditions which favor cancer growth.

WHY ME AND WHY NOW?

Y ou may ask, "What qualifies Patrick Quillin to write such a book on nutrition and cancer?" I have earned my bachelor's, master's, and doctorate degrees in nutrition, taught college nutrition for 9 years, worked with the Scripps Clinic and La Costa Spa in southern California, am a registered dietitian, have written 5 books, 10 articles and contributed a chapter to a medical textbook. I am a member of the American College of Nutrition and New York Academy of Sciences, as well as being a grant reviewer for the National Institutes of Health, Office of Alternative Medicine. I have my own access code to computer search the 7 million scientific documents in the National Library of Medicine and the 500 other computer-accessed data bases around the world through Dialog and other services.

More importantly, I have studied the subject of nutrition in cancer as intensively as anyone. I organized the first scientific conference on nutrition for the cancer patient, held in November of 1992 with 26 speakers and 300 scientists and clinicians from around the world in attendance. Even more critical, I have been privileged to use nutrition in a formal clinical setting with hundreds of cancer patients. The scientific studies are important, but even more crucial is what is happening to the patients in front of me. This stuff works. You will read a few patient profiles from patients that I have worked with.

Some critics might say,"The evidence is very preliminary for you to be making any recommendations." I disagree. The evidence is substantial and points toward an inexpensive and low-risk method for extending the quality and quantity of life for cancer patients, many of whom have no options left. As poetically stated by Arthur Janov, PhD: "Research is a necessity for scientists, but a luxury for suffering humanity who cannot wait for final statistical proofs. For them, waiting may be a fatal disease." It can be an absurdly long wait for this or any field to become "politically correct", which requires people overcoming their reluctance to change. Traditional cancer therapies *alone* offer almost no hope for many cancer patients, especially lung, pancreas, liver, bone, and advanced colon and breast cancer. These people need supportive therapies to dovetail with traditional therapies. They need options and hope. There are too many lives at stake, and nothing to lose in implementing the nutrition program presented in this book.

In the 1970s, amidst heavy criticism, two Canadian physicians, the Shute brothers, began writing about their clinical success using vitamin E supplements to reverse heart disease and relieve the symptoms of angina and leg pain. A multi-nation study was begun in Europe to examine this issue. As reported at the University of California, Berkeley conference on Antioxidants and Free Radicals in 1989 by Dr. Fred Gey, the best predictor of developing heart disease was low vitamin E levels in the blood. The Shute brothers were right. Since then, other work has shown that a low intake of vitamin E can also lead to suppressed immune functions, cancer, Alzheimer's disease and cataracts. How many people suffered and died needlessly while the authorities tried to make up their minds about whether to endorse non-toxic and inexpensive nutrients? Where is the downside to this equation?

In the early 1980s, I would ask scientists at professional meetings, "How many of you are taking supplements?" The answer was about 5%, with the remainder being sarcastic about the subject. At a recent meeting, 80% of the scientists polled admitted to taking therapeutic levels of supplements to protect their health. Over three decades ago, free radicals were discovered to be the cause of degenerative diseases by Denom Harmon, MD, PhD of the University of Nebraska. This crucial area was then popularized by Dirk Pearson and Sandy Shaw in their 1982 book, LIFE EXTENSION, and fully supported by the world's most prestigious group of nutrition scientists in the American Journal of Clinical Nutrition conference held in 1990. A half century had produced more evidence and explanations, but had wasted many lives in the process.

America is a consumer driven society. You who will create the momentum for change. Don't wait for some government organization, or new law, or general endorsement from one of the major health care organizations to implement nutrition as part of comprehensive cancer treatment. It has been said that all truth must go through three stages: first, it is rejected; second, it is violently opposed; third, it is accepted as self-evident. Nutrition in cancer treatment currently resides on stage two, and is moving swiftly toward stage three. When is the evidence enough? Right now.

HOW IS THIS BOOK DIFFERENT?

■ **Attacking cancer on many levels.** A hammer, pliers and screwdriver belong in any good tool box, just as chemo, radiation and surgery have their place in cancer treatment. But that tool box is far from complete. There are many alternative cancer therapies which can be valuable assets in cancer treatment.

This book offers other "tools" to support the basic but incomplete toolbox that we currently use against cancer.

There are a number of books on the market that offer alternative advice for cancer patients. Many of these books have served a valuable purpose and have helped cancer patients to be aware of cancer treatment options. This book offers a unique multi-disciplinary approach to treating cancer that is based on both scientific studies and actual clinical experience. My basic strategy is a two-pronged attack on cancer:

1. **External medicine.** To reduce cancer burden and symptoms with chemo, radiation and surgery.
2. **Internal medicine.** To use nutrition, exercise, attitude and detoxification to elevate the body's own internal healing abilities.

■ **Avoid tunnel vision.** It is important to avoid the mistakes of the past; which is to focus on one aspect of cancer treatment and forget the other potentially valuable therapies. Avoid mono-mania, or obsession with one "magic bullet" idea. This book pays homage to the complexities of the human body and mind and draws on many fields to provide maximum firepower against cancer. We need all the weapons we can muster, for cancer is no simple beast to kill.

■ **Individualize treatment plans.** I recognize the diversity of the human population. There are well over 5 billion people on the planet earth. We are as different as we are alike. There is no one perfect diet. The macrobiotic diet is truly a major improvement over the typical American diet, yet was developed by a Japanese physician who was drawing heavily on his ancestral Oriental diet. Eskimos eat 60% of their calories from high fat animal food, with very little vitamin C, fiber, fruit or vegetables in their diet. Yet they have a very low incidence of cancer and heart disease. There are groups of people in Africa and Asia that rely on their dairy herds for their dietary staples and others that are vegans, or pure vegetarians. Each of these groups has adapted to a unique diet that strongly influences their health. Rather than give you one set diet to follow, I am going to work with you to find a diet that reflects your ancestral heritage and your unique biochemical needs.

Also, we need to fix the problem(s) that may have triggered the cancer. If low thyroid and milk allergies were the initial problems, then you will never really resolve the cancer until the problems have been fixed. I will present a logical flow later in the book that will help you to detect common problems that can be the original insult which triggered the cancer.

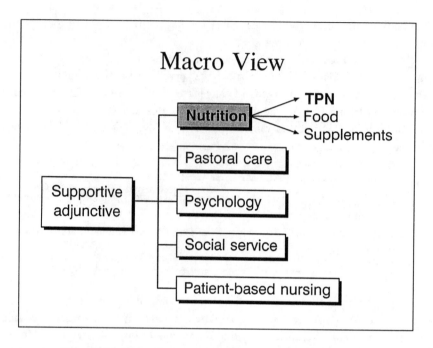

Macro View

RE-ENGINEERING CANCER TREATMENT

I t is a brave new world out there. The "iron curtain" has fallen. Environmentalism is "in". Women have earned their way into boardrooms and the highest political offices. Indians are now called Native Americans and considered the good guys. And health care is in a state of major transition. America spent $950 billion on disease maintenance in 1992, which is 12% of our gross national product–twice the expense per capita of any other health care system on earth. Notice that I said "disease maintenance", because we certainly do not support health care in America, and "health insurance" is neither related to health nor solid actuarial insurance. Just to put that into perspective, 10% of the cost of that new car you bought was for health insurance for factory workers. And Richard Lamm, visiting professor at Dartmouth College, has estimated that inefficient and unnecessary health care expenditures add $100 billion annually to the cost of American goods and services, which jeopardizes our ability to compete in the emerging global economy.

The most expensive disease in America is cancer, which cost Americans $110 billion in 1992, which is greater than 11% of the total spent on all diseases. These opulent expenses would be easier to swallow if we were obtaining impressive results. But many experts argue that we have made limited progress

In Search of: the "magic bullet" nutrient

HUMAN REQUIREMENTS:
Physical:
50+ essential nutrients
200 minor dietary constituents
18 conditionally essential
nutrients
others: gravity, EMF, light

Intangible:
spiritual
mental
emotional
exercise

NUTRIENTS IMPLICATED CANCER:
Vitamins: A, E, C, D, K, riboflavin,
niacin, pyridoxine, folacin
Minerals: Ca, K, Na+?, Mg, Zn, Fe+?,
Cu, I, Mn, Fl, Se
Carb: refined sugar+?, natural CHO
Fat: Omega 6+?, omega 3, quant,
qual
Pro: quant+?, tyro & phe+?, arg, orn
MDCs: flavonoids, carotenoids,
allicin, isothiocyanates
Cond.Ess.Nutr.:Coenzyme Q-10

in the costly and lengthy "war on cancer". Annually in America, there are more than 50 million cancer-related visits to the doctor; one million cancer operations and 750,000 radiation treatments.

By 1971, cancer had become enough of a nuisance that President Richard Nixon launched the long awaited "war on cancer", confidently proclaiming that we would have a cure within 5 years, before the Bicentennial celebration in 1976. Two decades later, with over $35 billion spent on research, $1 trillion spent on therapy, 7 million casualties, and no relief in sight from traditional therapies, it is blindingly obvious that we must re-examine some options in cancer prevention and treatment.

One in three Americans will get cancer and one in four will die from it. Breast cancer has increased from one out of 20 women in the year 1950 to one out of 9 women in 1990. With some cancers, notably liver, lung, pancreas, bone and advanced breast cancer, our five year survival rate from traditional therapy alone is virtually the same as it was 30 years ago. Cancer kills more Americans each year than three times the total 150,000 American AIDS casualties since the discovery of HIV.

This book is about options. If our current results from traditional cancer treatment were encouraging, then there would be no need for alternative therapies against cancer. Unfortunately, traditional cancer therapies have plateaued–some might say that they hit a dead end brick wall. In many instances, the treatment is worse than the disease, with chronic nausea and vomitting, hair loss, painful mouth sores, extreme fatigue and depression as common side effects of therapy and minimal improvements in lifespan. Long term complications include toxicity to the heart, kidneys and bone marrow. While many children may recover from cancer, they are placed at much higher risk for getting cancer later in life from their cancer therapy. And if the cancer patient recovers from the disease, which is no small task, then recovering from the therapy may be even more challenging. Obviously, if what we are doing isn't working, then we need to look at some sensible, scientific, non-toxic and cost effective options that can amplify the tumor-killing abilities of traditional therapies. Nutrition is at the top of that list.

Be prepared as you read this book for a new way of looking at cancer. Think of how strange it must have been for:

- the first person to inject extract of bread mold, or penicillin, into a patient to relieve an infection.
- the first American oncologist who ground up the plant periwinkle, now called the drug vincristine, and injected it into a cancer patient.
- the first awkward attempts to inject chemical warfare mustard gas into a cancer patient for the crude beginnings of chemotherapy.

Nutrition therapy should seem no stranger than anything else in health care. Hopefully, nutrition seems a whole lot more logical than some other common practices.

The best selling cancer drug in the world is a mushroom extract, PSK, manufactured in Japan and sold throughout Europe and Japan. Only 30% of cancer therapy in Japan is from the "big three" of radiation, chemo and surgery. The bark of the yew tree, Taxol, holds promise as a potent cancer drug. Digestive enzymes and mistletoe (Iscador) are government approved prescription cancer drugs in Germany. Evening primrose oil is an accepted cancer therapy in England. Do not discount any possibilities in this "war on cancer". While America is considered one of the world's heavy weight champions at developing new industrial technologies and patents, we are lagging well behind the rest of the world in cancer treatment. In order to make any progress, we will have to examine new therapies, some of which, admittedly, sound more like Woody Allen invented them.

As you enter this watershed era of nutrition therapy for cancer, perhaps a few words of encouragement are in order from some of humanity's greatest thinkers:

- If we worked on the assumption that what is accepted as true really is true, then there would be little hope for advance. *Orville Wright*
- If everyone is thinking alike, then no one is thinking. *Benjamin Franklin*
- We live in a world of problems which can no longer be solved by the level of thinking which created them. *Albert Einstein*
- Progress is impossible without change, and those who cannot change their minds cannot change anything. *George Bernard Shaw*

PATIENT PROFILE

J. B. Marsh, male, 65 years old. My first cancer was colon cancer, diagnosed in April 1990. The doctor removed my rectum and put in a permanent colostomy (bag on my side). The doctor assured me, "We got it all." Just before Christmas of 1990, I began spitting up chunks of blood and black things. My doctor told me I had lung cancer and removed most of my right lung. They told me that I was lucky that my case was operable, but I didn't feel too lucky. I cried a bit, then went to my doctor with the question,: "If my immune system was working right, then I wouldn't have cancer. Right?" He said, "Right." So I asked him, "Then how do I get my immune system working?" He said,"Either it works or doesn't, there's nothing you can do about it." My two other doctors gave me the same strange answers. I told my wife, "I got to take control of my health, or I'm going to die." I spent time in the library, bookstores and health food stores reading about cancer and nutrition.

I started eating right and jogging and began feeling great. But in August of 1991 I used a lot of pesticides to start my garden. I mean I had this stuff caked on my arms by the end of the day. My dog started digging in the pesticide sack to get after some animal and by the end of the day, my dog was dead.

By October of 1991 I knew I had cancer again, this time somewhere near my testicles. My doctors wanted to remove my testicles to slow the spread of my prostate cancer. By then, I said no to surgery. I read an article by Dr. Quillin which talked about nutrition as part of full spectrum cancer treatment. I went to Dr. Quillin's hospital in Tulsa, Oklahoma where they gave me a high quality organic diet, high doses of supplements and radiation therapy for my prostate cancer. I am pleased to report that my doctors find no trace of cancer in my body after 4 months of therapy. I am going to stay on my diet and exercise program because I feel great and can jog 2 miles each day.

CHAPTER 1

CANCER AND ITS CAUSES— KNOW YOUR ENEMY

Y ou are your best physician. No one knows your body better than you. Only you can fully appreciate and interpret your symptoms. Only you can make lifestyle changes that will improve your outcome. You are the one who will benefit or suffer from choices regarding therapy. This book provides you with more than a sense of empowerment regarding your treatment. This book is your map to help guide you through the "mine field" of choices that await the cancer patient.

In the terrifying film, "The Predator", a chameleon-like beast from outer space descends upon the sweltering jungles of Central America to hunt humans, including Arnold Schwartzenager. If you sweated through this film, then you have an idea of how hard it is to kill cancer. The Predator wore a shield which allowed it to blend into the surrounding environment, making it almost invisible. Cancer mimics the chemistry of a fetus, and hence becomes invisible to the human immune system. Cancer also mutates by changing its DNA composition almost weekly, which is a major reason why many cancers develop a drug resistance that often limits the value of chemotherapy. Cancer also weakens its host by installing its own abnormal biochemistry, including:

- changes in the pH, or acid base balance, making the environment more favorable for cancer growth and less favorable for host recovery
- creation of anaerobic (oxygen deprived) pockets of tissue which resist radiation therapy like someone hunkered into a bomb shelter
- blunting the immune system, which is the primary means of fighting cancer
- elevating metabolism and calorie needs while simultaneously lowering appetite and food intake to slowly starve the host
- ejecting by-products that create weakness, apathy, pain and depression in the host
- siphoning nutrients out of the bloodstream like a parasite.

With its invisible, predatory and every-changing nature, cancer is truly a tough condition to treat. Cancer is essentially an abnormal cell growth. It is a piece of the cancer patient that was once normal, but somehow developed altered DNA blueprints and began growing wildly. Its unchecked growth tends to overwhelm other functions in the body until death comes from:

1. Organ failure, i.e. the kidneys shut down
2. Infection, i.e. pneumonia because the immune system has been blunted
3. Malnutrition, because the parasitic cancer shifts the host's metabolism into high gear through inefficient use of fuel while also inducing a loss of appetite.

There is a basic flaw in our thinking about health care in this country. We treat symptoms, not the underlying cause of the disease. Yet, the only way to provide long-lasting relief in any degenerative disease, like cancer, arthritis and heart disease, is to reverse the basic cause of the disease. For example, let's say that you developed a headache because your neighbor's teenager is playing drums too loudly. You take an aspirin to subdue the headache, then your stomach starts churning. So you take some antacids to ease the stomach nausea, then your blood pressure goes up. And on it goes. We shift symptoms with medication, as if in a bizarre "shell game", when we really need to deal with the fundamental cause of the disease.

A more common example is heart disease. There are over 60,000 miles of blood vessels in the average adult body. When a person develops blockage in the arteries near the heart, open heart bypass surgery will probably be recommended. In this procedure, a short section of vein from the leg is used to replace the plugged up vessels near the heart. But what has been done to improve the other 59,999 miles left that are probably equally obstructed? A Harvard professor, Dr. E. Braunwald, investigated the records from thousands of bypass patients in the Veteran's Administration Hospitals and found no improvement in lifespan after this expensive and risky surgery.[1] Why? Because the underlying cause; which could be a complex array of diet, exercise, stress, and toxins; has not been resolved. Bypass surgery treats the symptoms of heart disease like chemo and radiation treat the symptoms of cancer. Each provide temporary relief, but no long term cure.

Meanwhile, Dr. Dean Ornish has spent years developing a program that both prevents and reverses heart disease, something that drugs and surgery cannot do. His program recently was found effective in a clinical study. When you deal with the underlying causes of a degenerative disease, you are more likely to get long term favorable benefits. When you allow the fundamental causes to continue and merely treat the symptoms that surface, then the outlook for the patient is dismal. In dozens of diseases and millions of patients, this

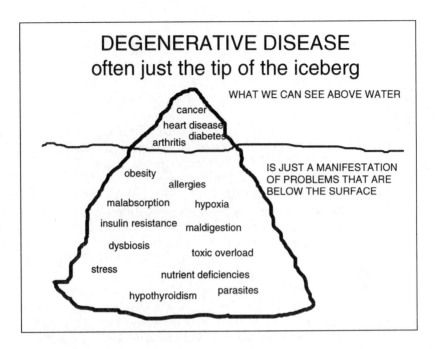

DEGENERATIVE DISEASE
often just the tip of the iceberg

WHAT WE CAN SEE ABOVE WATER

cancer
heart disease
diabetes
arthritis

IS JUST A MANIFESTATION
OF PROBLEMS THAT ARE
BELOW THE SURFACE

obesity
allergies
malabsorption   hypoxia
insulin resistance   maldigestion
dysbiosis
toxic overload
stress
nutrient deficiencies
hypothyroidism   parasites

obvious law holds true.

The crucial missing link in most cancer therapy is stimulating the patient's own healing abilities. Because the best medical equipment cannot detect one billion cancer cells. Imagine leaving behind only one billion dandelion seeds on your lawn after you thought you got them all. After a lifetime of battling bacteria as the root of all infectious diseases, Pasteur claimed on his deathbed, "the terrain [host environment] is everything." We have developed an equally illogical "war on farm pests", in which we blast the food crop with lethal doses of pesticides in an attempt to kill the bugs. Yet, the bugs adapt to the poison, while the natural predators of these bugs die off. The net effect with both chemical warfare on our food crop is the same as chemical warfare on the cancer patient: we oftentimes make the situation worse.

Most experts now agree that the war on bugs can be won by using the time-tested laws of nature: food crops develop their own pest resistance when grown on well-nourished soil, early preventive intervention to stop problems before they become overwhelming, rotating crops and using natural predators to eat insects. Similarly, the "war on cancer" is an internal microscopic war that can only be won by working within the laws of nature: stimulating the patient's own abilities to fight cancer while changing the abnormal conditions that allow cancer to grow. All other therapies are doomed to disappointing results. Combined together, these treatments of external medicine coupled with stimulating the cancer patient's internal healing abilities hold great promise for dramatically improving your chances of success against cancer.

WHAT CAUSES CANCER?

Most degenerative diseases, including cancer, do not have a readily identifiable enemy. In a bacterial infection, you can attack the "cause" of the disease with an antibiotic. Cancer seems to be caused by a collection of lifestyle and environmental factors that accumulate over the years. Since success against any degenerative disease requires getting to the root of the problem, let's examine the accepted causes of cancer.

■ **Toxic overload.** Of the 5 million registered chemicals in the world, mankind comes in contact with 70,000, of which at least 20,000 are known carcinogens, or cancer-causing agents. Each year, America alone sprays 1.2 billion pounds of pesticides on our food crops, dumps 90 billion pounds of toxic waste in our 55,000 toxic waste sites, feeds 9 million pounds of antibiotics to our farm animals to help them gain weight faster and generally bombards the landscape with questionable amounts of electromagnetic radiation.

Bruce Ames, PhD of the University of California at Berkeley has estimated that each of the 60 trillion cells in your body undergoes from 1,000 to 10,000 DNA "hits" or potentially cancer-causing breaks every day. Yet somehow for most of us, our DNA repair mechanisms and immune system surveillance are able to keep this storm of genetic damage under control. Wallowing in our own high tech effluvia is a major cause of cancer in modern society, since carcinogens add to the fury of the continuous assault on the DNA. Noted authority, Samuel Epstein, MD of the University of Illinois, says that a major thrust of cancer prevention must be detoxifying our earth. Toxins not only cause DNA breakage, which can trigger cancer, but also subdue the immune system, which then allows cancer to become the "fox in the chicken coop", with no controlling force.

Early research indicated that once cancer has been upregulated, or " the lion is out of the cage", then no amount of detoxification is going to matter. Newer evidence says otherwise. Cancer growth can both be slowed and even reversed under the right conditions. According to the National Cancer Institute, there are 7 million Americans alive today who have lived 5 or more years after their cancer diagnosis. Cancer is reversible. If toxins caused the problem, then detoxification is the solution. Detoxification includes expelling accumulated:

- wastes that are natural by-products of living
- toxins from our heavily polluted environment
- dead cancer cells from the battle within.

Detoxification involves accelerating the excretion of poisons out of the body via urine, sweat, and feces, including the use of chelation, herbal purgatives, hot baths and enemas.

■ **Distress**. It was the Canadian physician and researcher, Hans Selye, MD, who coined the term "the stress of life" as he could document the physiological changes that took place in lab animals when exposed to noise, bright lights, confinement and electric shocks. The thymus gland is a pivotal organ in immune system protection against infections and cancer. Dr. Selye noted that stress would induce thymus gland shrinkage, increases in fats in the blood (for the beginnings of heart disease) and erosion of the stomach lining (ulcers).

Since the 1920s, scientific evidence has been gathering that emotional stress can depress the immune system and make that individual more vulnerable to infections and cancer. It was Norman Cousins' book, ANATOMY OF AN ILLNESS, which thrust this mind-body principle in front of the public. After 10 years of lecturing and researching at the University of California at Los Angeles, Cousins' theories held valid under scientific scrutiny.

Carl Simonton, MD, a radiation oncologist, found that his mental imagery techniques seemed to produce better results with fewer side effects for his cancer patients. Bernie Siegel, MD, a Yale surgeon, found that certain mental characteristics helped his cancer patients to recover. Candace Pert, PhD, a celebrated researcher at the National Institutes of Health, discovered endorphins in human brains and led the charge toward unravelling the chemical mysteries of the mind. Dr. Pert says that the mind is a pharmacy and is continuously producing potent substances that either improve or worsen health. Since the mind can create cancer, it should seem a logical leap that the mind can help to prevent and even subdue cancer. Many alternative therapists use a wide variety of psychological approaches to help rid the body of cancer.

According to Dr. Arthur Janov, the anaerobic cancer may stem from the suffocating experience of being born from a heavily sedated mother. Primal therapy coaxes the near-death suffocation experience out of the adult patient to theoretically eliminate the cause of cancer.[2] Clearly, there is some mental link in the development of cancer for many patients.[3] I have worked with many cancer patients whose major hurdle was spiritual healing. While dietary changes are difficult for many people, it is far easier to change the diet or take some nutrient pills than change the way we think. Pulling emotional splinters are an essential and painful experience. Not only is there a metaphysical link to cancer, but the site of the cancer may provide clues regarding how to fix the problem. Many breast cancer patients have experienced a recent divorce, which results in the loss of a femine organ. One patient of mine suffered from cancer of the larynx, which began one year after his wife left him with the thought "there's nothing you can say that will make me stay." If spiritual wounds started the cancer, then spiritual healing is an essential element for a cure.

■ **Nutrition**. The human body is built from, repaired by and fueled by substances found in the diet. In the most literal sense, "we are what we eat...and think, and breath, and do." Nutrition therapy merely tries to re-establish "metabolic balance" in the cancer patients. Medical doctors Gerson, Moerman and Livingston have each provided their own nutrition programs to treat cancer.

Other schools of thought include macrobiotics, vegetarianism, acid/alkaline balancing, fasting, fruit and vegetable juicing and others. I will assess all of these therapies in more detail later. After decades of living outside the accepted realm of cancer therapies, nutrition therapy has found a new level of scientific acceptance with the 1990 report from the Office of Technology Assessment, an advisory branch of Congress, whose expert scientific panel wrote in UNCONVENTIONAL CANCER TREATMENTS:

"It is our collective professional judgment that nutritional interventions are going to follow psychosocial interventions up the ladder into clinical respectability as adjunctive and complementary approaches to the treatment of cancer."[4]

■ **Exercise**. While one out of three Americans will eventually develop cancer, only one out of seven active Americans will get cancer. Exercise imparts many benefits, including oxygenation of the tissues to thwart the anaerobic needs of cancer cells. Exercise also helps to stabilize blood glucose levels, which can restrict the amount of fuel available for cancer cells to grow. Exercise improves immune function, lymph flow and detoxification systems. Exercise helps us better tolerate stressful situations. For cancer patients who can participate, exercise improves tolerance to chemotherapy. Some therapists use hydrogen peroxide or ozone to oxygenate the tissue. Humans evolved as active creatures. Inactivity is an abnormal under-oxygenated metabolic state—so is cancer.

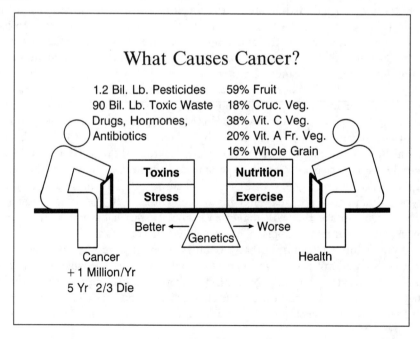

What Causes Cancer?

1.2 Bil. Lb. Pesticides	59% Fruit
90 Bil. Lb. Toxic Waste	18% Cruc. Veg.
Drugs, Hormones,	38% Vit. C Veg.
Antibiotics	20% Vit. A Fr. Veg.
	16% Whole Grain

Toxins	Nutrition
Stress	Exercise

Better ← /Genetics\ → Worse

Cancer
+ 1 Million/Yr
5 Yr 2/3 Die

Health

PATIENT PROFILE

DV, female, 51 years old. In July of 1990 she underwent a hysterectomy and extensive chemotherapy after a diagnosis of uterine cancer. DV was admitted to our facility in March of 1991 with metastases to both lungs and extensive pain in the bones and joints. Narcotics only aggravated her constipation and did not help the bone pain. In addition to a chemo regimen administered in fractionated dosage, DV began a vegetarian diet while taking nutritional supplements, including a broad spectrum vitamin and mineral product, beta-carotene, vitamin C, vitamin E, selenium, fish oil (EPA) and Wobenzym digestive enzymes. Within 2 months, her general condition improved markedly. Her pain diminished and her quality of life was quite good. She renewed her interest in gardening and involvement in her daughter's life. As of July 1993, DV remains in very good condition.

REFERENCES

1. Braunwald, E., New England Journal Medicine, vol.309, p.1181, Nov.10, 1983
2. Janov, A., THE NEW PRIMAL SCREAM, Enterprise, Wilmington, DE,1991
3. Newell, GR, Primary Care in Cancer, p.29, May 1991
4. Office of Technology Assessment, UNCONVENTIONAL CANCER TREATMENTS, p.14

CHAPTER 2

TREATMENTS CURRENTLY
USED FOR CANCER

I n order to know where we are going in cancer treatment, it is important to know where we have been and how we got where we are. This chapter looks at both conventional and alternative cancer treatment methods to give you a better understanding of our "roots" in cancer treatment options. For a more thorough discussion of conventional therapies, read CANCER THERAPY by Mallin Dollinger, MD; for alternative therapies, read CANCER THERAPY by Ralph Moss, PhD.

CONVENTIONAL THERAPIES

■ **Chemotherapy** is a spin-off product from the chemical warfare of World Wars I and II and is now given to 75% of all American cancer patients. Yale University pharmacologists who were working on a government project during World War II to develop an antidote for mustard gas noted that bone marrow and lymphoid tissue were heavily damaged by these poisons. That observation led to experiments in which mustard gas was injected into mice with lymphomas (cancer of the lymph glands) and produced remission. In 1943, researchers found that mustard gas had a similar effect on human Hodgkins disease.[1] Chemo has also become a useful agent against testicular cancer, which is now 92% curable. Most proponents of chemo now recognize the limitations of using chemo as sole therapy against many types of cancer.

Shortly after these initial exciting discoveries, progress on chemo cures quickly plateaued and forced the innovative thinkers into creative combinations of various chemo drugs, which is now the accepted practice. In the 1980s, oncologists began using chemo by "fractionated drip infusion" in the hospital rather than one large (bolus) injection in the doctor's office. The fractionated method was not only more effective against the cancer but also less toxic on the patient. Think of the difference in toxicity between taking 2 glasses of wine with dinner each night, or guzzling all 14 glasses at one time at the end of the week. Also, fractionated drip infusion is more likely to catch the cancer cells in their growth phase, while bolus injections are a random guess to coincide with the growth phase of cancer. In the next evolutionary step, borrowing from technology developed for heart disease, oncologists began using catheters (thin tubes) that could be inserted into an artery (called intra-arterial infusion) to deliver chemo at the site of the tumor, once again improving response and reducing overall toxicity.

■ **Radiation therapy** is given to about 60% of all cancer patients. In 1896, a French physicist, Marie Curie discovered radium, a radioactive metal. For her brilliance, Madam Curie was eventually awarded two Nobel prizes and was considered one of the founders of radiation therapy and the nuclear age. For her unprotected use of radioactive materials, she eventually died while still young of leukemia. Cancer patients were soon being treated with a new technique developed by the German physicist, Wilhelm Roentgen, called radiation therapy. This technique relies on regional destruction of unwanted tissue through ionizing radiation that disrupts the DNA of all bombarded cells. Radiation therapy can be externally or internally originated, high or low dose and delivered with uncanny computer-assisted precision to the site of the tumor. Brachytherapy, or interstitial radiation therapy, places the source of radiation directly into the tumor, as an implanted seed. New techniques use radiation in combination with heat therapy (hyperthermia).

■ **Surgery** is the first treatment of choice for about 67% of cancer patients. By 1600 B.C., Egyptian physicians were excising tumors using knives or red-hot irons.[2] By physically removing the obvious tumor, physicians feel that they have the best chance for overall success. Unfortunately, many tumors are so entwined with delicate body organs, such as brain and liver, that the tumor cannot be resected (cut out). Another concern is that partial removal of a cancer mass may open the once-encapsulated tumor to spread, like opening a sack of dandelion seeds on your lawn.

■ **Biological therapies,** as with most other discoveries, were the product of accidents being observed by a bright mind. William B. Coley, MD, a New York cancer surgeon scoured the hospital records around 1890 looking for some clue why only a minority of patients survived cancer surgery. He found that a high percentage of survivors had developed an infection shortly after the surgery to remove the cancer. This observation led Dr. Coley to inject a wide variety of bacteria, known as Coley's cocktail, into his cancer patients, who then underwent the feverish recovery phase, with noteworthy cancer cures produced. Infections were found to induce the immune system into a higher state of activity, which then helped to destroy tumors. From this crude beginning, molecular biologists have found brilliant ways of producing injectable amounts of the immune factors that can theoretically fight cancer.

Even amidst our polluted, overstressed and poorly nourished society, most people do not die of cancer—due to the protection afforded by our immune systems; which is a well-orchestrated army of specialized cells that kill invaders, like cancer, bacteria and viruses. An over-reactive and out of balance immune system creates auto-immune diseases, such as allergies, asthma, Crohn's disease and arthritis. An under-reactive immune system leaves the person open to cancer, infections and premature aging.

Biological therapies attempt to fine tune and focus the immune system into a more vigorous attack on the cancer. Lymphokines are basically "bullets" produced by the immune system to kill invading cells, such as cancer. Lymphokine activated killer cells (LAK) are incubated in the laboratory in the presence of a stimulator (interleukin-2) and then injected back into the cancer patient's body for an improved immune response.[3] In some lab tests, LAK cells swarm on the tumor like ants on honey.

Interferon, interleukin, monoclonal antibodies and tumor necrosis factor are among the leading contenders as biological therapies against cancer. The downside of biological therapies is that most forms have extremely toxic side effects, and none can be legally used even in approved experiments unless that patient has been considered untreatable by the other three conventional means. The National Cancer Institute is beginning to place more emphasis on researching biological therapies.

■ **Heat Therapy (hyperthermia).** Cancer cells seem to be more vulnerable to heat than normal healthy cells. Since the time of Hippocrates and the Egyptian Pharoahs, heat therapy has been valued. Experts have shown that applying heat to the patient elevates immune responses. Temperatures of 42 degrees Celsius or 107 degrees Fahrenheit will kill most cancer cells, but can be quite stressful on the patient also. Could it be that exercise induces regular "hyperthermia" to kill off cancer cells before they can become a problem?

Whole body hyperthermia involves a very sophisticated hot tub device, general anesthesia and medical supervision. Regional hyperthermia can involve either a miniature waterbed-like device applied to the tumor or focused microwaves. Major cancer research centers, including Stanford and Duke, have found this therapy useful by itself, or used synergistically to improve the response to chemo and radiation therapy.

ALTERNATIVE THERAPIES

If you need emergency medical care, reconstructive surgery, orthopedic surgery or critical life support, then an American hospital is where you will get the world's best care. That's why alternative emergency care does not exist, because our current system is working just find, thank you very much. Unfortunately, not all areas of American medicine have such an impressive track record of success. Many patients with cancer, Chronic Fatigue Syndrome, arthritis, AIDS, multiple sclerosis, Alzheimer's, mental illness and muscular dystrophy find little help from traditional medicine. When the accepted approach does not work, the grounds are fertile for "alternative" approaches to develop.

Among the many advantages of living in America, we are blessed with abundant individual liberties as guaranteed by the Constitution and Bill of Rights. And we fight viciously to preserve these rights. The controversy of alternative cancer treatment basically centers around the question "Which is more important: the patient's right to choose whatever health care they want, or the responsibility of the government to protect the unwarey consumer from fraudulent practices?" This question is heated, polarized and regularly doused with the emotional testimonies of someone who was cured through alternative therapy after conventional therapy told he or she to "go home and get your affairs in order."

Studies now show that up to 50% of all cancer patients use some form of unconventional cancer therapy, with most of these people being of above-average income and education.[4] A newer study reported in the New England Journal of Medicine from David Eisenberg, MD of Harvard Medical School shows that Americans make more visits to alternative therapists than to family physicians. Since the patient usually pays for alternative therapists while insurance pays for most expenses in a family physician visit, these numbers are quite astonishing. People don't keep going back and paying out of pocket expenses unless they are getting some relief for their health problem. This information somewhat debunks the theory that the government is protecting poor uneducated minority consumers from predatory, dangerous and unproven health care specialists.

While critics brand alternative cancer therapies as "unproven, questionable, dubious, quackery and fraudulent"; proponents prefer the labels "complementary, comprehensive, innovative, nontoxic, holistic, natural and noninvasive." Meanwhile, the American Cancer Society has kept a list of about 100 cancer therapies that the ACS calls "unproven". This blacklist has become the "gatekeeper" in cancer treatment in America. Insurance companies will not reimburse for "unproven or experimental" therapies.

Yet, are we using dual standards in judging our health care options? According to the Office of Technology Assessment, only 10-20% of all surgical procedures practiced in the United States have been "proven" to be effective by controlled clinical trials.[5] Much of what Americans do throughout medicine, law, education and even business are more based on a "Grandfather clause" or tradition, rather than being the best way to do things. We oftentimes "pave cow paths" which are usually inefficient routes from point A to point B, then consider these sacred and inviolable. If 50% of cancer patients this year will seek alternative cancer care, which is non-reimburseable, imagine the stampede toward alternative cancer treatment if people could choose their own therapies.

Improvement in cancer treatment options may be coming soon. Retired Iowa Congressman Berkley Bedell could only find cures for his Lyme disease, then advanced and untreatable prostate cancer from alternative therapists. Mr. Bedell told his powerbroker friends on Capitol Hill of his experiences. Senator Tom Harkin, chairman of the subcommittee on health issues, then convinced his colleagues to allocate $2 million to form the Office of Alternative Medicine as a branch of the National Institutes of Health. Many insurance companies are awakening to the profitability of alternative cancer therapy because: 1. the public wants it and is willing to pay for it, 2. alternative cancer therapy costs about 10% of conventional cancer care and therefore can be more profitable. Some pioneering insurance companies now reimburse for alternative cancer treatment.[6]

The medical freedom advocates argue that a person afflicted with a terminal disease deserves a chance at whatever therapies offer hope. Meanwhile, the Food and Drug Administration cites examples in which premature permission to use newly discovered therapies ended in disaster—like the Thalidomide situation. However, lets compare the risk to benefit ratio of Thalidomide and alternative cancer treatment:

THALIDOMIDE

- **Benefits:** an entirely elective drug used to relieve the mild symptoms of nausea.
- **Risks:** taken during an extremely vulnerable phase of life, pregnancy. We know, for instance, that small amounts of alcohol will not harm most healthy adults, but the same amount of alcohol could create permanent birth defects when consumed by pregnant women.

The results of Thalidomide use were catastrophic, with thousands of newborn infants suffering irremedial birth defects.

ALTERNATIVE CANCER THERAPIES

- **Benefits:** has been demonstrated to improve quality and quantity of life for many cancer patients; especially for patients who have no hope in conventional cancer treatment.
- **Risks:** in extremely unprofessional hands it may cause minor side effects. Costs money, but usually less than 10% of standard cancer therapies.

It is unconstitutional to think that protecting the end-stage and otherwise untreatable cancer patient from inexpensive and non-toxic therapies is a government obligation. AIDS patients have become models of political activism and have won this logic debate as the Food and Drug Administration now allows many "compassionate use" variances for otherwise unapproved drugs in AIDS therapy. Cancer patients, also, need a broader scope of treatment options. To quote Hippocrates, the father of modern medicine, 2400 years ago: "Extreme diseases call for extreme measures." Nutrition therapy, surely, is no more extreme than chemo, radiation therapy or surgery.

Alternative cancer therapies would best be categorized as:

- *Physical*, which includes botanicals, nutrition, biochemical vaccinations, anti-neoplastons, biologically guided chemotherapy, eumetabolic, laetrile, DMSO, cellular treatment, oxygen therapy, hydrazine sulfate, immuno-augmentative therapy and more.
- *Metaphysical* (meaning "above physical"), which includes psychoneuroimmunology (PNI), guided imagery, relaxation therapy, primal therapy, faith healing and other methods that use the mind or spirit to elevate the body out of cancer.

It is clear that humans are a complex interplay of physical and metaphysical forces. Many documented cases of paranormal psychology have shown that people can alter autonomic bodily functions by entering suspended animation, walking on hot coals without any burns, reading minds and living outside the laws of nutrition. As humans become more spiritual or metaphysical, we tend to transcend physical laws. Hence, the ultimate cancer cure may come from this relatively untapped area of healing.

PIONEERS AND THEIR ALTERNATIVE CANCER THERAPIES

T he alternative therapists are at a serious disadvantage in the battle of documentation. Even after $35 billion spent on government-funded research and thousands of researchers working for decades, scientists are hard pressed to prove efficacy in the assortment of conventional cancer treatment. Alternative therapists don't publish results for a number of reasons:

- poorly financed and cannot support research efforts
- poorly organized and shy away from cooperative pooled data
- outlawed in the U.S. and ineligible for government research grants
- leery of reporting their data in the U.S. for fear of medical license revocation and/or imprisonment.

There have been efforts recently to examine certain alternative cancer therapies. Harold Foster, PhD at the University of British Columbia showed some rather promising results from alternative cancer treatment. "Spontaneous regression" is that elusive miraculous cure that comes to a few cancer patients after traditional therapists have given up. It seems wise to study these "winners" and see if there is something that they have in common. Of the 200 cancer patients that Foster studied who had experienced "spontaneous regression", 87% made serious dietary changes which were mostly vegetarian in nature, and many others underwent some detoxification program or used nutritional supplements.

All of the following alternative cancer therapies are practiced somewhere in the world. My most humble apologies to the pioneers or therapies that have been left out of this brief overview. For more information, read:

- THIRD OPINION by John Fink, Avery Press, NY, 1988
- UNCONVENTIONAL CANCER TREATMENTS by the Office of Technology Assessment of the U.S. government printing office, 1990
- CANCER THERAPY by Ralph Moss, PhD, Equinox Press, 1992
- OPTIONS by Richard Walters, Avery, 1993.

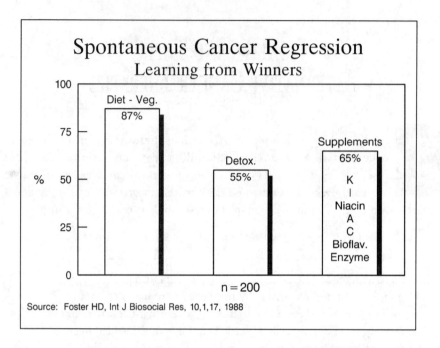

Spontaneous Cancer Regression
Learning from Winners
Source: Foster HD, Int J Biosocial Res, 10,1,17, 1988

■ **Max Gerson, MD** emigrated from Europe to the United States in 1936 and began practicing medicine in New York. Gerson was labelled by the famous missionary doctor, Albert Schweitzer, as "I see in Gerson one of the most eminent geniuses in medical history." Gerson was treating cancer patients with a diet and toxin purgative approach. Gerson's program included a diet that was high in raw unprocessed plant food, low in fat, included raw liver injections, thyroid extract, pancreatin (digestive aids), and supplements of minerals and vitamins, especially high doses of vitamin C.

One of the more intriguing aspects of Dr. Gerson's therapy was an emphasis on foods and supplements high in potassium. Realize that we evolved on a "caveman" diet which was high in potassium from fresh plant food and low in sodium (pre-salt shaker era). Our modern American diet reverses this ratio from an ideal of 4 to 1 (potassium to sodium) to our current 1 to 4, a full 16 fold deterioration in this crucial balance of electrolytes. All of your cells are bathed in a salty ocean water, with higher concentrations of potassium inside the cell to create the "battery of life."

Birger Jansson, PhD at the University of Texas finds a strong link between dietary sodium to potassium ratio and cancer.[7] Stephen Thompson, PhD researcher at the University of California San Diego, found that increasing sodium content could accelerate the metastasis of colon cancer in animals. Maryce Jacobs, PhD, former research director of the American Institute of Cancer

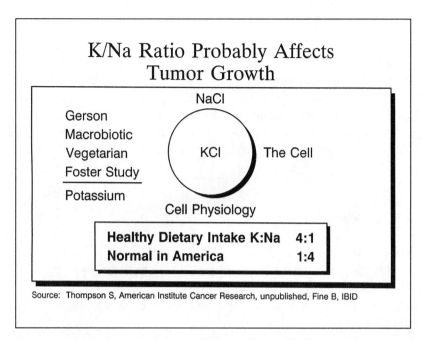

K/Na Ratio Probably Affects
Tumor Growth

NaCl

Gerson
Macrobiotic
Vegetarian
Foster Study
_____
Potassium

KCl   The Cell

Cell Physiology

Healthy Dietary Intake K:Na	**4:1**
Normal in America	**1:4**

Source: Thompson S, American Institute Cancer Research, unpublished, Fine B, IBID

Research, has written an extensive technical chapter on the link between the sodium to potassium ratio and cancer progression.[8]

When the National Cancer Institute reviewed Gerson's book which illustrated his 30 years of clinical experience with 50 patients who recovered from end-stage cancer, the NCI felt that the evidence was inadequate. The American Cancer Society heavily criticized Gerson for several decades and did not recognize a nutrition cancer link until the 1980s. The modern ACS anti-cancer diet looks remarkably similar to Dr. Gerson's diet.

■ **William D. Kelley, DDS** was a dentist who claimed to have healed himself of pancreatic cancer with his own therapy in 1964. Kelley's program included metabolic typing to provide a patient-specific dietary program, detoxification (coffee enemas, etc.), neurological stimulation through chiropractic adjustment and supplements of vitamins, minerals and enzymes. Until 1977, the MERCK MEDICAL MANUAL, considered the "bible of physicians", included coffee enemas as an accepted means of detoxification and constipation relief. Yet coffee enemas became the focal point of critics who considered the Kelley program unscientific.

Meanwhile, there has been an abundance of scientific studies in Europe showing that enzymes (protease, amylase, lipase) can improve the general course of the cancer patient.[9] Kelley's work is carried on by a Sloan-Kettering trained oncologist, Dr. Nicholas Gonzales, in New York City. In his 1970s trial, Kelley was ordered by a federal judge never to speak or write about cancer again. Kelley has since become a recluse.

■ **Macrobiotics**. This program is based on the writings of a Japanese physician, Sagen Ishizuka (1850-1910) who cured himself of cancer by abandoning the refined diet of affluent Japan and reverting back to the unpurified Japanese diet of brown rice, soybeans, fish, miso soup, sea vegetables and other traditional Oriental foods. When you read the "laws of nutrition" later in this book, you will notice the importance of consuming one's ancestral diet. Some proposed mechanisms why the macrobiotic diet helps some cancer patients:

- low in fat
- high in fiber
- high vegetable intake
- improved sodium to potassium ratio
- ability to change an acid (cancer) environment back toward alkaline (healthy)
- potent anti-cancer agents found in soybeans, sea vegetables and other fresh produce
- thyroid stimulating substances found in sea vegetables.

Macrobiotics includes an Eastern philosophy of balancing yin and yang, which are opposing forces. Michio Kushi established a macrobiotic center in Boston in 1978 and has gained a noteworthy following. Kushi has publicly encouraged cancer patients to continue with conventional care.

There are varying levels of intensity in complying with macrobiotic principles, with the ultimate level (+7) being a diet of 100% whole cereals. An American physician, Anthony Sattilaro, cured himself of advanced prostatic cancer with the macrobiotic diet and wrote a book to further popularize this approach. While the macrobiotic lifestyle is certainly a major improvement over the typical American diet, certain aspects of this program are a bit mystifying:

- unlimited access to miso and pickles, which are high in sodium
- limited intake of fruit and fish
- potential for protein and B-12 malnutrition.

This program includes cotton clothes, fresh air and exercise.

■ **Herbal Therapies**. Plant extracts are mankind's oldest medicines. One third of all prescription drugs in the U.S. are based on plant extracts. There is a desperate scramble among drug companies and even the National Cancer Institute to develop *patentable variations* of the many anti-cancer agents found in plants. Many of the people listed below have staked their claim to herbal cures of cancer, including Caisse, Hoxsey, Winters, and others. Periwinkle plant is now the very acceptable cancer drug, vincristine. Undoubtedly, plant extracts will become a major source of cancer drugs in the future. James Duke, PhD, a well respected botanist with the United States Department of Agriculture, has written textbooks on the anti-cancer ingredients in many plants. If you have seen the movie "Medicine Man", then you can appreciate the complexities of trying to find the active ingredient(s) in plant extracts. Botanicals used to fight cancer include Pau D'Arco (LaPacho), ginseng, green tea, mistletoe, polyphenols, carotenoids, bioflavonoids, echinecea, astragalus, chaparral, blood root, garlic and various mushroom extracts.

■ **Rene Caisse,** a Canadian public health nurse, was told by a patient in 1922 that an Indian herbal tea had saved her life from breast cancer. Caisse obtained the recipe, reportedly used it successfully on a few of her patients and then named the therapy "Essiac", or Caisse spelled backward. Her troubles with the government waxed and waned for the coming decades until 1978, shortly before her death, when she signed over the rights to her secret formula to a Canadian manufacturing firm.

■ **Harry Hoxsey** (1901-1974) popularized his great-grandfather's herbal formula which had reputedly cured horses of cancer. Harry Hoxsey's father was a veterinary surgeon who also used the formula on both animals and people with cancer. Yet Harry is the man who made the formula famous. Hoxsey's flamboyant and controversial style led to many encounters with federal officials and the American Medical Association. At his zenith in the U.S., Hoxsey had thousands of very happy cancer patients going to his 17 clinics across the country. After uncountable arrests, he closed his Dallas clinic in the late 1950s and moved to Mexico to continue practicing. Hoxsey's formula included bloodroot, burdock, buckthorn, cascara, barberry, licorice, red clover, pokeroot, zinc chloride and antimony trisulfide. Hoxsey's general formula has ended up in many escharotics, or topically applied ointments that successfully burn away surface cancers.

■ **Rudolph Steiner, PhD** popularized the use of mistletoe in the early 20th century. A certain lectin in mistletoe has been found to inhibit the growth of proliferating cells. By the 1980s, about 40,000 patients worldwide were receiving Iscador, a fermented form of mistletoe that is injected. Iscador and its variations are licensed in Germany as drugs.

■ **Stanislaw R. Burzynski, MD, PhD** theorized that certain anti-neoplastons, or naturally occurring peptides, could inhibit the growth of tumor cells without interrupting normal cell growth. Burzynski first isolated his anti-neoplastons from human urine and later synthesized these compounds in the laboratory. Dr. Burzynski uses about 10 types of anti-neoplastons in both oral and intravenous fashion. Government authorities have restricted Burzynski to administering his cancer therapy only in his clinic in Houston, Texas, and now even that narrow scope of practice is in jeopardy.

■ **Paul Niehans, MD** developed his "cell therapy" techniques in Switzerland in the 1930s. The principle is that "something" in young tissue is able to regenerate old and sick tissue. Hence, injecting cells derived from whole fetuses is supposed to make old people feel younger and sick people get well. Cell therapy has been used for a wide range of otherwise untreatable conditions, most notably for aging wealthy people to feel younger.

■ **Joseph Gold, MD** of the Syracuse Cancer Research Institute reported good results in the 1970s using hydrazine sulfate to inhibit the growth of tumors in animals. While there certainly are some less effective approaches among alternative cancer therapies, hydrazine sulfate has been found in human clinical studies at the University of California at Los Angeles to reduce lean tissue wasting (cachexia) and improve the abnormal glucose and insulin levels which are common among end stage cancer patients.[10] Hydrazine sulfate, for some unknown reason, has become a tainted subject among traditional cancer researchers, which is a real travesty for millions of cancer patients worldwide.

■ **Ernst Krebs, Sr., MD, and Ernst Krebs, Jr.** were the developers of laetrile, which is amygdalin, a cyanide-containing compound first isolated from the seeds of pit fruit, like apricots. The ancient Egyptians, Chinese, Greeks, and Romans all used seed pits, or amygdalin, as their "sacred seeds" against cancer. Since the 1970s, 70,000 people have used laetrile to treat cancer. Laetrile has become an irrational "head butting contest" between the conventional and unconventional cancer communities.

Ralph Moss, PhD was the science writer for the Sloan-Kettering cancer hospital in New York when research was being conducted by a celebrated scientist, Dr. Kanematsu Sugiura, on laetrile. Dr. Moss writes of a disturbing coverup that basically ended any legitimate assessment of laetrile.[11] Dr. Sugiura found that laetrile did not destroy primary tumors in animals, but did inhibit the growth of tumors and signficantly retarded lung metastases. A San Antonio physician, Dr. Eva Lee Sneak wrote a letter to the editor printed in a publication of the American Medical Association: "Laetrile, properly used, has had, in my hands at least, as good a success as chemotherapy with far fewer side effects."[12]

In 1982, the National Cancer Institute funded a laetrile cancer study conducted by Charles Moertel, MD of the Mayo Clinic. Dr. Moertel's results, published in the prestigious New England Journal of Medicine, played "Taps" for laetrile, claiming that it neither helped cancer nor the symptoms of cancer. About 21 states still allow the use of laetrile in cancer treatment, while other states have revoked medical licenses for the same.

A curious footnote to laetrile is that young plants develop their own naturally occurring pesticides to provide some protection against insects and rodents. This "pesticide" is rich in nitrilosides, which are similar in chemical structure to laetrile. Could it be that a diet high in young fresh plants, like alfalfa sprouts, is like having continuous non-toxic chemotherapy to kill pockets of cancer cells before they can flourish?

■ **Virginia Livingston-Wheeler, MD** felt that cancer was caused by a specific pathogen, Progenitor cryptocides (PC), a cousin of the bacteria that causes leprosy and tuberculosis. Treatment includes immunologic vaccines of PC, pharmacologic therapies and nutritional components. Dr. Livingston helped many cancer patients with her nutritional approaches, which included avoidance of foods that contain PC, like chicken and eggs. However, most cancer patients are immune suppressed and subject to nearly every opportunistic infection that comes along, including PC.

While this bacteria and many others are present in most cancer patients, linking cause and effect is another matter. For instance, fire engines are present at most fires, but they do not cause fires. Yet, other researchers are equally intrigued with the theory that cancer is caused by a bacteria.[13] It is known that older people are at greater risk for both developing cancer and experiencing a reduced output of stomach acid. Since the acid bath of the stomach is supposed to destroy many invading organisms, the theory of "cancer caused by a pathogen" would help to explain the prevalence of cancer in older adults.

■ **I. William Lane, PhD** has been the forerunner in the use of shark cartilage to inhibit angiogenesis and stop tumor growth. Dr. Lane's use patent on cartilage, bestselling book, *Sharks Don't Get Cancer*, and appearance on the TV series "60 Minutes" have heralded a modern champion for non-toxic cancer therapy.

■ **Hans Nieper, MD** is a European physician who uses conventional and unconventional drugs, vitamins, minerals (many of his own design), plant and animal extracts, a certain diet, and avoidance of "geopathogenic zones" which may incite disease.

■ **Otto Warburg, PhD** was awarded two Nobel prizes and first discovered the link between low oxygen levels and cancer growth. Other scientists have proven that cancer becomes more resistant to therapy as the tumor mass becomes more acidic and anaerobic.[14] Warburg's theories provided the foundation for ozone and hydrogen peroxide therapies, which are given intravenously, orally and rectally. While the efficacy of these therapies is controversial, experts caution against drinking hydrogen peroxide, since it is such a potent free radical generator.

■ **Emmanuel Revici, MD** based his treatment on correcting an imbalance between fatty acids and sterols in the cancer patient; called "biological dualism". Revici was considered a very dedicated physician and developer of selenium as an anti-cancer agent.

■ **Ewan Cameron, MD**, a Scottish surgeon first popularized the use of high dose vitamin C in terminal cancer patients. Linus Pauling, PhD, twice Nobel laureate, furthered this cause with studies and writings. While vitamin C is far from a "magic bullet" against cancer, many cancer patients have been found to have clinical scurvy. Both in studies and my experience, high dose vitamin C does improve the quality and quantity of life for most cancer patients.

■ **J.H. Lawrence,** a British scientist during World War II, found that something in urine seemed to have anti-tumor activity in animals. His work has since been refined and carried on by numerous disciples throughout the world.

■ **Lawrence Burton, PhD** developed Immuno-Augmentative Therapy by injecting various blood products into cancer patients to stimulate the immune system. Once a well-respected researcher, Burton was ridiculed by his colleagues and forced to practice in the Bahamas.

■ **714X & Gaston Naessens**. Naessens was driven out of France in the 1950s when he developed a treatment for leukemia called Anablast. He settled in French Quebec in Canada and developed a microscope that supposedly has a much better resolution than other conventional microscopes. Naessens claims to have found "somatids" or "elementary particles endowed with movement and possessing a variable life cycle of many forms." Pleomorphism is the theory that inanimate objects can change into living pathogens and back again. If this principle is true, then traditional microbiologists will have to add a new axiom to their texts: "Ignore all previous axioms." Naessens invented 714X, a compound of camphor and nitrogen, which is injected directly into the lymph system of the cancer patient to bring nitrogen to starving cancer cells.

■ **CanCell (Entelev)** was developed by an analytical chemist and patent attorney, Jim Sheridan. The basics of this formula came to Sheridan in a dream, in which he visualized interrupting the respiratory energy chain of cancer cells. Cancell contains a catechol, a natural chemical that can inhibit respiration. By 1942, Sheridan claimed to be getting better than 70% tumor response in mice studies. In 1953, human clinical trials with Cancell were blocked by the American Cancer Society. In 1961, Sheridan tried proving his theories to the government, which needed to see results in 5 days, while Cancell supposedly takes 28 days to show effect. In 1982, Cancell was put into "handcuffs" when the Food and Drug Administration gave Sheridan an Investigative New Drug (IND) number, then put the project on "clinical hold". By then, Sheridan gave up and turned the formula over to Ed Sopcak, a foundry owner, who has since given away 20,000 bottles of Cancell.

WHERE DO WE GO FROM HERE?

As you can see, alternative therapists have been busy developing their own versions of cancer remedies. There is a serious problem with this long menu of alternative therapies for cancer: the gatekeepers of the Food and Drug Administration, the insurance industry, the American Medical Association and the American Cancer Society have been quick to "throw out the baby with the bathwater". That is, some of these approaches warrant further study, yet they have all been lumped together under the tainted reputation of "fringe" and either discouraged or outlawed. We need to separate the chaff from the grain in these therapies and expose them to some much needed research scrutiny.

It is obvious that no unqualified cure for cancer exists, either in conventional or unconventional circles. Given the disappointing results of traditional cancer therapy, it only makes sense to expand our horizons and look at other possibilities. As cancer is about to become the primary cause of death in Western society and as the "war on cancer" drags into its third decade, we need to ponder the inspirational words from one of history's greatest minds, Benjamin Franklin: "If everyone is thinking alike, then no one is thinking."

PATIENT PROFILE

Mary Schriendl, female, 57 years. I first discovered that I had breast cancer in October of 1989. I had the traditional treatment of mastectomy, followed by seven months of chemotherapy. A year and a half later, I had a recurrence and had radiation and more surgery. No mention was ever made of proper nutrition or the value of nutritional supplements.

In October of 1992, I had another recurrence. This time it had metastasized to the bone. At this time, I went to Cancer Treatment Centers of America. One of the first things that I learned here was the importance of proper nutrition and how vital the right supplements are. I had no idea that sugar actually fed the tumors and how destructive salt and fat are. I have changed my diet drastically and take all of the nutritional supplements recommended.

I am doing well while taking chemo. I feel great and have lots of energy. Everyone finds it hard to believe that I have cancer.

REFERENCES

1. Romm, S, Washington Post, p.Z14, Jan.9, 1990
2. Herman, R., Washington Post, p.Z14, Dec.3, 1991
3. Boly, W, Hippocrates, p.38, Jan.1989
4. Family Practice News, vol.10, Sept.1990
5. Office of Technology Assessment, ASSESSING THE EFFICACY AND SAFETY OF MEDICAL TECHNOLOGIES, U.S. Govt. Printing Office,Washington, DC, 1978
6. American Western Life, 100 Foster City Blvd, Foster City, CA 94404-1166; ph. 415-573-8041; see also Sidha National Insurance Group, Box 122, Fairfield, IA 52556; ph. 800-383-9108; see also Alternative Health Insurance, Box 9178, Calabasas, CA 91372; ph. 818-509-5742
7. Jansson, B., Cancer Detection and Prevention, vol.14, no.5, p.563, 1990
8. Jacobs, MM (ed.), VITAMINS AND MINERALS IN THE PREVENTION AND TREATMENT OF CANCER, CRC Press, Boca Raton, FL, 1991
9. Wrba, H., Therapie Woche, vol.37, p.7, 1987
10. Chlewbowski, RT, et al., Cancer Research, vol.44, p.857, 1984
11. Moss, RW, THE CANCER INDUSTRY, Paragon, NY, 1989
12. American Medical News, Jan.15, 1982
13. White, MW, Medical Hypotheses, vol.32, no.2, p.111, June 1990
14. Newell, K, et al., Proceedings of the National Academy of Science, USA, vol.90, no.3, p.1127, Feb.1990; see also White, MW, Medical Hypotheses, vol.39, no.4, p.323, Dec.1992

CHAPTER 3

PROGRESS REPORT IN THE WAR ON CANCER

C ancer is not a new phenomenon. Archeologists have discovered tumors on dinosaur skeletons and Egyptian mummies. From 1600 B.C. on, historians find records of attempts to treat cancer. In the naturalist Disney film, "Never Cry Wolf", the biologist sent to the Arctic to observe the behavior of wolves found that the wolves would kill off the easiest prey, which were sometimes animals suffering from leukemia. Cancer is an abnormal and rapidly growing tissue which, if unchecked, will eventually smother the body's normal processes. Cancer may have been with us from the beginning of time, but the fervor with which it attacks modern civilization is unprecedented.

President Richard Nixon declared "war on cancer" on December 23, 1971. Nixon confidently proclaimed that we would have a cure for cancer within 5 years, by the 1976 Bicentennial. However, by 1991 a group of 60 noted physicians and scientists gathered a press conference with the message: "The cancer establishment confuses the public with repeated claims that we are winning the war on cancer... Our ability to treat and cure most cancers has not materially improved."[1] The unsettling bad news is irrefutable:

- newly diagnosed cancer incidence continues to escalate, from 1.1 million Americans in 1991 to an anticipated 1.3 million in 1993
- deaths from cancer in 1992 are projected at 520,000, up from 514,000 in 1991
- since 1950, the overall cancer incidence has increased by 44%, with breast cancer and male colon cancer up by 60% and prostate cancer by 100%
- for decades, the 5 year survival has remained constant for non-localized breast cancer at 18% and lung cancer at 13%
- only 5% of the $1.8 billion annual budget for the National Cancer Institute is spent on prevention

- grouped together, the average cancer patient has a 50/50 chance of living another five years; which are the same odds he or she had in 1971
- claims for cancer drugs are generally based on tumor response rather than prolongation of life. Many tumors will initially shrink when chemo and radiation are applied, yet tumors often develop drug-resistance and are then unaffected by therapy.
- by the turn of the century, cancer is expected to eclipse heart disease as the number one cause of death in America. It is already the number one fear.

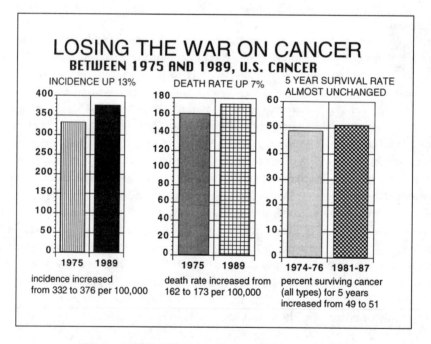

LOSING THE WAR ON CANCER
BETWEEN 1975 AND 1989, U.S. CANCER

INCIDENCE UP 13%   DEATH RATE UP 7%   5 YEAR SURVIVAL RATE ALMOST UNCHANGED

1975   1989

1975   1989

1974-76   1981-87

incidence increased from 332 to 376 per 100,000

death rate increased from 162 to 173 per 100,000

percent surviving cancer (all types) for 5 years increased from 49 to 51

HAVE WE MADE ANY PROGRESS?

D epending on which expert you subscribe to, the war on cancer has been either "a qualified failure" or "is progressing slowly". No one is willing to spread the propaganda that it has been a victory. According to the National Cancer Institute (NCI), five year survival rates (definition of a cure) have increased from 20% of cancer patients in 1930 to 53% of adults and 70% of children today.[2] Critics of the NCI claim that living 5 years after diagnosis has nothing to do with being cured, and that earlier diagnosis alone could account for the improvement in survival.

There are 7 million Americans living today who have been cured of cancer. Twenty years ago, surgery for breast cancer routinely removed the entire breast, lymph nodes and chest muscles in a procedure called radical mastectomy. New methods favor a "lumpectomy" or removal of merely the lump, followed by radiation and/or chemotherapy. In other words, surgeons are becoming more rational and restrained in their efforts to surgically remove the cancer.

Richard Adamson, PhD, Chief of Cancer Etiology at the National Cancer Institute, says that progress has been made against cancer as death rates from colon and rectal cancer have fallen 15-20% in the last 20 years; and other death rates have dropped, including 20% for ovarian, 30% for bladder and 40% for cervical cancer.

LOSING THE WAR ON CANCER— TIME FOR EXAMINING OPTIONS

The purpose of this section is not to blast the National Cancer Institute, but rather to make it blatantly obvious that our current cancer treatment methods are inadequate and incomplete and that we need to examine some options—like nutrition. A growing body of dissidents cite data to refute the NCI's confident numbers. Among the skeptics is John Bailar, MD, PhD of Harvard University, whose outspoken article in the prestigious *New England Journal of Medicine* ushered in a champion for the many strident critics of the National Cancer Institute.[3] Bailar, as a member of the National Academy of Sciences and former editor of the Journal of the National Cancer Institute, cannot be ignored. Dr. Bailar confronts the NCI's unfounded enthusiasm with "We are losing the war against cancer" and has shown that the death rate, age-adjusted death rate and both crude and age-adjusted incidence rate of cancer continues to climb in spite of efforts by the NCI. Non-whites are excluded from the NCI statistics for vague reasons. Blacks, urban poor, and the 11 million workers exposed to toxic substances have all experienced a dramatic increase in cancer incidence and mortality. Less than 10% of patients with cancer of the pancreas, liver, stomach and esophagus will be alive in five years.[4]

As a percentage of total annual deaths in America, cancer has escalated from 3% in 1900 to 22% of today's deaths. Many experts have been quick to explain away this frightening trend by claiming that our aging population is responsible for the increase in cancer incidence—older people are more likely to get cancer.

But aging does not entirely explain our epidemic proportions of cancer in America.

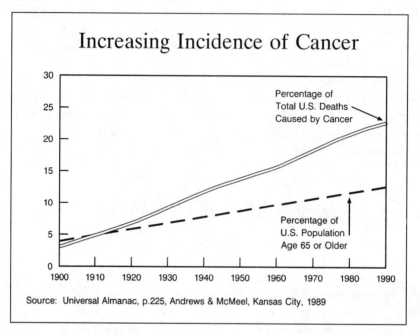

Increasing Incidence of Cancer

Source: Universal Almanac, p.225, Andrews & McMeel, Kansas City, 1989

Perhaps the most tragic "pawns" in this game are the children. The NCI admits to a 28% rise in the incidence of childhood cancers from 1950 through 1987, much of which is due to the ubiquitous presence of environmental pollutants.[5] On the other side of the coin, progress in pediatric oncology has produced cure rates in some forms of childhood cancer of up to 90%, which makes chemotherapy for childhood cancers an NCI victory, of sorts. However, while these patients do survive longer, they have a much higher risk for developing bone cancer later in life as a result of the chemo and/or radiation therapy.[6]

Not that money should be a top priority when health and life are at stake, but our health costs are out of control. We spend about $950 billion per year or 12% of our Gross National Product on health care, compared to Sweden at 8%, a socialistic country with free health care for all, and our former American level of 3% in the year 1900. Even after adjusting for inflation, we spend twice as much money on health care for the elderly as we did prior to the inauguration of Medicare.[7] Cancer care is the most expensive of all diseases, costing Americans about $110 billion annually.

Albert Braverman, MD, a full professor of oncology at the State University of New York, has published in the prominent medical journal, *Lancet,* a biting review of chemotherapy as sole therapy against cancer: "Many medical oncologists recommend chemotherapy for virtually any tumour, with a hopefulness undiscouraged by almost invariable failure."[8] And if Bailar started all this rancor, then Ulrich Abel, PhD of the Heidelberg Tumor Center in Germany has brought the issue to a fever pitch. Abel, a well-respected biostatistics expert, published a controversial 92 page review of the world's literature on survival of chemotherapy-treated cancer patients; showing that chemotherapy alone can help only about 3% of the patients with epithelial cancer (such as breast, lung, colon and prostate) which kills 80% of total cancer patients. "...a sober and unprejudiced analysis of the literature has rarely revealed any therapeutic success by the regimens in question."[9]

A prominent scientist from the University of Wisconsin, Johan Bjorksten, PhD, has shown that chemotherapy alone destroys the immune system beyond a point of return, which increases the risk for early death from infections and other cancers in these immunologically-naked people.[10] Critics of American cancer treatment point out that the therapy may sometimes be worse than the condition. Researchers reported in the *New England Journal of Medicine* that the risk of developing leukemia from chemotherapy treatment of ovarian cancer outweighs the benefits of the therapy.[11]

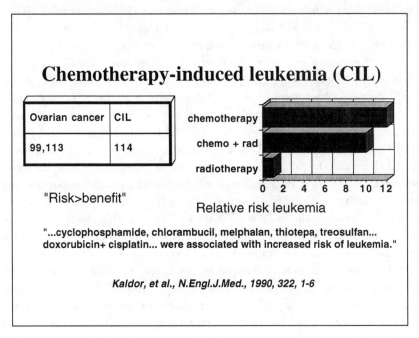

Chemotherapy-induced leukemia (CIL)

Ovarian cancer	CIL
99,113	114

"Risk>benefit"

chemotherapy
chemo + rad
radiotherapy

0 2 4 6 8 10 12

Relative risk leukemia

"...cyclophosphamide, chlorambucil, melphalan, thiotepa, treosulfan... doxorubicin+ cisplatin... were associated with increased risk of leukemia."

Kaldor, et al., N.Engl.J.Med., 1990, 322, 1-6

Breast and prostate cancer have recently surfaced in the press as "forgotten cancers" due to their intimate nature. While one out of 20 women in 1950 were hit with breast cancer, today that number is one in nine. Even with early detection and proper treatment, a "cured" breast cancer patient will lose an average of 19 years of lifespan. Breast cancer kills about 45,000 women each year.[12] Lack of faith in cancer treatment has led a few physicians to recommend that some women with a high incidence of breast or ovarian cancer in their family undergo "preventive surgery" to remove these high risk body parts.[13] Life and health insurance companies now refer to healthy intact women as "with organs" and at high risk, therefore forced to pay higher health insurance premiums.

And while breast cancer is tragic, prostate cancer is equally prevalent in men and even more lethal. The NCI spends one fourth the amount on prostate cancer research as on breast cancer research. There are no good early screening procedures for prostate cancer, which means that in 85% of the prostate cancers found, the cancer has spread beyond the prostate gland and is difficult to treat. Comparing the outcome of 223 patients with untreated prostate cancer to 58 patients who underwent radical prostatectomy, the 10 year disease-specific survival was 86.8% and 87.9% respectively. There was essentially no difference in survival between the treated and untreated groups.[14]

While tamoxifen is being administered to thousands of cancer patients and trials are underway to eventually use tamoxifen as a chemo-preventive agent for millions of high risk breast cancer patients, other data shows that tamoxifen is carcinogenic, with a 60% increase in cancer in the tamoxifen-treated humans.[15]

According to an extensive review of the literature, there has been no improvement in cancer mortality from 1952 through 1985.[16] These authors state: "Evidence has steadily accrued that [cancer therapy] is essentially a failure." There are no good screening tests for colon cancer. Meanwhile, we spend millions researching molecular biology in a futile quest for a "magic bullet" against cancer.[17] A London physician and researcher has provided statistical backing for his contention that breast cancer screenings in women under age 50 provides no benefit in 99.85% of the premenopausal women tested.[18] The average cancer patient still has only a 40-50% chance of surviving the next five years, same odds as 30 years ago. A gathering chorus of scientists and clinicians proclaim that success from chemo and radiation therapy has plateaued and we need to examine alternative therapies.[19]

A 1971 textbook jointly published by the American Cancer Society and the University of Rochester stated that biopsy of cancer tissue may lead to the spread of cancer.[20] Although encapsulated cancer can be effectively treated with surgery and 22% of all cancer can be "cured" through surgery[21], 30% or more of surgery patients with favorable prognosis still have cancer recurrences.[22] A study of 440,000 cancer patients who received chemotherapy or radiation showed that those treated with radiation had a significantly increased risk for a type of leukemia involving cells other than the lymphocytes.[23] Long term effects of radiation include: birth defects and infertility. Short term effects include: mouth sores and ulcers which can interfere with the ability to eat, rectal ulcers, fistulas, bladder ulcers, diarrhea and colitis.

Analysis of over 100 clinical trials using chemotherapy as sole treatment in breast cancer patients found no benefits and significant damage from the chemotherapy in post-menopausal patients.[24] A member of the National Cancer Advisory Board, Dr. Rose Kushner, pointed out that toxic drugs are "literally making healthy people sick" and are "only of marginal benefit to the vast majority of women who develop breast cancer."[25] While some scientists and clinicians argue that chemotherapy does not cure breast cancer but can add a few years to the patients' lives; other experts counter that chemotherapy actually shortens the life of breast cancer patients.[26]

According to a psychologist writing in the *American Cancer Society Journal*, "the side effects of cancer chemotherapy can cause more anxiety and distress than the disease itself."[27] A well-recognized side effect of chemotherapy is suppression of bone marrow, which produces the white blood cells that fight infection. This common immune suppression leads to the all-too-common death from infection.[28]

According to the literature which comes with each chemotherapeutic agent, methotrexate may be "hepatotoxic" (damaging to the liver) and suppresses immune function. Adriamycin can cause "serious irreversible myocardial toxicity (damage to heart) with delayed congestive heart failure often unresponsive to any cardiac supportive therapy." Cytoxan can cause "secondary malignancies" (cancer from its use). It is widely known among health care professionals that just working around chemotherapy agents can cause birth defects.[29]

In spite of $35 billion in research at the NCI and billions more spent in private industry, there have been no new chemotherapy drugs discovered in the past 20 years.[30] Not even NCI official, Dr.Daniel Ihde, can conjur up any enthusiasm for the failure of chemotherapy drugs against lung cancer.[31] Given the limited successes in traditional cancer treatment, it is not surprising that 50% of all American cancer patients seek "alternative therapies".

Biological therapies, such as interferon and interleukin, are extremely toxic, with treatment requiring weeks of hospitalization, usually in intensive therapy, with multiple transfusions, severe bleeding, shock, and confusion as common side effects.[32] Interferon causes rapid onset of fever, chills, and severe muscle contractions that may require morphine.[33]

WHERE DID WE GO WRONG?

T here has been a lot of finger pointing since the war on cancer was so heavily criticized. For starters, it would be easy to blame bread mold, from which springs penicillin, which was discovered by Alexander Fleming in 1928 and gave us hope that there was a "magic bullet" against every disease. We could rest equal blame on Jonas Salk, inventor of the polio vaccine in 1952, for such a tremendous show from his medicine bag. With a simple vaccine, one of the most tragic pandemic plagues of history was felled. Again, more reasons to believe that a "magic bullet" against every disease must exist.

Another scapegoat is good old patriotic pride. After all, it was the Americans who rode into World Wars I and II to rescue the world. Americans stepped in to finish the Panama Canal after the French had failed. Americans have more patents and Nobel laureates than any other nation on earth. We had good reasons to be confident of curing cancer.

Some of our problem lies in scientific research models. Using animals with induced leukemia, a non-localized disease of the blood-forming organs, is not a realistic representation of how well a cancer drug will work against a solid human tumor. We have also made the erroneous assumption that "no detectable cancer" means no cancer. A million cancer cells are undetectable by even the most sensitive medical equipment. A billion cancer cells become a tiny and nearly undetectable "lump".[34] When the surgeon says,"We think we got it all."— that is when the war on cancer must become an invisible battle involving the patient's well-nourished immune system.

We also have wrongly guessed that "response rate", or shrinkage of the tumor, is synonymous with cure. As mentioned, chemotherapy works on cancer cells like pesticides work on insects. Spraying pesticides on a field of plants may kill 99% of the bugs in the field, but the few insects that survive this baptism of poison have a unique genetic advantage to resist the toxicity of the pesticide. These "super bugs" then reproduce even more rapidly without competition, since the pesticides killed off biological predators in the field and reduced the fertility of the soil for an overall drop in plant health. Similarly, blasting a typically malnourished cancer patient with bolus (high dose once per week) injections of chemotherapy alone may elicit an initial shrinkage of the tumor, but the few tumor cells that survive this poison become resistant to therapy and may even accelerate the course of the disease in the now immune-suppressed patient. Meanwhile, the once marginally malnourished patient becomes clinically malnourished since nausea becomes a prominent symptom in bolus chemo usage. An expert in cancer at Duke University, Dr. John Grant, has estimated that 40% or more of cancer patients actually die from malnutrition.[35]

We also made the mistake of becoming enamored with a few tools that we thought could eradicate cancer. We focused all of our energies in these three areas and ridiculed or even outlawed any new ideas. Because the real reason for our failure lies in our error in thinking. The wellness and illness of our bodies is almost entirely dependent on what we eat, think, drink, move, and breath. These forces shape our general metabolism, which is the sum total of bodily processes. Our metabolism then either favors or discourages the growth of both infectious and degenerative diseases. Cancer is a degenerative disease of abnormal metabolism throughout the body—not just a regionalized lump or bump.

Our health is composed of a delicate interplay of nutrients consumed, and toxins expelled, coupled with mental and spiritual forces that influence metabolism. We are a product of our genes, lifestyle and environment. We are not dumb automobiles to be taken to the mechanic and fixed. We are physical and metaphysical beings who must become part of the cure, just as surely as we are a part of the disease process. Healing is a joint effort between patient, clinician, and that mysterious and wonderful Force which most of us take for granted. The days of "magic bullet" cures are over. The days of cooperative efforts between patient and clinician are here to stay.

ONLY TEAMWORK WILL BEAT CANCER

Shortly before the turn of the millenia, cancer will become the number one cause of death in Western society.[36] Cancer is a cruel disease that infiltrates the body with abnormal tissue growth and finally strangles its victims with malnutrition, infections or multiple organ failure. We need teamwork in cancer treatment because of the formidable "Predator" that we face. We cannot discard any cancer therapy, no matter how strange or perpendicular to medical theories, unless that therapy does not work. There are no "magic bullets" against cancer, nor can we anticipate such a development within our lifetime. We need to join the forces of traditional oncology with the ancillary fields of nutrition, psychology, detoxification, exercise physiology, botanical extracts and others to develop a more complete arsenal against cancer.

Chemotherapy has its role, especially for certain types of cancer and when administered in fractionated dose or via intra-arterial infusion to a therapeutically nourished patient. Radiation therapy has its place, especially as the highly targeted brachytherapy. Surgery has its place, especially when the tumor has been encapsulated and can be removed without bursting the collagen envelope. Hyperthermia can be extremely valuable in about 4% of all cancer cases. Combinations of these traditional therapies are becoming better accepted in medical circles. Later in this book, you will see the synergism in creative combinations of conventional and unconventional cancer therapies, like quercetin (a bioflavonoid) and heat therapy or niacin with radiation therapy. The take home lesson here is: "Just because traditional medicine has failed to develop an unconditional cure for cancer, doesn't mean that we should categorically reject all traditional approaches."

Our reigning allopathic medical system has maintained a philosophy that most diseases have a readily identifiable enemy that can be surgically removed or blasted into submission with chemo and radiation. Comprehensive cancer treatment uses traditional cancer therapies to reduce the tumor burden, while concurrently building up the "terrain" of the cancer patient to fight the cancer on a microscopic level. That is the "one-two punch" that will eventually bring the Predator of cancer to its knees.

PATIENT PROFILE

M.H., female, admitted to our hospital at age 65 years. M.H. came to our center in September of 1990 with a diagnosis and biopsy showing cancer of the pancreas with pulmonary lesions (spread to the lungs). Her tumor marker CEA was 9.6 (very high, extensive cancer) and CA19-9 was 3300 units. In her hometown, M.H. was told that there was no treatment of any benefit. M.H. was treated at our facility with chemotherapy, parenteral nutrition for her weight loss, and aggressive nutrition supplements, including enzymes.

Her condition improved markedly within 2 months. She maintained an excellent quality of life for the next 27 months. At that time, February 1993, she was in for a check up in her hometown hospital, caught the flu and passed away within 48 hours.

M.H. is included to show the reader that even untreatable cancers often respond to adjuvant nutrition therapy. M.H. savored her last 27 months of life, which was largely a gift of nutrition therapy, since all other oncologists had given up on her. Nutrition did not cure M.H., but it did dramatically improve her quality and quantity of life.

REFERENCES

1.   Ingram, B., Medical Tribune, vol.33, no.4, p.1, Feb.1992
2.   Mayo Clinic Health Letter, vol.10, no.2, , p.1, Feb.1992
3.   Bailar, JC, New England Journal of Medicine, vol.314, p.1226, May 1986
4.   Squires, S, Washington Post, p.Z19, Dec.3, 1991
5.   Epstein, SS, and Moss, RW, The Cancer Chronicles, p.5, Autumn 1991
6.   Weiss, R., Science News, p.165, Sept.12, 1987
7.   Stout, H, Wall Street Journal, p.B5, Feb.26, 1992
8.   Braverman, AS, Lancet, vol.337, p.901, Apr.13, 1991
9.   Abel, U., CHEMOTHERAPY OF ADVANCED EPITHELIAL CANCER: A Critical Survey, Hippokrates Verlag Stuttgart, 1990
10. Bjorksten, J, LONGEVITY, p.22, JAB Publ., Charleston, SC, 1987
11. Kaldor, JM, et al., New England Journal of Medicine, vol.322, no.1, p.1, Jan.1990
12. Neuman, E, New York Times, Insight, p.7, Feb.9, 1992
13. Bartimus, T., Tulsa World, p.B3, Dec.22, 1991
14. Johansson, JE, et al., Journal American Medical Association, vol.267, p.2191, Apr.22, 1992
15. Ralof, J., Science News, vol.141, p.266, Apr.25, 1992
16. Temple, NJ, et al., Journal Royal Society Medicine, vol.84, p.95, 1991
17. Temple, NJ, et al., Journal Royal Society of Medicine, vol.84, p.95, Feb.1991
18. Shaffer, M., Medical Tribune, p.4, Mar.26, 1992
19. Hollander, S., et al., Journal of Medicine, vol.21, p.143, 1990
20. Rubin, P., (ed), CLINICAL ONCOLOGY FOR MEDICAL STUDENTS AND PHYSICIANS: A MULTI-DISCIPLINARY APPROACH, 3rd edition, Univ. Rochester, 1971
21. American Cancer Society, "Modern cancer treatment" in CANCER BOOK, Doubleday, NY, 1986
22. National Cancer Institute, Update: Primary treatment is not enough for early stage breast cancer, Office of Cancer Communications, May 18, 1988
23. Curtis, RE, et al., Journal National Cancer Institute, p.72, Mar.1984
24. New England Journal Medicine, Feb.18, 1988; see also Boffey, PM, New York Times, Sept.13, 1985
25. Kushner, R., CA-Cancer Journal for Clinicians, p.34, Nov.1984
26. Powles, TJ, et al., Lancet, p.580, Mar.15, 1980
27. Redd, WH, CA-Cancer Journal for Clinicians, p.138, May1988
28. Whitley, RJ, et al., Pediatric Annals, vol.12, p.6, June 1983; see also Cancer Book, ibid.
29. Jones, RB, et al., California Journal of American Cancer Society, vol.33, no.5, p.262, 1983
30. Hollander, S., and Gordon, M., Journal of Medicine, vol.21, no.3, p.143, 1990
31. Ihde, DC, Annals of Internal Medicine, vol.115, no.9, p.737, Nov.1991
32. Moertel, CG, Journal American Medical Association, vol.256, p.3141, Dec.12, 1986
33. Hood, LE, American Journal Nursing, p.459, Apr.1987
34. Dollinger, M., et al., EVERYONE'S GUIDE TO CANCER THERAPY, p.2, Somerville House, Kansas City, 1990
35. Grant, JP, Nutrition, vol.6, no.4, p.6S, July 1990 supl
36. Meyskens, FL, New England Journal of Medicine, vol.23, no.12, p.825, Sept. 1990

Chapter 4

The Link Between Nutrition and Cancer

C ancer is a disease of metabolic imbalance. It could originate in a thousand different ways. Yet the body has many built-in mechanisms to thwart the progress of cancer. Scientists agree that nearly all individuals develop undetectable cancer about six times in a 70 year lifespan. Yet only one of three people actually develops overgrown and detectable cancer. With built-in biological check points for detoxification, genetic correction, immune stimulation, and sealing off an abnormal cell growth, the body is equipped to deal with cancer. But all of these biological check points rely heavily on nutrition, which is a serious problem for the typically malnourished American.

■ **Preventing and reversing cancer.** It has now been well accepted that proper nutrition could prevent from 50-90% of all cancer.[1] It has also been well documented that various nutrients can reverse pre-malignant conditions, including: folic acid and cervical dysplasia (abnormal cells in the cervix), vitamin A and oral leukoplakia (mouth lesions), vitamin E and fibrocystic breast disease, folic acid and bronchial metaplasia (abnormal cells leading to the lungs). Each of these conditions are "regionalized cancers" that have not yet sprung forth into the rest of the body. The next step is for metastasizing cancer.

What is truly remarkable is the apparent inter-relationship of nutrients against cancer. Betel nuts provide a tobacco-like chew for hundreds of millions of people in third world countries. The effects of betel nuts includes a pre-cancerous condition called oral leukoplakia, in which there is a white film over the mouth surface, which can mature into full blown cancer. Years ago, researchers showed that vitamin A or beta-carotene can reverse oral leukoplakia. In a quest for a patentable version of vitamin A that would have the same results, researchers dabbled with 13-cis retinoic acid in oral leukpoplakia, yet found severe toxicity reactions. Now we find that vitamin E may do what vitamin A did, without any side effects, and that beta-carotene coupled with vitamin E shows the greatest synergistic and non-toxic combination of all.

Researchers at M.D. Anderson Hospital in Houston gave 800 iu of vitamin E daily to 43 patients with oral leukoplakia for 24 weeks of treatment. Twenty of the 43 subjects, or 47%, had clinical responses, which means at least 50% disappearance of lesions, and 9 more had histological improvements (can be seen on a microscope). Given the toxicity of 13-cis-retinoic acid, it seems that vitamin E deserves further attention as a chemopreventive agent.[2]

So nutrition is definitely a potent weapon at preventing cancer, and has been scientifically demonstrated to reverse certain pre-cancerous conditions. The question then becomes: "How far downhill can this cancerous process roll before nutrition is no longer effective?" No one knows.

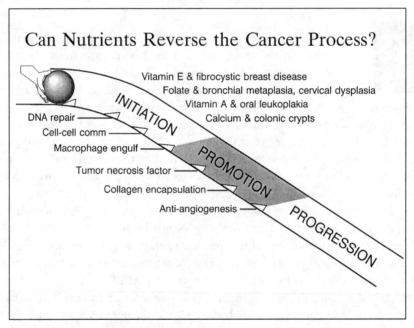

Can Nutrients Reverse the Cancer Process?

■ **Long History.** There is a long history in the link between nutrition and cancer. Over 2000 years ago, Chinese medical texts referred to "an immoderate diet" increasing the risk for esophageal cancer.[3] Throughout the early 20th century, epidemiological and animal lab data continued to accumulate showing that a diet high in fat and/or low in vitamin A elevated the risk for cancer. By 1964, the evidence was sufficient for the World Health Organization panel, headed by the noted authority Sir Richard Doll, to issue a tidy little pamphlet on the causes of cancer, including nutrition. All of the cancer risk factors listed in this booklet still ring surprisingly true today. By 1982, the National Academy of Sciences in America endorsed the nutrition to cancer link with their technical book that began with an unscientifically exuberant proclamation: "Spread the good news that cancer is not as inevitable as death and taxes."

■ **Negative image**. Unfortunately, the nutrition to cancer link also has a negative connotation that must be overcome. Some of the early efforts at using nutrition in cancer treatment centered around starving the patient with the intent of starving the cancer out of the body. Didn't work. As experts in parasitology know, the host usually dies before the parasite. Next came drugs that interfered with nutrient pathways in the body, such as the folic acid inhibitor, methotrexate. These early scientists reasoned: "Obviously, if drugs that inhibit vitamin pathways can slow cancer, then high dose supplements will only make matters worse". Also, not so. The scant evidence that was provided by proponents of nutrition in cancer treatment consisted of emotional testimonials. A few researchers labored intensely on a Holy Grail quest for one nutrient that might cure cancer—with no results.

■ **Nutrients feed cancer?** Then physicians tried to use the fledgling field of parenteral nutrition, involving feeding liquid nutrients through a vein, to prevent wasting cancer patients from starving to death. The nourishment accelerated the disease. Once again, the cancer specialists reasoned, "If you feed the patient, then you also feed the tumor." However, in recent research, scientists found that the standard high sugar, low protein parenteral formula used to feed these cancer patients does indeed accelerate tumor growth, while a newly developed disease-specific formula of low sugar and high protein may selectively starve the tumor.[4]

Case closed, thought the pioneer oncologists. Not only does nutrition not help the cancer patient, but it may accelerate the course of the disease. Even in 1992 after extensive research, it is entirely possible that some nutrients–notably iron, salt, sugar, and omega 6 fats like corn oil–may accelerate tumor growth. With such a dubious beginning, it would take a miracle to resurrect medical interest in nutrition for cancer patients. But miracles are happening.

■ **Paradigm shift**. Nutrition is a science, born out of the related disciplines of biochemistry, anatomy, physiology, pharmacology, and medicine. Historically, early nutrition scientists looked at nutrients to prevent clinical deficiency syndromes. A newer paradigm examines secondary functions of nutrients when given at "higher-than-normal" intake levels:

- Various nutrients have been shown to reverse pre-malignant lesions.
- Vitamin C intake at 300 mg daily, which is 500% of the RDA, provides an extra 6 years of life in men.
- Folacin supplements at 200% of the RDA can virtually eliminate neural tubes defect, a common birth defect also called spinal bifida. The Center for Disease Control, a branch of the federal government, has issued a

statement encouraging women of childbearing years to take supplements of folacin. Meanwhile, another branch of the federal government, the Food and Drug Administration, is making serious efforts to make nutrition supplements only available by prescription.

- Various nutrients at above RDA levels, including B-6, zinc, selenium, and vitamin E, have been shown to elevate immune function beyond what is accepted as "normal", which provides for 6 colds per year and a 33% chance of eventually getting cancer.
- Vitamin E supplements at 600% of the RDA lowers the risk for heart disease dramatically.
- Niacin supplements becomes a potent and non-toxic agent to lower serum cholesterol when given at 1000% of RDA levels.
- Certain inherited mental problems, including autism (with B-6 & magnesium), schizophrenia (many nutrients), and bipolar (phosphatidylcholine and tyrosine) are improved and sometimes cured with therapeutic levels of nutrients.[5]

Essentially, nutrients are emerging as the "biological response modifiers" of choice when considering side effects, efficacy and cost. For a more in-depth look at the thousands of studies which document the therapeutic value of nutrients, see:

- my book HEALING NUTRIENTS
- NUTRITIONAL INFLUENCES ON ILLNESS by Melvyn Werbach, MD
- THE REAL VITAMIN AND MINERAL BOOK by Shari Lieberman, PhD,RD
- THE ENCYCLOPEDIA OF NATURAL MEDICINE by Michael Murray, ND
- THE DOCTOR'S VITAMIN AND MINERAL ENCYCLOPEDIA by Sheldon Hendler, MD, PhD.

There is a clear and unmistakable trend in the scientific literature showing that high dose nutrients have potent therapeutic benefits and have very few side effects.

■ **Synergy with medicine.** The synergy between adjuvant nutrition and traditional oncology will likely blossom throughout the 1990s into the accepted mode of humane, cost effective, and clinically effective comprehensive cancer treatment. I have yet to find any valid data showing that proper nutrition therapy will reduce the therapeutic value of medical approaches to cancer. Briefly, the advantages of implementing nutrition as part of cancer therapy include:

1. *Avoiding malnutrition.* Cancer is a major stress on the body, often causing lean tissue wasting (cachexia) as the body "cannabolizes" its own protein reserves (catabolism) to stay afloat. Tumors are major parasites that drain nutrient reserves from the host. Often, the first symptom of cancer is weight loss. Many tumors can induce loss of appetite in the host. Malnutrition leaves the patient even more vulnerable to tumor progress, infection, reduced response to medical therapy and significant loss in quality of life. Nutrition therapy is the only treatment for malnutrition.

2. *Mitigating the symptoms of conventional medical treatment.* Properly nourished patients experience less nausea, malaise, hair loss and organ toxicity than patients on routine oncology programs. Cancer patients will sometimes give up therapy because of hair loss, which happens in nearly all chemo patients. Yet studies show that loading the patient with 1600 iu of vitamin E daily for 1 week prior to beginning therapy will allow 69% of patients to keep their hair.[6] When high dose anti-oxidants are given to cancer patients for a week prior to beginning chemo or radiation therapy, the resultant fatigue and nausea can be dramatically reduced. Another common side effect of chemotherapy is mucositis, or mouth sores, which are painful and can limit food intake. In a double blind study, 67% of patients given topical vitamin E on their mouth sores improved in the 5 day test period, while only 11% of patients on placebo showed improvement.[7] Beta-carotene has shown a similar ability to prevent these nasty mouth sores.[8] For over 20 years, scientists have known that by improving the overall quality of the diet prior to and during radiation therapy, patients had a better response to radiation treatment.[9]

3. *Synergistic action with medical treatments.* Certain nutrients, like beta carotene, vitamin C, vitamin E, and selenium appear to enhance the effectiveness of chemo, radiation, and hyperthermia while minimizing damage to the patient's normal cells. See the many references in the last chapter for more information.

4. *Anti-proliferative factors.* While nutritionists often speak of nutrients for proper growth, rarely does anyone mention when growth should taper off. Just like a furnace that keeps cranking out the heat without any shutoff mechanism, cancer is unregulated growth. There is evidence that certain nutrients, like selenium and the fatty acid EPA, have the ability to slow down unregulated growth. Various nutrition factors, including vitamin A, D, folacin and soybeans, have been shown to influence DNA expression in both healthy and tumor tissue.

5. *Anti-tumor agents*. There are numerous factors in our diet that directly fight tumor cells. Garlic, yogurt, seaweed, cruciferous vegetables, seed foods (like soybeans), dark green leafy vegetables, and tomatoes all contain factors that kill tumor cells and/or stimulate the immune system to produce other anti-tumor components, like interferon or natural killer cells. Many components of dark green leafy vegetables have been found to stimulate immune activity while protecting against the damage from radiation therapy.[10] There is also evidence that the individual nutrients of beta-carotene and selenium may be directly toxic to tumor cells. In a landmark study, researchers at Harvard University found that injections of vitamin E, canthaxanthin (a carotenoid compound much like beta-carotene), and extract of spirulina algae *reversed* cancer of the mouth in hamsters.[11]

6. *Prevention*. Most medical treatments for cancer are carcinogenic themselves. We use deadly poisons to hopefully kill off more cancer cells than host cells. Yet, cancer patients have already demonstrated their genetic vulnerability to cancer. For this reason, a major problem in cancer treatment is dealing with the impending tumors that are likely to develop in the patient even if they recover from this current bout with cancer. Proper nutrition minimizes the risk for future tumors.

7. *Guidance*. Many cancer patients are tempted by foods that would lessen their chances of recovery due to altered taste buds from therapy. Chemotherapy kills rapidly dividing cells, of which about 80% will be cancer cells and 20% will be healthy rapidly growing body cells, primarily the lining of the tongue, lining of the gastro-intestinal tract, hair, nails and the immune system. Because of the damage to the taste buds, cancer patients often have unusual cravings for high sugar, high fat, nutrient-depleted junk food. Their taste buds have temporarily shut down and only foods with strong flavors sound good. To submit to this temptation would be a bad idea. Another problem is that cancer cells are sugar-feeders and tend to siphon glucose out of the bloodstream, thus leaving the patient with lower blood glucose levels and the appetite mechanism in the brain lobbying for the person to eat high sugar foods. Yet to submit to these cravings would be like throwing gasoline on a spark.

NUTRITION AFFECTS THE IMMUNE SYSTEM

I n the classic thriller from H.G. Wells, WAR OF THE WORLDS, a highly advanced Martian army descends on the earth to take over. The Martian war machines completely overwhelm the paltry defenses of earthlings, when suddenly, all of the Martian war machines topple over with dead occupants. As the author explains, the Martians had long since developed such an advanced society that they had eliminated all disease-causing organisms from their environment, with the resulting effect that their immune systems atrophied for lack of use. Once on earth, amidst our teeming sea of lethal microorganisms, the Martians were no match for tenacious humans. Though the earthlings may have lost the outside war to the Martians, just as medicine is losing the visible war against cancer, our sturdy inner soldiers of the immune system can win the overall battle—against the Martians and cancer.

Most of the great pandemic plagues of history have been preceded by either a war or a crop failure. Take a major dose of psychological stress, whip in widespread malnutrition and sprinkle generously with foreigners innoculating the local people with new diseases for which there is no acquired immunity. Such a situation killed 75 million people, or half the known world, in the 14th century in Europe. Another 21 million people died from the flu epidemic that followed World War I. Historians are only beginning to estimate the millions of Native Americans and Polynesians who died when Europeans brought their new diseases, stress and malnutrition to the New World. From the 16th to 19th centuries, natives from Africa and the Americas were nearly exterminated, not unlike the Martians, by a barrage of infectious diseases.

While there is plenty of evidence linking blatant malnutrition with blatant immune problems, the immune system loses efficiency with even slight malnutrition, or negative emotions or exposure to poisons. The typical American lifestyle of bad diet, stress and exposure to endless pollutants is like making a checklist on how to get cancer.

The trillions of specialized warriors in our immune system are on 24 hour duty, vigilantly destroying and mopping up virus, bacteria, yeast, tumor cells, toxins from both inside and outside the body and even dead cells. When the immune system is crippled by a virus, AIDS may be the result. When the immune system goes awry and begins attacking its own friendly host tissue, then auto-immune diseases may set in, like arthritis, Crohn's disease and allergies. When the immune system is not functioning at peak efficiency, we may get a cold or an infection. And when the immune system is subdued for any extended period of time, cancer may result.

Immune soldiers are produced in the bone marrow (called B-cells), the thymus gland (called T-cells), the spleen and lymphoid tissue. Among the more crucial immune factors that fight cancer are interleukin, interferon, lymphocytes, Natural Killer cells (NK) and tumor necrosis factor (TNF). Immune soldiers work by literally swallowing the cancer cells (phagocytosis) or spraying toxic chemicals on the cancer cells (chemotaxis). Arginine supplements help kill cancer cells, possibly by providing "bullets" for the immune system, since arginine is so heavily laddened with amine groups which can be dumped on cancer cells as nitric acid. Supplements of arginine and thymus extract also increase the output of the thymus gland to make more T-cells.

One of the main thrusts of this book is to maximize your immune capabilities. Unfortunately, most medical treatments, like chemotherapy and radiation, are serious immune depressants. These therapies also induce a loss of appetite which further depresses the immune system with malnutrition. When nutritional support of the immune system is dovetailed with medical treatments, there is often a synergistic tumor kill rate that neither nutrition nor medicine can attain alone. The results are increased chances for recovery with minimal side effects from medical treatment.

The immune system is literally a scoreboard of a person's nutrient intake, since dietary nutrients provide the raw materials (precursors) to build and maintain the immune system The bulk of immune bodies are composed of protein, which explains why a protein deficiency often leads to depressed immune function. Many cancer warriors, including interleukin and interferon are all measurably reduced in protein malnutrition.

Basically, scientists have shown that "normal" nutrition in America leads to a "normal" immune system, while above-normal nutrient intake provides above-normal immune response. For instance, B-6 supplements at 50 mg per day provided a measurable improvement in immune functions (T3 and T4 lymphocytes) for 11 healthy well fed older adults.[12] Both in animals and humans, normal vitamin E intake is not adequate to optimize immune functions.[13], but modest supplements of vitamin E do enhance the immune response. Various B vitamins have been linked to the proper functioning of antibody response and cellular immunity. Folate deficiency decreases production of communication substances in the immune system, called mitogens. Deficiency of vitamin C impairs phagocyte functions and cellular immunity, for lowered ability to engulf cancer cells.. Vitamin E deficiency decreases antibody response to T-dependent antigens, all of which gets worse when you add in a selenium deficiency.

Zinc exerts a major influence on the immune system. Lymphocyte function is seriously depressed and lymphoid tissues undergo general atrophy in zinc-deficient individuals. The lymphocytes in zinc-deficient animals quickly lose their killing abilities (cytotoxicity) and engulfing talents (phagocytosis) for tumor cells and bacteria. Natural killer cell and neutrophil activity is also reduced. Copper plays a key role in the production of superoxide dismutase and cytochrome systems in the mitochondria, hence, a deficiency of copper is manifested in a depressed immune system. Iodine allows immune soldiers to make lethal substances to kill invaders. Boron deficiency in chicks creates immune abnormalities like arthritis. Toxic trace minerals, like cadmium, arsenic, and lead all blunt the immune system.

Selenium works in conjunction with vitamin E to shield immune warriors from the toxins dumped on tumor cells. This process allows an increased efficiency of the immune system. Instead of one immune factor killing one cancer cell, then dying in a suicidal pool of toxins; the immune soldier lives on to kill other cancer cells.

In magnesium deficiency, all immunoglobulins (except IgE) are reduced, along with the number of antibody forming cells. Magnesium is crucial for lymphocyte growth and transformation of immune soldiers in response to mitogens sounding the "battle call". Prolonged magnesium deficiency in animals leads to the development of lymphomas and leukemia.

Many of the trace minerals relate to immune competence. Iron presents a particularly unusual case because:

1. iron deficiency anemia is one of the most common malnutritive conditions in the world
2. iron deficiency will depress the immune system
3. iron excess may stimulate tumor growth
4. unbound iron can trigger free radical destruction, which can suppress immune functions, attack the delicate DNA or accelerate aging.

Just as the iron in your car can rust, the iron in your body can rust, or oxidize, and damage delicate tissue and blood vessel walls. Good research shows that higher iron reserves in the body will elevate the risk for both cancer and heart disease.[14] Unbound iron, which is an oxidizing metal, coupled with low level anti-oxidants may create a "dynamite and blasting cap" situation in the body to trigger cancer. You need enough nutrients to make adequate red blood cells, requiring folacin, B-12, B-6, zinc, iron, copper and protein. You also need enough anti-oxidants, like beta-carotene, vitamin C, E, and selenium, to ensure that iron will not oxidize and damage the precious DNA. Also, the oxidized iron salts (ferric chloride) used to fortify white flour should be avoided.

Cancer can bind up iron supplies for its own growth and also use the iron like a battering ram to barge through cell membranes. Hence, many cancer patients have very low blood levels of iron. Yet giving a cancer patient high doses of non-heme iron may accelerate tumor growth. We have found that patients' serum iron levels will spike up precipitiously when the medical therapy starts killing the tumor, which causes the tumor to release its iron stores. The liver will then begin to store the excess iron from the bloodstream and anemia goes away. Iron intake needs to be well regulated—not too much, and not too little and always in the presence of anti-oxidants to check the destructive internal "rusting" of iron.

Too much fat or the wrong kind of fat in the diet will depress the immune system. A deficiency of the essential fatty acid (linoleic acid) will lead to atrophy of lymphoid tissue and a depressed antibody response. And yet excess intake of polyunsaturated fatty acids, like soy and corn oil, will also diminish T-cell immune responsiveness. Intake of protein, carbohydrate and fat influences insulin levels which drive the prostaglandin pathways, which have a major impact on immune performance. Sustained high blood sugar levels, such as occurs in the high sugar diet of most Americans, will depress immune function. Oxidized cholesterol is highly immuno-suppressive. Cholesterol is less likely to oxidize while in the presence of anti-oxidants, like vitamin E, C, and beta-carotene.

Basically, nutrition plays a critical role in the effectiveness of the immune system. A healthy immune system is better able to join in the battle to rid the body of tumor cells.

NUTRIENTS AS BIOLOGICAL RESPONSE MODIFIERS

While many very bright people have labored intensely, extensively and expensively to develop some "magic bullet" substance that would cure cancer, Nature has been patiently working on the same project for a couple of billion years. The National Cancer Institute has dedicated much time and resources to creating "biological response modifiers (BRM)", such as interferon, tumor derived activated killer cells (TDAK) and interleukin in an effort to use biological agents to kill cancer. Thus far, this work has been disappointing, since the side effects are so dramatic, the cost so high, and results are good in only a few types of cancers, like kidney cancer.

However, you can take effective, inexpensive and non-toxic BRM agents— available now at your grocery and health food store. Americans choose their food for reasons of taste, cost, convenience and psychological gratification. All of those reasons are fine as long as the top priority in food selection is its BRM activity. Everything that you put into your mouth will eventually have an impact on your health—for better or for worse.

Biologists are fascinated with the different levels of cancer incidence in animals. Most creatures don't live long enough to get cancer. A majority of chickens will get cancer if allowed to live beyond 3 years. Many cattle carry a virus that has been linked to leukemia. Several epidemiological studies show that cat owners have a slightly elevated risk for cancer, perhaps due to the feline leukemia virus carried by many cats. Sharks will not get cancer, even if bathing in cancer causing agents, due to the special proteins in shark cartilage that inhibit cancer growth. While other fish usually don't live long enough to get cancer, in some polluted streams and lakes in America, two out of three fish have cancer from industrial carcinogens.

Among humans, cancer incidence is 33% in heavily polluted America, but 7% in underdeveloped nations, while archeologists speculate that 0.1% of our primitive ancestors got cancer. The reason for this major difference in cancer incidence is that our level of stress, pollution and refined diets have overloaded, underfed or shut down the BRMs developed by Nature to squelch cancer growth in humans.

Think of your built-in cancer protective mechanisms like a defensive football line, arranged in hierarchical pattern. If the cancer (runner) breaks through the front line tackles and guards (primary defense), then the linebackers (secondary defense) are supposed to shut down the cancer. If secondary defense mechanisms are overwhelmed, then the defensive backs (tertiary defense) are called upon. More on this subject in chapter 7, which explains the strategy of why my program works.

The more I study Nature and the human body, the more reverence I develop for the Great Engineer who designed us. There are elaborate and elegant systems in place in your body to prevent and even reverse the growth of cancer. While cancer is certainly taking its toll in suffering and lives, cancer is not our predetermined fate. We have chosen to ignore the laws of nature which provide substantial cancer protection. Americans live in a treacherous environment of stress, toxins and non-nutritive food. When, not if, our bodies begin to fail, then we try surgery or poisons to get rid of the defective parts. Just as surely as the law of gravity pulls us to earth, the law of BRMs is inescapable. Our current system is not working. The answers to cancer lie patiently waiting for humans to swallow our pride and accept the protective mechanisms which have evolved over eons. In a later chapter, the action plan shows you how to use readily available foods and supplements to restore these protective mechanisms back into optimal functioning.

From this brief explanation, you can see that humans are not entering the arena unprepared to fight cancer. Cancer has been with us long enough that we have evolved various procedures to thwart cancer. What you put in your mouth can have a major bearing on the quality and quantity of life for cancer patients. Food, water, oxygen and supplements can be potent BRMs in cancer treatment.

RISK TO BENEFIT TO COST RATIO OF NUTRITION THERAPY

Modern medicine is founded on principles of allopathic drugs and surgery, which are unsurpassed methods in emergency medicine. Although these techniques are very risky, not applying them may be even more risky. Hence, the modern physician and nurse develop a very skeptical approach to any treatments that claim to help. If the treatment helps, then it must carry with it a long list of complications and side effects. With nutrition, that is usually not the case.

To illustrate, Henry Turkel, MD, both a physician and scientist, found that a certain collection of nutrients improved the overall condition of Down's syndrome. He was able to demonstrate changes in IQ, immune capacity, appearance and even X-rays by using his nutrition formula. He applied for a drug patent on his "Eutrophic" formula in 1959, but was denied FDA approval because there was no toxicity level for his formula.[15] The FDA will only allow therapeutic claims to be made on any substance after the applicant has proven both the effective dose and the toxic dose, called the lethal dose required to kill half the rats (LD-50). Since Dr. Turkel's formula had no toxicity, it could not be granted a drug patent. Many Americans still have the misconception: "If it can't hurt you, then it can't help you either."

There are major differences between drugs and nutrients. Hence, the risk to benefit paradigm is dramatically different. To contrast drugs and nutrients:

DRUGS	NUTRIENTS
non-essential	essential for life
most are created in a lab	created in nature
minimal time for adaptation	long term adaptation
many are toxic and dangerous	few are toxic
excess can do harm	excess usually excreted
valuable in acute care	valuable in chronic care
work quickly, forcefully	work slowly, subtly
accelerate or inhibit pathways	precursors for pathways
many are addictive	none are addictive
many have side effects	no side effects at useful dose
	rare side effects at high dose
drug/nutrient interactions	nutrient/nutrient interactions
narrow window of effectiveness	wide window of effectiveness

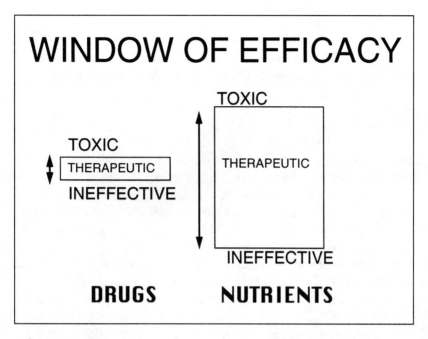

There are a few nutrients that can be toxic when used indiscriminately. Preformed vitamin A, from animal sources or as retinyl palmitate, can be toxic when pregnant women consume as little as 10 times the RDA, or when others consume as little as 200 times the RDA. The plant version of vitamin A (beta-carotene) is non-toxic in humans. Vitamin D can create calcium and heart abnormalities in some sensitive individuals when consumed at levels of 5 times the RDA for many months. Iron toxicity is possible in adult males, since they have no monthly outlet for excess iron stores. Acute iron toxicity is possible and happens at least 6 times each year when some child eats an entire bottle of adult formulated vitamins with iron. Selenium toxicity may start as low as 25 times the RDA in some sensitive adults. Show me a prescription drug which is safe for anyone at 25 times the recommended intake.

Although vitamin and mineral supplements can be abused, they are rarely harmful and almost never fatal. Compare the safe track record of nutrients to the estimated 300,000 annual deaths in America from drug and surgery complications, called iatrogenic deaths. According to the Food and Drug Administration, Center for Disease Control and Public Citizen Health Research Group, one year of adverse prescription drug reactions included:

- 61,000 people with induced parkinsonism
- 32,000 hip fractures, including 1,500 deaths
- 16,000 injurious car crashes

- 163,000 with memory loss
- 659,000 hospitalizations
- 28,000 cases of life-threatening or fatal reactions to digoxin (digitalis)
- 41,000 hospitalizations, including 3,300 deaths from aspirin-like compounds
- all together, 9.6 million older adults each year suffer adverse drug reactions

Meanwhile, there has not been a fatality from vitamins, minerals, herbs or homeopathic remedies in the past 10 years. You can see why the risk to benefit ratio indicates that nutrients may help and rarely do any harm.

For the cancer patient, nutritional supplements can cost up to $20 per day with a full regimen of vitamins, minerals, amino acids, shark cartilage and herbal extracts. Enteral feedings can cost up to $40 per day and parenteral feedings (nutrients injected into the veins) can cost $600 per day. Compare these cancer costs to $900 per day for drugs, $3400 per day for hospitalization and $100,000 for bone marrow transplant operation. Many cancer patients outlive their insurance, which often is a $200,000 maximum that the insurance company will pay. Not only is nutrition therapy effective and safe, but about as cost effective as it gets in health care.

THE AUTHORITIES' VIEWPOINT OF NUTRITION AND CANCER

The data on nutrition and cancer has become so overwhelming that the National Cancer Institute has instigated a "Designer Foods Division" which is charged with researching the various known anti-cancer substances in food, like indoles from cabbage. The National Institute of Health has been pressured into opening a new branch, called the Office of Alternative Medicine, which will provide research grants to further examine some of the topics discussed in this book. The National Cancer Institute is now spending about $100 million annually to investigate the prospects of using nutrition to prevent cancer. The Office of Technology Assessment, an advisory branch of Congress, listed nutrition as one of the few credible alternative cancer approaches.

Both the Surgeon General of the United States and the National Academy of Sciences, which include our most decorated scientists, have endorsed the nutrition to cancer link. Even the American Dietetic Association has offered their recommendations for using nutrients to help prevent cancer: 12,500 iu. for vitamin A, 200-800 iu. for vitamin E, 1000 mg for vitamin C, and 200 mcg for selenium.[16] All of these doses are well above Recommended Dietary Allowances

(RDA) levels and constitute an enlightened change of policy for the ADA.

Professors at Harvard University have published considerable evidence in the prestigious *New England Journal of Medicine* showing that 90% of all cancer is environmentally caused and therefore preventable. Our incidence of breast cancer is 500% higher than Japan and is related to our diet. These experts highlight the power broker nutrients in cancer: fat, selenium, vitamin A, C, E, and fiber.[17]

While most of these groups strongly endorse the ability of nutrition to prevent cancer, they are less enthusiastic about using nutrition as part of comprehensive therapy. Yet, in degenerative diseases, like heart disease and cancer, the cause is directly linked to the cure. The same diet that Dr. Gerson used to help reverse cancer is now endorsed by the American Cancer Society to help prevent cancer. If allergies caused the arthritis, then only allergy avoidance will cure the arthritis. If chromium deficiency caused the adult onset diabetes, then only chromium supplements will cure the diabetes. While 15,000 iu of beta carotene can dramatically cut the risk for getting cancer, it may take 100,000 iu of beta carotene in the cancer patient to provide therapeutic stimulation of the immune system. While the numbers may change, there is a common thread running between a nutrition program to prevent cancer and one to buttress traditional cancer therapy.

WHY DON'T MORE HOSPITALS USE NUTRITION IN CANCER TREATMENT?

Many patients come to me with the same misinformation: "My doctor told me that nutrition has nothing to do with cancer outcome, so I should eat whatever I want". I then must spend considerable time explaining to these patients that their doctors are providing the best information available from their peer groups and mean no harm to the patient in this "sin of omission". If the data in my book is so solid, non-toxic, and cost-effective, then why don't all hospitals use it? There are a number of obstacles.

1. Physicians are not trained in nutrition. An old saying goes: "What you are not up on, you are down on." Physicians are very bright and capable individuals who have saturated their brains with over a decade of rigorous and expensive college education. Doctors are quick to delegate patient care to the ancillary specialists of respiratory therapists, physical therapists, occupation therapists, and psychologists. Yet, in spite of the fact that physicians are not trained in nutrition, they insist on controlling nutrition. This illogical hierarchy leads to inadequate patient care and needs to be remedied. Let the experts of various fields work together in a cooperative venture to heal the patient. Let's not make the patient's illness a forum for power struggles.

2. Time lags. It takes decades if not centuries to implement proven findings. It was two thousand years after the Greek astronomer, Eudoxus, discovered that the earth was not at the center of the solar system before his findings were finally accepted. Spanish explorers in the 17th century brought potatoes back to Europe, and, in spite of the fact that an advanced Incan culture had thrived on potatoes for centuries, the European scientists proclaimed the potatoes only acceptable as animal feed. In the early 1900s, gold and aspirin were acceptable treatments for arthritis. Then someone proposed that arthritis was an infectious disease, hence aspirin and gold were discarded as worthless therapies, even though they worked. In the past decade, evidence was re-established that arthritis is a degenerative disease, and that aspirin and gold are effective treatment. It was fifty years after limes were positively proven to prevent and cure scurvy that limes were finally mandated aboard all English vessels. It was twenty years after niacin was proven to both prevent and treat pellagra that scientists finally accepted the fact. Time lags are an unfortunate aspect of life and can be a fatal aspect of cancer treatment.

3. Nutrition therapy is often not reimburseable. Patients are nearly totally dependent on their insurance companies for paying health bills. Many insurance companies will not pay claims for nutrition therapy, sometimes even for life-saving nutrition support for starving patients. It has been proven beyond argument that the well-nourished patient is better able to manage any disease, including cancer. Insurance companies will pay $3,000 per day for cancer patients to be hospitalized, but balk at the idea of paying $20 per day for therapeutic supplements to dramatically improve quality and quantity of life for the cancer patient.

PRIORITIZING NUTRITIONAL NEEDS OF THE CANCER PATIENT

Not all nutritional intervention is of equal value for the cancer patient. For instance, if you wanted your car to go faster, it would be much more effective to put in a bigger engine, rather than remove the outside mirrors for less wind resistance. Similarly, I have met people who were more concerned with the pesticides residues on their food supply than the 2 packs of cigarettes they were smoking. We need to keep our fears and risk factors in the proper perspective. I have ranked the main nutrition approaches used to treat cancer in descending order: those listed first are most critical. Don't waste time with something minor, when a major issue has been neglected.

■ **Avoid malnutrition.** Up to 40% of all cancer patients die from malnutrition[18]. It is crucial to provide quality calories and protein to slow down the wasting that often occurs in cancer. Cancer elevates calorie needs, while chemotherapy often causes nausea and poor eating habits. The metabolic by-products of cancer can blunt the appetite. End result: the patient ends up eating less and needing more. The consequences can be catastrophic. For patients who cannot or will not eat, nutrients can be infused into the patient's veins, a medical process called total parenteral nutrition, or TPN.

■ **Immune stimulation.** There is an abundance of data linking nutrient intake to the quality and quantity of immune factors that fight cancer. Therapeutic levels of vitamins C, E, A, beta-carotene, zinc, selenium and others are crucial to nourish the microscopic battle within.

■ **Protection from therapy.** While chemo and radiation therapy can significantly reduce tumor burden, they can also be carcinogenic. By loading the patient with therapeutic levels of anti-oxidants (vitamins E, C, beta-carotene, selenium, and some botanicals), the oncologist can make medical therapy more of a "selective toxin". Tumor cells do not absorb anti-oxidants as efficiently as do healthy cells. The net effect is to first give "bullet proof vests to the good cells", then "spray the area with machine gun fire" (i.e. chemo and radiation) to kill more cancer cells. Secondary tumors, a serious problem in various cancers, can be prevented with optimal nutrient loading during cancer therapy.

■ **Selectively starve the tumor.** Tumors are primarily "sugar feeders", meaning that they are fueled by blood glucose, not fats or protein. Americans not only consume about 20% of their calories from refined sugar, but also ride the roller coaster of wild swings in blood glucose levels. This constant intravenous infusion of cancer fuel is a primary reason for our cancer incidence. By maintaining lower levels of blood glucose, the patient can selectively starve the tumor while also reaping the benefits of lower insulin output which favorably steers prostaglandin synthesis. Also, the sodium to potassium ratio in the American diet favors the growth of tumors. It has been speculated that a high salt diet changes the dynamics of all cell membranes and makes the passage of oxygen and nutrients more difficult across the membrane barrier. The atmosphere then becomes ideal for cancer growth.

■ **Feed Biological Response Modifiers.** Provide optimal support for the internal biological mechanisms that help us all fight cancer all of the time.

DOES NUTRITION REALLY HELP CANCER PATIENTS?

Y es. There have been many efforts to pinpoint any number of "magic bullet" nutrients for cancer patients. Yet, only a few scientists have conducted more realistic research using a comprehensive blend of a healthy diet coupled with high dose nutrition supplements. Drs. Hoffer and Pauling instructed patients to follow a reasonable cancer diet, similar to what is outlined in this book, coupled with therapeutic doses of vitamins C, A, E, niacin, and a broad spectrum vitamin and mineral supplement. All 129 patients in this study received the best oncology care available in North America—whatever his or her doctor felt was most appropriate. The results of this study are nothing short of headlines material. The group of 31 patients who did not receive nutrition support lived an average of less than 6 months. The group of 98 cancer patients who did receive the diet and supplement program were categorized into 3 groups:

- Poor responders (n=19) or 20% of treated group. These people may have been nearly unsalvageable with their advanced cancer. They had an average lifespan of 10 months, or a 75% improvement over the group not on nutrition. Some cancer patients have exhausted their "cellular reserve" or ability to recover from disease.
- Good responders (n=47), who had various cancers, including leukemia, lung, liver, and pancreas; had an average lifespan of 6 years.
- Good female responders (n=32), with involvement of reproductive areas (breast, cervix, ovary, uterus); had an average lifespan of over 10 years. Many were still alive at the end of the study.

In another study, Dr. Marc Goodman and colleagues at the University of Hawaii examined the diet and lifespan of 675 lung cancer patients over the course of 6 years. The more vegetables that women consumed, the longer they lived; with a 33 month lifespan for best veggie eaters and 18 months for veggie haters.[19] A separate group of researchers provided high doses of vitamins A, C, and E to cancer patients who were being treated by traditional oncologists. Of the 20 patients evaluable for a response after one year, 7 had a complete response (35%), 8 had a partial response (40%) and 5 failed therapy (25%).[20] A particularly intriguing patient in this study had advanced pancreatic cancer with metastasis to the liver. He recovered completely with no sign of disease, which happens in

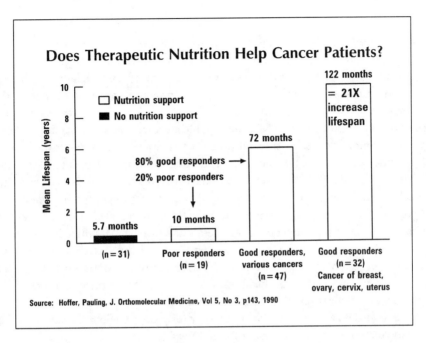

Does Therapeutic Nutrition Help Cancer Patients?

- □ Nutrition support
- ■ No nutrition support

122 months
= 21X increase lifespan

72 months

80% good responders →
20% poor responders

5.7 months

10 months

(n = 31)

Poor responders
(n = 19)

Good responders,
various cancers
(n = 47)

Good responders
(n = 32)
Cancer of breast,
ovary, cervix, uterus

Mean Lifespan (years)

Source: Hoffer, Pauling, J. Orthomolecular Medicine, Vol 5, No 3, p143, 1990

less than 2% of pancreatic patients.

Professor Harold Foster of the University of British Columbia examined lifestyle changes in patients who experienced "spontaneous regression" from cancer, which is a euphemism for "these people should have died". Anything that we can learn from these cancer victors who beat the odds may be valuable. Of these survivors, 87% made a major change in diet, mostly vegetarian in nature, 55% used some form of detoxification and 65% used nutritional supplements.[21] Researchers compared survival in macrobiotic followers versus patients who continued with their standard Western lifestyle. Of 1467 pancreatic patients who made no changes in diet, 142 (10%) were alive after one year, while 12 of the 23 matched pancreatic patients (52%) consuming macrobiotic foods were still alive after one year.[22] Similar benefits were seen in 9 prostate cancer patients adhering to macrobiotic foods (median survival 228 months) versus 9 matched controls who made no changes in diet (medium survival 45 months).

Nick Gonzales, MD is a Sloan-Kettering trained oncologist who uses a comprehensive nutrition program to treat cancer patients. Dr. Gonzales reports far better than average results in his advanced cancer patients.

Cancer Treatment Centers of America has been using nutrition as part of a comprehensive cancer therapy program for 18 years. Thousands of our patients have enjoyed a marked improvement in quality and quantity of life due to adjuvant nutrition therapy. Many were given a death sentence by other clinics.

I have personally worked with hundreds of cancer patients who have made dramatic recoveries through adjuvant nutrition therapy.

Cornelius Moerman, MD was a Dutch physician who lived to the ripe age of 95, during which he spent 40 years developing a nutrition program that helped hundreds of cancer patients. Dr. Moerman's program is now accepted by the Dutch government as a legitimate cancer therapy.[23] A physician wrote about his use of the macrobiotic diet to beat untreatable advanced prostatic cancer.[24] Anne Frahm, a young mother of three children, battled advanced breast cancer for 2 years with surgery, chemo, radiation and bone marrow transplant. When her physicians finally gave up on her, she used the macrobiotic diet to beat her cancer.[25] Another book has compiled 30 cancer victors who triumphed over advanced cancer with nutrition and mental changes after failing medical therapy.[26] One of the founders of this field, Max Gerson, MD highlighted his 30 years of clinical experience with 50 exemplary cancer victors who used his nutrition program to beat cancer.[27] Charles Simone, MD is one of the few oncologists in the world who has been trained in all three medical therapies to fight cancer: medical oncology, tumor immunology and radiation therapy. Dr. Simone has used aggressive nutrition therapy for years to help hundreds of cancer patients, including former president Ronald Reagan.

The odds of all these successes being nothing but random occurrence are about the same odds as you being struck by a meteor while sleeping tonight. A professionally managed nutrition program not only improves the quality and quantity of life for nearly all cancer patients, but also improves the odds of complete remission—a cure.

THE COMPONENTS OF A NUTRITION PROGRAM

Providing proper nutrient intake levels requires a multi-faceted approach to nutrition:

1. Food. If the gut works and if the patient can consume enough food through the mouth, then this is the preferred route for nourishing the patient. We are only beginning to understand the elegant symphony of anti-cancer substances in our diet. Food is a high priority item in the nutrition program for cancer. When the GI tract is not used, it can atrophy or bacteria can cross from the intestines into the bloodstream to cause infections.

2. Supplements. Additional vitamins, minerals and other supplements in both pill and powder form can make significant contributions to the patient's nutrient intake.

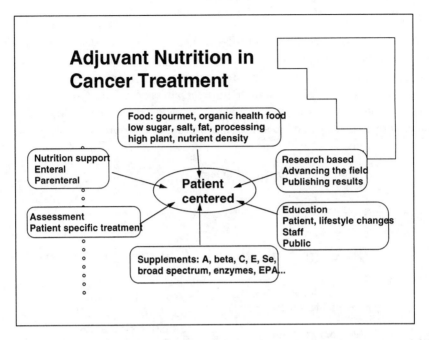

3. Total parenteral nutrition (TPN). There are many cancer patients who are so malnourished that we must interrupt this deterioration with "tube feedings". TPN allows the Metabolic Support Team of physician, nurse, dietitian and pharmacist to provide quality nutrient intake in spite of the patient's inability to eat. TPN can be an invaluable life raft during the crisis phase of cancer treatment.

4. Assessment. It is important to determine the patient's nutrient status through:

- Computer diet analysis to provide a nutrient breakdown of what the patient has been eating.
- Allergy testing to find problems in immune function.
- Functional vitamin assays to determine how close to saturation blood vitamin levels are.
- Provocative mineral assays to detect sub-optimal levels.
- Health history form, including habits and environmental exposure to health hazards, which offers clues regarding the origin of the cancer.
- Physician's examination of skin, eyes, grip strength, tongue, and other external signs can provide vital clues to the patient's nutrient status.
- Percent body fat via skinfold or Futrex infrared analysis is a key indicator of cachexia (lean tissue wasting) or obesity.
- Calorimeter measures the oxygen consumed and carbon dioxide exhaled to provide exact information regarding the patient's calorie needs.

5. *Education*. The patient needs a sense of involvement and control in their condition, which can improve the chances for recovery. Just as much as the patient's lifestyle may have contributed to the problem, an involved patient can help reverse the problem. We need to convert the patient into a valuable ally, rather than trying to force unwanted lifestyle habits onto an unwilling person.

6. *Research*. Those who advance the knowledge base have a responsibility to properly gather data and report their findings to the world.

PROGRESS SLOW–BUT SWEET

Adjuvant Nutrition in Cancer Treatment

THEN:	NOW:
-Starve tumor out of patient??	-Textbook from AICR
-Vitamin inhibitors slow cancer...?	-Am.J.Clin.Nutr. AOX
-TPN, high dextrose, low protein...?	-Pres.Reagan treated with adj.nutr.
-Nutrients^ tumor: Fe, Na, glu, n-6	-NIH new office "Alternative Medicine"
-Little/no research from alternatives?	-popular press: NY Times, Time Mag.
-Theoretical: AOX vs Pro-ox. vit. K vs. anti-coag.	-OTA report: "Unconventional Ca.Treat"
-Western science: one variable???	-NIH conference: "Vitamin C & cancer"
-Phase 1 vs 2 in nutrition science	

I n the 1950s, Dr. Max Gerson, was ostracized and defrocked in the U.S. for his notion that eating properly might help the course of otherwise untreatable cancer patients. Today, the American Cancer Society has endorsed a diet that is remarkably similar to Gerson's diet. In the 1970s, twice Nobel laureate and member of the prestigious National Academy of Sciences, professor Linus Pauling, was ostracized for suggesting that vitamin C may improve the quantity and quality of life for cancer patients. Pauling's work eventually inspired a conference held at the National Institute of Health in 1990 on the subject of vitamin C and cancer. Recently, a prominent cancer journal featured Pauling's face on the cover. In the early 1980s, it was difficult to get any credible scientists to attend meetings that looked at nutrition to prevent cancer. In November of 1992, the world's finest researchers from the best universities gathered to cross-pollinate their findings on using nutrients as "non-toxic chemotherapy". The time's they are a changin'.

PATIENT PROFILE

Valeri Radcliffe, female, 55 years. On November 7, 1992, I entered the hospital for tests since I could barely breath. After numerous tests, the diagnosis was stage IV cancer. Primary breast cancer with massive lung metastasis had left me little room for breathing. I was a very sick lady. Many doctors thought that I would never leave the hospital. My doctor thought it was too late for chemo and I probably couldn't tolerate it anyway.

I made a choice. I chose life and the Jesus that I had praised. The Lord gave me a peace about cancer. I asked my doctor what I should eat. He said to eat whatever I could keep down. My spirit rebelled and I called Dr. Quillin, a good friend. He sent me information on diets and what nutrients to take, which I am still on. I find now that I am unable to return to my old way of eating, which was not the best. I have a new energy now, even though I am still on chemo. As of March 19, 1993, my blood work shows no tumor. The tumor that was once the size of a grapefruit cannot be felt at all. My last X-ray showed that my lungs are clear of fluid. My doctor marvels at my recovery. He calls me a walking wonder.

REFERENCES

1. Quillin, P, HEALING NUTRIENTS, Random House, NY, 1987
2. Benner, SE, et al., Journal National Cancer Institute, vol.85, p.44, 1993
3. U.S. Dept. Health Human Services, THE SURGEON GENERAL'S REPORT ON NUTRITION AND HEALTH, p.177, GPO # 017-001-00465-1, Washington, DC, 1988
4. Rothkopf, M., Nutrition, vol.6, no.4, p.14S, July/Aug 1990 suppl.
5. Werbach, M., NUTRITIONAL INFLUENCES ON MENTAL ILLNESS, Keats, New Canaan, CT, 1990
6. Wood, L, New England Journal Medicine, vo.312, no.16, p.1060, 1985
7. Wadleigh, RG, American Journal of Medicine, vol.92, p.481, May 1992
8. Mills, EE, British Journal of Cancer, vol.57, p.416, 1988
9. Cheraskin, E., et al., Acta Cytologica, vol.12, no.6, p.433, 1968
10. Lau, BH, International Journal of Clinical Nutrition, vol.12, no.3, p.147, July 1992
11. Shklar, G., et al., European Journal Cancer and Clinical Oncology, vol.24, no.5, p.839, 1988

12. Talbott, MC, et al., American Journal of Clinical Nutrition, vol.46, p.659, 1987
13. Bendich, A., et al., Journal of Nutrition, vol.116, p.675, 1986
14. Nutrition Reviews, vol.47, no.6, p.176, June 1989; see also Stevens, RG, et al., New England Journal of Medicine, vol.319, p.1047, 1988
15. Turkel, H., Journal of Orthomolecular Psychiatry, vol.4, no.2, p.102, 1975
16. Watson, RR, and Leonard, TK, Journal of the American Dietetic Association, vol.86, p.505, Apr.1986
17. Willett, WC, and MacMahon, B., New England Journal of Medicine, vol.310, p.633, Mar.8, 1984; and again p.697, Mar.15, 1984
18. Grant, JP, Nutrition, vol.6, no.4, p.7S, July 1990 supplement
19. Goodman, MT, et al., European Journal of Cancer, vol.28, no.2, p.495, 1992
20. Sakamoto, A, et al., in MODULATION AND MEDIATION OF CANCER BY VITAMINS, p.330, Karger, Basel, 1983
21. Foster, HD, International Journal Biosocial Research, vol.10, no.1, p.17, 1988
22. Carter, JP, et al., Journal American College of Nutrition,vol.12, no.3, p.209, 1993
23. Jochems, R., DR. MOERMAN'S ANTI-CANCER DIET, Avery, Garden City, NY, 1990
24. Sattilaro, AJ, RECALLED BY LIFE, Avon, NY 1982
25. Frahm, AE, et al., A CANCER BATTLE PLAN, Pinon Press, Colorado Springs, 1992
26. East West Foundation, CANCER FREE, Japan Publ, NY 1991
27. Gerson, M., A CANCER THERAPY, Gerson Institute, Bonita, CA 1958

CHAPTER 5

MALNUTRITION AMONG
CANCER PATIENTS

H oward Hughes, the multi-billionaire, died of malnutrition. It is hard to believe that there can be malnutrition in this agriculturally abundant nation of ours—but there is. At the time of the Revolutionary War, 96% of Americans farmed while only 4% worked at other trades. Tractors and harvesting combines became part of an agricultural revolution that allowed the 2% of Americans who now farm to feed the rest of us. We grow enough food in this country to feed ourselves, to make half of us overweight, to throw away enough food to feed 50 million people daily, to ship food overseas as a major export, and to store enough food in government surplus bins to feed Americans for a year if all farmers quit today. With so much food available, how can Americans be malnourished?

The answer is: poor food choices. Americans choose their food based upon taste, cost, convenience and psychological gratification—thus ignoring the main reason that we eat, which is to provide our body cells with the raw materials to grow, repair and fuel our bodies. The most commonly eaten foods in America are white bread, coffee and hot dogs. Based upon our food abundance, Americans could be the best nourished nation on record. But we are far from it.

Malnutrition in typical "healthy" American

average annual consumption of low nutrient foods:

756 doughnuts

60 pounds cakes & cookies

23 gallons ice cream

7 pounds potato chips

22 pounds candy

200 sticks gum

365 servings soda pop

90 pounds fat

134 pounds refined sugar

CAUSES OF NUTRIENT DEFICIENCIES

And there are many reasons for developing malnutrition:

1. **DON'T EAT IT.** Due to poor food choices, loss of appetite, discomfort in the gastro-intestinal region, or consuming nutritionally bankrupt "junk food"; many people just don't get enough nutrients into their stomach.
2. **DON'T ABSORB IT.** Just because you eat it, does not necessarily mean that it will end up in your body. Malabsorption can occur from loss of digestive functions (including low hydrochloric acid or enzyme output), allergy, "leaky gut" or intestinal infections.
3. **DON'T KEEP IT.** Increased excretion or loss of nutrients can be due to diarrhea, vomiting or drug interactions.
4. **DON'T GET ENOUGH.** Increased nutrient requirements can be due to fever, disease, aging, alcohol or drug interactions.

Overwhelming evidence from both government and independent scientific surveys shows that many Americans are low in their intake of:[1]

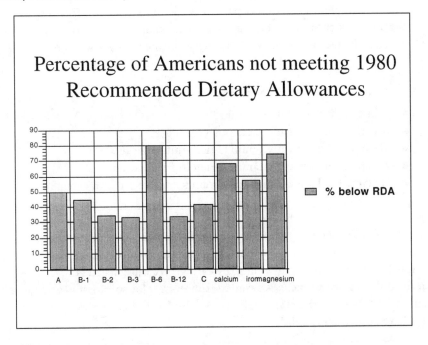

- **VITAMINS:** A, D, E, C, B-6, riboflavin, folacin, pantothenic acid
- **MINERALS:** calcium, potassium, magnesium, zinc, iron, chromium, selenium; and possibly molybdenum and vanadium. With many common micronutrient deficiencies in the western diet, it makes sense that a major study in Australia found that regular use of vitamin supplements was a protective factor against colon cancer.[2]
- **MACRONUTRIENTS:** fiber, complex carbohydrates, plant protein, special fatty acids (EPA, GLA, ALA), clean water

Meanwhile, we also eat alarmingly high amounts of: fat, salt, sugar, cholesterol, alcohol, caffeine, food additives and toxins.

This combination of too much of the wrong things along with not enough of the right things has created epidemic proportions of degenerative diseases in this country. The Surgeon General, Department of Health and Human Services, Center for Disease Control, National Academy of Sciences, American Medical Association, American Dietetic Assocation, and most other major public health agencies agree that diet is a major contributor to our most common health problems, including cancer.

The typical diet of the cancer patient is high in fat while being low in fiber and vegetables—"meat, potatoes, and gravy" is what many of my patients lived on. Data collected by the United States Department of Agriculture from over 11,000 Americans showed that on any given day:

- 41 percent did not eat any fruit
- 82 percent did not eat cruciferous vegetables
- 72 percent did not eat vitamin C-rich fruits or vegetables
- 80 percent did not eat vitamin A-rich fruits or vegetables
- 84 percent did not eat high fiber grain food, like bread or cereal[3]

The human body is incredibly resilient, which sometimes works to our disadvantage. No one dies on the first cigarette inhaled, or the first drunken evening, or the first decade of unhealthy eating. We misconstrue the fact that we survived this ordeal to mean we can do it forever. Not so. Malnutrition can be blatant, as we see in the starving babies in third world countries. Malnutrition can also be much more subtle.

SEQUENCE OF EVENTS IN A DEVELOPING VITAMIN DEFICIENCY

1. **Preliminary.** Reduction of tissue stores and depression of urinary excretion.
2. **Biochemical.** Reduction of enzyme activity due to insufficient coenzymes (vitamins). Urinary excretion at minimum levels.
3. **Physiological.** Behavioral effects, such as insomnia or somnolence. Irritability accompanied by loss of appetite and reduce body weight. Modified drug metabolism and reduced immune capabilities.
4. **Clinical.** Classical deficiency syndromes as recognized by the scientific pioneers in the developmental phases of nutrition science.

It was the Framingham study done at Harvard University that proclaimed: "Our way of life is related to our way of death." Typical hospital food continues or even worsens malnutrition. While many Americans are overfed, the majority are also poorly nourished. If proper nutrition could prevent from 30 to 90% of all cancer, then doesn't it seem foolish to continue feeding the cancer patient the same diet that helped to induce cancer in the first place?

MALNUTRITION AMONG CANCER PATIENTS

From 25-50% of hospital patients suffer from protein calorie malnutrition. Protein calorie malnutrition leads to increases in mortality and surgical failure, with a reduction in immunity, wound healing, cardiac output, response to chemo and radiation therapy, plasma protein synthesis and generally induces weakness and apathy. Many patients are malnourished before entering the hospital and another 10% become malnourished once in the hospital. Nutrition support, as peripheral parenteral nutrition, has been shown to reduce the length of hospital stay by 30%. Weight loss leads to a decrease in patient survival. Common nutrient deficiencies, as determined by experts at M.D. Anderson Hospital in Houston, include protein, calorie, thiamin, riboflavin, niacin, folate and K.

So nutrition therapy has two distinct phases:

1. Take the clinically malnourished patient and bring them up to "normal" status.
2. Take the "normal" sub-clinically malnourished person and bring them up to "optimal" functioning. For at least the few nutrients tested thus far, there appears to be a "dose-dependent" response— more than RDA levels of intake provide for more than "normal" immune functions.

Not only is malnutrition common in the "normal" American, but malnutrition is extremely common in the cancer patient. A theory has persisted for decades that one could starve the tumor out of the host. That just ain't so. The tumor is quite resistant to starvation and most studies find more harm to the host than the tumor in either selective or blanket nutrient deficiencies.[4] Pure malnutrition (cachexia) is responsible for at least 22% and up to 67% of all cancer deaths. Up to 80% of all cancer patients have reduced levels of serum albumin, which is a leading indicator of protein and calorie malnutrition.[5] Dietary protein restriction in the cancer patient does not affect the composition or growth rate of the tumor, but does restrict the patient's well being.[6]

A commonly used anti-cancer drug is methotrexate, which interferes with folate (a B vitamin) metabolism. Many scientists guessed that folate in the diet

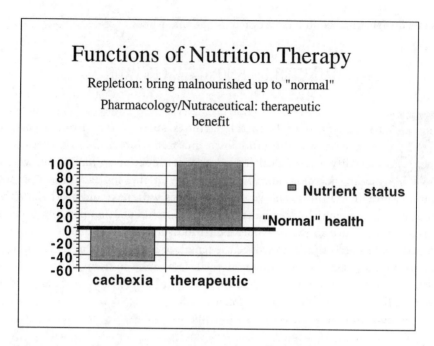

Functions of Nutrition Therapy

Repletion: bring malnourished up to "normal"

Pharmacology/Nutraceutical: therapeutic benefit

might accelerate cancer growth. Not so. Depriving animals of folate in the diet allowed theirs tumor to grow anyway.[7] Actually, in starved animals, the tumors grew more rapidly than in fed animals, indicating the parasitic tenacity of cancer in the host.[8] Other studies have found that a low folate environment can trigger "brittle" DNA to fuel cancer metastasis.

There is some evidence that tumors are not as flexible as healthy host tissue in using fuel. A low carbohydrate parenteral formula may have the ability to slow down tumor growth by selectively starving the cancer cells.[9] Overall, the research shows that starvation provokes host wasting while tumor growth continues unabated.[10]

A position paper from the American College of Physicians published in 1989 basically stated that TPN had no benefit on the outcome of cancer patients.[11] Unfortunately, this article excluded malnourished patients, which is bizarre, since TPN treats malnutrition, not cancer.[12] Most of the scientific literature shows that weight loss drastically increases the mortality rate for most types of cancer, while also lowering the response to chemotherapy.[13]

Parenteral feeding improves tolerance to chemotherapeutic agents and immune responses.[14] Of 28 children with advanced malignant disease, 18 received parenteral feeding for 28 days with resultant improvements in weight gain, increased serum albumin, and transferrin and major benefits in immune functions. In comparing cancer patients on TPN versus those trying to nourish themselves by oral intake of food, TPN provided major improvements in calorie, protein, and nutrient intake but did not encourage tumor growth. Malnourished cancer patients who were provided TPN had a mortality rate of 11% while the group without TPN feeding had a 100% mortality rate.[15] Pre-operative TPN in patients undergoing surgery for GI cancer provided general reduction in the incidence of wound infection, pneumonia, major complications and mortality.[16] Patients who were the most malnourished experienced a 33% mortality and 46% morbidity (problems and illness) rate, while those patients who were properly nourished had a 3% mortality rate with an 8% morbidity rate. In 49 patients with lung cancer receiving chemotherapy with or without TPN, complete remission was achieved in 85% of the TPN group versus 59% of the non-TPN group.[17] A TPN formula that was higher in protein, especially branched chain amino acids, was able to provide better nitrogen balance in the 21 adults tested than the conventional 8.5% amino acid TPN formula.[18]

A finely tuned nutrition formula can also nourish the patient while starving tumor cells. Enteral (oral) formulas fortified with arginine, fish oil and RNA have been shown to stimulate the immune system, accelerate wound repair and reduce tumor burden in both animals and humans. Diets with modified amino acid content, low tyrosine (2.4 mg/kg body weight) and low phenylalanine (3.5 mg/kg body weight), were able to elevate natural killer cell activity in 6 of 9 subjects tested.[19]

In 20 adult hospitalized patients on TPN, the mean daily vitamin C needs were 975 mg, which is over 16 times the RDA, with the range being 350-2250 mg.[20] Of the 139 lung cancer patients studied, most tested deficient or scorbutic (clinical vitamin C deficiency).[21] Another study of cancer patients found that 46% tested scorbutic while 76% were below acceptable levels for serum ascorbate.[22] Experts now recommend the value of nutritional supplements, especially in patients who require prolonged TPN support.[23] The Recommended Daily Allowance (RDA) is inadequate for many healthy people and nearly all sick people.

The take-home lesson here is that:

1. At least 20% of Americans are clinically malnourished, with 70% being sub-clinically malnourished (less obvious), and the remaining "chosen few" 10% in good to optimal health.
2. Once these malnourished people get sick, the malnutrition oftentimes gets worse through higher nutrient needs and lower intake
3. Once at the hospital, malnutrition escalates another notch
4. Cancer is one of the more serious wasting diseases known
5. A malnourished cancer patient suffers a reduction in quality and quantity of life, with higher incidences of complications and death
6. The only solution for malnutrition is optimal nutrition

PATIENT PROFILE

J im Bauder, male, 62 years. In February of 1993, I was diagnosed with a tumor of the parotid gland (under my tongue). This was removed immediately, along with lymph nodes on both sides of the neck. About a month later, I started radiation treatments. After 26 of 33 total radiation treatments, I developed a burning on the right side of my neck. The treatments had to be stopped until my neck could heal from its blisters and seeping fluid. I went to Dr. Quillin for a nutrition consult and he put me on a regimen of high doses of vitamins C, E, beta-carotene and selenium. Within four days, all the redness and open sores were gone. My doctor even remarked how fast I recovered.

REFERENCES

1. Quillin, P., HEALING NUTRIENTS, p.43, Vintage Books, NY, 1989
2. Kune, GA, and Kune, S., Nutrition and Cancer, vol.9, p.1, 1987
3. Patterson, BH, and Block, G., American Journal of Public Health, vol.78, p.282, Mar.1988
4. Axelrod, AE, and Traketelis, AC, Vitamins and Hormones, vol.22, p.591, 1964
5. Dreizen, S., et al., Postgraduate Medicine, vol.87, no.1, p.163, Jan.1990
6. Lowry, SF, et al., Surgical Forum, vol.28, p.143, 1977
7. Nichol, CA, Cancer Research, vol.29, p.2422, 1969
8. Norton, JA, et al., Cancer, vol.45, p.2934, 1980
9. Dematrakopoulos, GE, and Brennan, MF, Cancer Research, (sup.),vol.42, p.756, Feb.1982
10. Goodgame, JT, et al., American Journal of Clinical Nutrition, vol.32, p.2277, 1979
11. Annals of Internal Medicine, vol.110, no.9, p.735, May 1989
12. Kaminsky, M. (ed.), HYPERALIMENTATION: A GUIDE FOR CLINICIANS, Marcel Dekker, NY, Oct.1985
13. Dewys, WD, et al., American Journal of Medicine, vol.69, p.491, Oct.1980
14. Eys, JV, Cancer, vol.43, p.2030, 1979
15. Harvey, KB, et al., Cancer, vol.43, p.2065, 1979
16. Muller, JM, et al., Lancet, p.68, Jan.9, 1982
17. Valdivieso, M., et al., Cancer Treatment Reports, vol.65, sup.5, p.145, 1981
18. Gazzaniga, AB, et al., Archives of Surgery, vol. 123, p.1275, 1988
19. Norris, JR, et al., American Journal of Clinical Nutrition, vol.51, p.188, 1990
20. Abrahamian, V., et al., Journal of Parenteral and Enteral Nutrition, vol.7, no.5, p.465, 1983
21. Anthony, HM, et al., British Journal of Cancer, vol.46, p.354, 1982
22. Cheraskin, E., Journal of Alternative Medicine, p.18, Feb.1986
23. Hoffman, FA, Cancer, vol.55, 1 sup.1, p.295, Jan.1, 1985

CHAPTER 6

KNOW THE LAWS OF NUTRITION

When sailing instructors teach you how to sail, they cannot show you around the world. They show you how to use the instruments of navigation— a sextant, compass and map—and hope you can fare well on your own. So, too, I cannot follow you around for the rest of your life and make nutritional decisions for you. But I can condense the volumes of nutrition information into several easy-to-follow rules that become your navigation instruments in choosing the right foods. I have tried giving cancer patients a detailed 2 week food intake program. By day 2, this patient is out of some food, then eats with a friend at a restaurant, then has dinner with the cousins—all of which throws the patient off their diet without any idea of knowing how to "wing it" or improvise. Use this chapter as a shortcut toward building good nutrition judgment in choosing foods and supplements that will fight cancer.

THE KISS (KEEP IT SIMPLE STUDENT) METHOD OF OPTIMAL NUTRITION

■ **Go natural.** Eat foods in as close to their natural state as possible. Refining food often adds questionable agents (like food additives, salt, sugar and fat), removes valuable nutrients (like vitamins, minerals, and fiber) and always raises the cost of the food.

■ **Expand your horizons.** Eat a wide variety of foods. By not focusing on any particular food, you can obtain nutrients that may be essential but are poorly understood while also avoiding a buildup of any substance that could create food allergies or toxicities.

■ **Nibbling is better.** Eat small frequent meals. Nibbling is better than gorging. Our ancestors "grazed" throughout the day. Only with the advent of the industrial age did we begin the punctual eating of large meals. Nibbling helps to stabilize blood sugar levels and minimize insulin rushes; therefore has been linked to a lowered risk for heart disease, diabetes, obesity and mood swings.

■ **Avoid problem foods.** Minimize your intake of unhealthy foods which are high in fat, salt, sugar, cholesterol, caffeine, alcohol, processed lunch meats and most additives.

■ **Seek out nutrient-dense foods.** Maximize your intake of life-giving foods, including fresh vegetables, whole grains, legumes, fruit, low fat meat (turkey, fish, chicken) and clean water. Low fat dairy products, especially yogurt, can be valuable if you do not have milk allergies or lactose intolerance.

■ **Monitor your quality of weight**, rather than quantity of weight. Balance your calorie intake with expenditure so that your percentage of body fat is reasonable. Pinch the skinfold just above the hipbone. If this skin is more than an inch in thickness, then you may need to begin rational efforts to lose weight. Obesity is a major factor in cancer. For a more exact way to track your percent body fat, use the Futrex (phone 800-545-1950), a device based on research done at the United States Department of Agriculture. This device measures the thickness of fatty tissue in the biceps region, which is most representative of total body fat. How much you weigh is not nearly as crucial as the percent of fat in the body. Of all the controversies that plague the nutrition field, one issue that all nutritionists will agree on is to eat less fat in your diet and store less fat in your body.

■ **Eat enough protein.** Cancer is a serious wasting disease. I have counselled far too many cancer patients who looked like war camp victims, having lost 25% or more of their body weight due to insufficient protein intake. Take in 1 to 2 grams of protein for each kilogram of body weight. Example: 150 pound patient. Divide 150 pounds by 2.2 to find 68 kilograms, multiply times 1 to 2, yields 68 to 136 grams of protein daily is needed to generate a healthy immune system. While a protein excess can have some harmful side effects, a protein deficiency is disastrous for the cancer patient.

■ **Use supplements in addition to**, rather than instead of, good food. Get your nutrients with a fork and spoon. Do not place undo reliance on pills and powders to provide optimal nourishment. Supplements providing micronutrients (vitamins and minerals) cannot reverse the major influence of foods providing macronutrients (carbohydrate, fat, protein, fiber, water). Foods are top priority in your battle plan against cancer.

■ **Shop the perimeter of the grocery store.** On the perimeter of your grocery store you will find fresh fruits, vegetables, bread, fish, chicken and dairy. Once you venture into the deep dark interior of the grocery store, nutritional quality of the foods goes way down and prices go way up. Organic produce is raised without pesticides and may be valuable in helping cancer patients. However, organic produce is unavailable or unaffordable for many people. Don't get terribly concerned about having to consume organic produce. Produce should be either peeled (like watermelon or bananas) or soaked for 5 minutes in a solution of one gallon lukewarm clean water with 2 tablespoons of vinegar.

■ **If a food will not rot or sprout**, then don't buy it or throw it out. Your body cells have similar biochemical needs to a bacteria or yeast cell. Foods that have a shelf life of a millenia are not going to nourish the body. Think about it: if bacteria is not interested in your food, then what makes you think that your body cells are interested? Foods that cannot begin (sprouting) or sustain (bacterial growth) life elsewhere, will have a similar effect in your body.

■ **Dishes should be easy to clean.** Foods that are hard to digest or unhealthy will probably leave a mess on plates and pots. Dairy curd, such as fondue, is both difficult to clean and very difficult for your stomach to process. Same thing with fried, greasy or burned foods.

ESSENTIAL NUTRIENT PYRAMID

We need to recognize the priority placed on essential nutrients. We can live for weeks without food, a few days without water and only a few minutes without oxygen. Keep in mind the relative importance of these essential nutrients.

Oxygen and water form the basis of human life. Make sure that your quality and quantity of intake pay homage to this fact. Protein, carbohydrate, fiber and fat form the next level of importance. Vitamins and minerals are the essential micronutrients required for health.

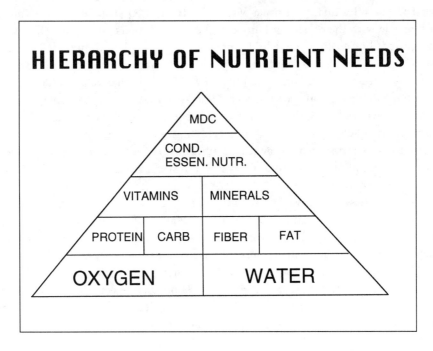

HIERARCHY OF NUTRIENT NEEDS

MDC

COND. ESSEN. NUTR.

VITAMINS | MINERALS

PROTEIN | CARB | FIBER | FAT

OXYGEN | WATER

Above these essential substances are two levels of quasi (meaning "as if it were") nutrients. Conditionally essential nutrients include Coenzyme-Q10, carnitine, EPA and GLA (fatty acids) and much more. Some people may require these nutrients in the diet during certain stressful phases of their lives. Minor dietary constituents (MDCs) include a wide variety of plant compounds that have shown remarkable anti-cancer abilities. Indoles in the cabbage family, lycopenes in tomatoes, allicin in garlic, immune stimulants in sea vegetables and others make up this new and exciting category. Eating a wide variety of unprocessed plant foods will help to insure adequate intake of these quasi-nutrients.

EXPECT THE EXISTENCE OF UNKNOWN ESSENTIAL NUTRIENTS

As laboratory equipment becomes more sophisticated, we keep finding more substances in the food supply that can help or hurt us. Macronutrients, which are found in large amounts in the diet, were discovered first, and micronutrients second. An entire universe of "sub-micro" nutrients await us as we look at substances found in the food supply in parts per trillion. Not until laboratory equipment could detect pesticide residues and minor dietary constituents could we begin to appreciate their importance in health.

For example, infant formulas were first tried 3000 years ago and became fashionable with the royalty in Europe in the past 500 years. By 1700 AD, it was recognized that feeding your child animal milk rather than human breastmilk brought nearly a 90% mortality rate. "Wet nurses" were peasant women brought in to breastfeed the children of nobility. By 1950, scientists felt confident that they could duplicate and even improve on breast milk. They were wrong. Since then, we have learned of the special fatty acids (EPA & GLA) contained in breast milk for brain development, the amino acid taurine for brain and sight, immune factors that share mother's acquired immunity with the newborn infant, nutrients that allow for maturation of the intestinal lining and the pancreatic cells and much more.

Studies show that breastfed infants later in life are at lower risk for heart disease, diabetes, allergies, sudden infant death (SID) and even emotional problems. Still, breastfeeding is only beginning to make a comeback, with less than 20% of American mothers nursing their young. We thought that we could duplicate mother's milk, but we really didn't understand the elegant symphony of "sub-micro" nutrients that it contained. Same applies with our foods. The more that we tamper with our food supply, the more hard lessons we learn regarding the ornate and subtle blend of potent nutrients offered by nature.

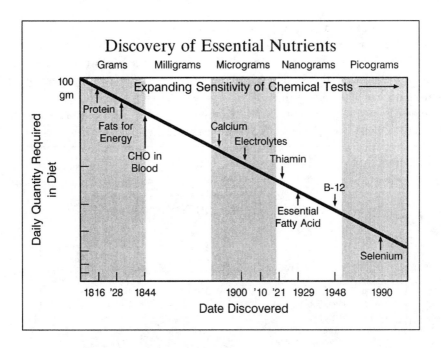

Discovery of Essential Nutrients

| Grams | Milligrams | Micrograms | Nanograms | Picograms |

Expanding Sensitivity of Chemical Tests ⟶

Daily Quantity Required in Diet

100 gm

Protein
Fats for Energy
CHO in Blood
Calcium
Electrolytes
Thiamin
Essential Fatty Acid
B-12
Selenium

1816 '28 1844   1900 '10 '21 1929 1948   1990

Date Discovered

THE CONTINUUM OF NUTRIENTS AND TOXINS

A continuum is a "continuous whole, whose parts cannot be separated." Most light switches only go on and off. But some lights have a dimmer switch which allows for a continuum of varying shades of light. Rarely are events in life as neatly classified as "you are pregnant or you aren't". The same complexities apply with nutrients.

When I was in undergraduate studies, my professors spoke of vitamin E as the "vitamin in search of a disease", because studies had shown that you could deprive a group of humans of all vitamin E for many months without any noticeable health problems surfacing. Today, it has been clearly demonstrated that the greatest nutritional risk factor for heart disease is a **long term** low intake of vitamin E. Vitamin E is certainly essential in the human diet, but it takes decades for deficiencies to surface.

Not all toxins are of equal toxicity and not all nutrients are equally essential. Some poisons, like botulism, are so potent that a tiny drop will kill a human quickly. For most toxins, it requires long term intake of larger amounts to create health problems. Professor Bruce Ames at the University of California Berkeley has created a HERP index (human exposure rodent potency) which illustrates the concept of varying degrees of toxicity. I have added to that idea the mirror image of a continuum of varying degrees of essential nutrients. A protein deficiency will surface within a few weeks of low intake. Most vitamin deficiencies take months to surface. Certain mineral deficiencies take years to surface, like chromium as heart disease or selenium as cancer. And it can take decades for some nutrient deficiencies to surface, such as riboflavin into cataracts, calcium into osteoporosis and vitamin E into Alzheimer's disease. These facts are known. From these facts, I am going to speculate on a critical issue in nutrition.

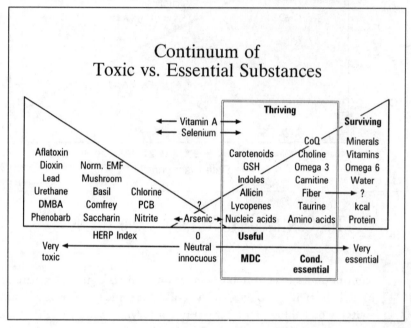

We used to have such a tidy definition of "essential nutrients": a substance that is not made in the body and is therefore required in the diet for health. So it was very unnerving when scientists discovered that we make niacin (essential vitamin B-3) in the body from the amino acid tryptophan and we make vitamin D from sunshine exposure on the skin. And there went the neat definition. The same applies for the special fatty acids EPA and GLA, the energy bridge nutrient Coenzyme Q-10 and the amino acid carnitine—we eat some of these nutrients in a good diet and we make some in our bodies from raw materials. Given that fact that during illness, aging, exposure to toxins and stress, we cannot make enough of these quasi-nutrients, scientists have argued to have these conditionally essential nutrients classified as essential for some people and during some "seasons" of our lives.

See the chart below. If your body depends on the precursor, meaning "raw materials", A plus enzymes D and E to get enough of the needed end-product C, then the supply line has become the rate limiting bottleneck in health.

Scientists have shown evidence that hypertension can surface in some people as a deficiency of GLA (a unique fatty acid) or EPA; and that heart disease arises in people who cannot manufacture enough carnitine or CoQ within. The answer to this riddle is to provide the ailing body with optimal amounts of end product C so that you don't have to depend on the tenuous and failing production line inside the body.

CONDITIONALLY ESSENTIAL NUTRIENTS
giving the body what it needs

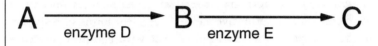

A ——————→ B ——————→ C
       enzyme D   enzyme E

A=raw materials (precursors) from the diet
B=intermediate
C=desired end product, conditionally essential nutrient
i.e. carnitine, EPA, CoQ, arginine

Some sensitive individuals with a limited internal production of quasi-nutrients may suffer cancer as a long term consequence of a deficiency. MDCs have potent disease-arresting capabilities and are known to exist mostly in unprocessed plant food. No one is willing to call these MDC substances "essential nutrients" yet because we don't know enough about them. But many cancer patients get better when they start eating properly, especially a diet high in unprocessed plant food. My contention is that, for some cancer victors, their disease resulted from a deficiency of a subtle but crucial nutrient that was not found in adequate quantities in a highly refined diet.

THE MORE COMPLEX THE ORGANISM, THE MORE COMPLEX THE NUTRIENT NEEDS

I n 1949, Professor Linus Pauling wrote of "orthomolecular medicine" as establishing the "right amounts" of molecules in the cell. In 1969, twice Nobel laureate Dr. Pauling wrote a brilliant paper on orthomolecular nutrition, or providing optimal amounts of nutrients to the cell. In complex chemical equations, he explained that a single cell organism has a very short "grocery list" of essential nutrients. These bacteria and yeast spend all of their time creating their own nutrients from just a few other essential molecules. As life evolved, organisms progressively lost the ability to make all of these essential nutrients inside the cell, and in doing so freed up cellular "machinery" to perform other functions beyond just survival. Eventually life evolved from primitive and self-sufficient forms into species that were highly dependent on the environment yet with complex thinking and movement.

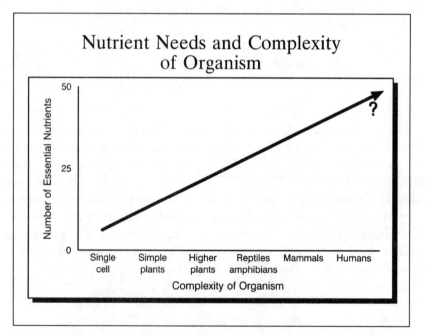

The movie "Jeremiah Johnson" with Robert Redford was a classic example of this principle. Jeremiah left the complex society of Boston in the 19th century to live in isolation in the mountain wilderness of Colorado. His isolationism forced him to spend all of his days just surviving: making his own clothes, capturing his meat, repairing things, etc. While Jeremiah had no need for society, he also made no contribution to society. Jeremiah was somewhat like a bacteria, since he had a short grocery list of essential supplies from his environment, yet he had no time for anything but survival.

Humans are the most complex organisms on earth. The downside of this equation is that we have the most extensive grocery list of essential nutrients. Yet the upside is our vast potential in thought and movement. We are more vulnerable to malnutrition than cockroaches, yet we can dance ballet and program a computer. An algae is better at surviving. A human is better at sophisticated movement and thought.

The take home lesson here is the complexity of human nutrition. Humans definitely have more extensive nutrient requirements than lower forms of life. We may need certain substances found only in liver (such as lipoic acid), or sea vegetables (such as a thyroid-stimulating factor), or fresh greens (such as chlorophyll and bioflavonoids), or garlic (allicin). We need to distinguish between facts and hunches, but my hunch is that some people get cancer because their sophisticated and complex bodily needs are not being met by the highly refined junk food diet of Western society.

DIFFERENCE BETWEEN SURVIVING AND THRIVING

Humans have survived car crashes at 200 miles per hour, falling out of jet planes without a parachute from five miles up, being fired out of cannons, inhumane treatment in prisoner of war camps, multiple gun shot wounds and a metal shaft fired cleanly through the head. While some people can survive a half century of smoking, no one thrives on it. Alcoholics can tolerate a suicidal lifestyle for decades. But their body and mind suffer and age rapidly in the process. None of these feats are good for the human body. Yet our tenacity is oftentimes our undoing. We assume that a diet that doesn't immediately kill us must be good for us. Not so.

The statistical picture of the average American is indicative of a tenacious survivor: overweight; 6 colds per year; chronic mild depression, constipation, and lethargy; dentures by age 45; chronic illness by age 60 with 6 different daily drugs needed; and death in the 70s from heart disease or cancer. None of this would be considered thriving—nor is our lifestyle "optimal". The fact that a person has cancer may be a clear indicator that "surviving" has deteriorated into illness. We need to pursue optimal health and "thriving" before the cancer will go away. The above graph shows that health and performance increase with increasing nutrient intake, until a plateau is reached—in pharmaceutical terms, there

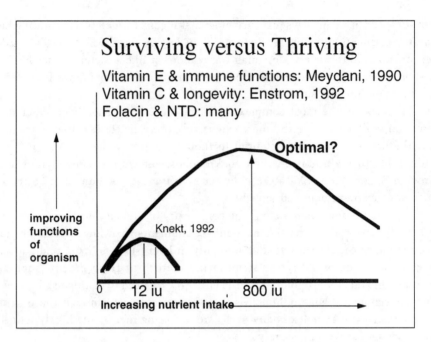

Surviving versus Thriving

Vitamin E & immune functions: Meydani, 1990
Vitamin C & longevity: Enstrom, 1992
Folacin & NTD: many

Optimal?

improving
functions
of
organism

Knekt, 1992

0   12 iu   ,   800 iu
Increasing nutrient intake

appears to be a "dose-dependent" response curve with the health benefits of many nutrients.

Think of the relative benefits of increasing daily intake of folate:

- Most people can live on 100 micrograms (mcg)
- Wound healing and overall health are improved at 400 mcg
- The risk for pregnant women having babies with neural tubes defect can be lowered dramatically at 1000 mcg
- Pre-cancerous conditions of the cervix and lungs can be reversed with 20,000 mcg.

Most people can survive for decades on 10 international units (iu) of vitamin E. Yet, 100 iu of E will improve lung resistance to air pollutants and lower the risk for heart disease, while 800 iu has been shown to measurably elevate immune functions. Humans can survive on 10 milligrams (mg) of vitamin C for decades. Yet, many experts recommend 400 mg as a healthier RDA, and 10,000 mg helps to fight AIDS, cancer and the flu. In a study reported in the May 1992 edition of *Epidemiology* by UCLA researcher Professor Enstrom, 300 mg of supplemental vitamin C daily lengthened lifespan in men by 6 years.

Clearly, survival levels of nutrient intake are not enough for the cancer patient. Elevating a cancer patient out of surviving and into thriving dramatically improves the patient's ability to manage the disease.

DISEASE IS A CLASH BETWEEN GENETIC VULNERABILITY & ENVIRONMENTAL INSULT

H eart disease is not the inevitable end for most people. Japanese people have a lower rate of heart disease, until they move to the U.S. and begin living our lifestyle, which equalizes the numbers quickly. Our genetic vulnerability collides with our risky lifestyle to create heart disease. Fair skinned people who are exposed to excessive sunlight run a higher risk of contracting skin cancer. Its not that their skin is defective, but rather these people have evolved to extract more vitamin D from a less sunny environment. Their weakness in a sunny setting is a survival advantage in a cloudy part of the world. Australians have the highest incidence of skin cancer in the world; as an example of northern European people who have been placed in a sun-drenched climate.

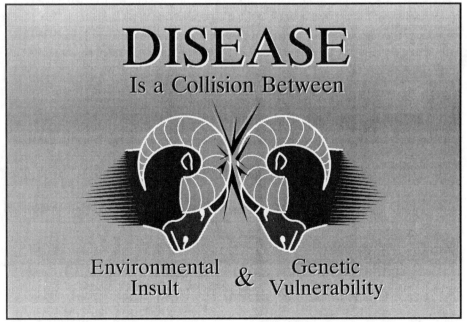

Cancer patients have demonstrated a genetic vulnerability toward cancer. Therefore, optimal nutritional protection is required to reduce the carcinogenic risks of chemo and radiation therapy. This means re-organizing the cancer patient's lifestyle to protect the obviously delicate cellular machinery from another bout with cancer. Quitting smoking improves the odds that the cancer patient will beat cancer. Continuing to smoke is a sure death sentence. In hundreds of patients, I have never seen an active smoker actually recover from cancer.

SIMPLE SOLUTIONS FOR COMPLEX PROBLEMS

Most biological therapies have been serious disappointments for cancer patients. After decades of work from brilliant scientists, there is always another unexpected obstacle around the bend that leads to toxic side effects and reduced therapeutic value from substances like interferon or interleukin. The reason for these frustrating results is our arrogance. We assume that we fully understand the interdependent and complex machinery of the human body. Yet we have only a vague grasp of how to optimally support the mind and body. We dump billions of pounds of known lethal poisons in our air, food and water supply; then subject ourselves to unprecedented levels of psychological distress; then fill our stomachs with nutritionally bankrupt food. When our health fails, we cut off the defective part or try some dramatic, invasive, expensive therapy that will combat the disease. Somehow, we ignore the obvious and easy answers. The solution to many health problems revolves around nourishing our own internal healing ability—the "life forces" within.

Our rapidly expanding technology has brought us trips to the moon, powerful notebook computers, laser surgery and satellite communications. But in spite of our accomplishments, we cannot make a baby, or an apple, or even a feather. Life is far more complex than many people are willing to admit. My guess is that 20 years from now, we will compare our current awkward efforts at cancer therapy to a gorilla trying to fix a computer with a hammer. Odds are, the gorilla is going to do more harm than good.

Let's look at an example. Waterwheel-driven clocks were invented in China in the 8th century AD. Mechanical clocks were invented in Europe by the 13th century. For the next 700 years, watchmakers furiously pursued the perfect timepiece, as the parts became smaller, more numerous, more fragile and made of precious gems and metals. Finally, by 1960 you could spend $20,000 on a "chronometer" watch which was accurate to within a minute a month. But the real breakthrough in timekeeping was a piece of sand. That's right, the key part in our modern timepieces is a quartz crystal of silicon dioxide with no moving parts, made for pennies, never needs winding, totally shockproof and keeps time to within a few seconds a month. The perfect timepiece has become surprisingly simple and gives us a preview of the simple elegance in the answer to cancer—

harness the forces in nature.

I have had fascinating discussions with researchers in biological therapies for cancer. Their brilliance and dedication is beyond dispute. Yet in their brilliance, they ignore the laws of nature. Since we cannot veto these laws, we need to better understand and work with them. It is unlikely that we will ever develop a "magic bullet" against all cancer. Too many people are living a lifestyle which induces cancer. Using some medicine to counteract the powerful and destructive tides created by the typical diet and lifestyle is like trying to sweep back the ocean. The simple answers to the complex cancer puzzle will involve nourishing the life forces while eliminating physical and metaphysical poisons from the body.

THE TREATMENT OF DEGENERATIVE DISEASE MUST DEAL WITH THE CAUSE

The same lifestyle factors which prevent heart disease—stress reduction (meditation), walking and a low fat vegetarian diet—can also reverse heart disease, as demonstrated by Dr. Dean Ornish. If your headache is caused by your teenager's drums, then no amount of aspirin, antacid, or tranquilizers will actually cure the problem until you stop the noise. Cancer follows this same paradigm. Drugs and surgery can provide temporary relief from symptoms, but cannot reverse the underlying mechanisms that brought about the disease. If a long term zinc deficiency blunted the immune system, which led to cancer; then only zinc supplements can reverse the condition. If a painful divorce caused depression which blunted the immune system, then resolution of the psychological stress is the only long term cure. If low thyroid output is the problem that led to cancer, then normalizing thyroid is the answer. For most cancer patients, cancer is a result of many combined negative forces. Pure and simple: reverse the cause and you have a much better chance for a cure.

Recall the tree fungus drawing from earlier in this book. You can cut, burn and poison the fungus off a tree bark. But until you alter the underlying conditions that encourage the abnormal growth, the fungus will return. Similarly, you can cut, burn and poison with surgery, radiation and chemotherapy to temporarily relieve tumor burden; but until you alter the conditions that spawned the cancer, it will return.

The parallel between cancer and fungus may be more than just a convenient metaphor. C.B. "Doc" Pennington is a wealthy oil magnate who developed untreatable colon cancer 20 years ago and was sent home to die. While battling cancer, Doc saw a TV story in which thousands of turkeys died from a fungal poisoning, aflatoxin, in their peanut meal. After a visit from Dr. Linus Pauling, Pennington began taking high doses of vitamins C and E coupled with his own theory of an anti-fungal medication(Grisactin 250 from Ayest Labs, NYC). His cancer went away and today Doc is 92 years young and has single-handedly launched the Pennington Biomedical Institute in Baton Rouge, Louisiana with $126 million of his personal funds to study the link between nutrition and cancer. Pennington may be on to something. One of the main causes of death in cancer is infection, with autopsies showing that 50% of infections are caused by yeast overgrowth, primarily Candida.

BIOCHEMICAL INDIVIDUALITY—WE ARE ALL DIFFERENT

Stroll through a big city zoo if you want to truly appreciate the diversity of life on earth. There are creatures that eat mostly meat, like cats, who would die on a vegetarian diet. There are creatures, like elephants and rabbits, that are strict vegetarians and would die on a carnivorous diet. There are many shades of gray in between these two extremes, like omnivorous humans. The five billion people on the planet earth comprise an incredible tapestry of biochemical and physical diversity. Eskimos eat a diet primarily composed of high fat fish, with almost no fruit, vegetables, or fiber to speak of. Yet they are an incredibly hardy group of people, nearly devoid of heart disease, cancer or diabetes. They are eating their "factory specification" diet to which they have adapted. Some groups of people have evolved to depend entirely on their dairy herds, while other groups are vegetarians. Scientists examined the Turkana, a nomadic group in Kenya, Africa who survived on their goat herds. When a splinter group of the Turkana settled along a pristine lake shore for a seemingly healthier life of fresh fish; they developed warts, diarrhea and infections because they were not eating their "factory specification" diet.

There have been many efforts to sub-classify humans into their special dietary needs:

- Elliott Abravanel, MD in his Metabolic Diet
- Donald Kelley, DDS in his Metabolic typing into sympathetic and parasympathetic dominant
- Nick Gonzales, MD in his 10 different diets as an elaboration of Kelley's work
- Ayurvedic medicine is a 2000 year old Hindu system of healing which sub-classifies East Indian people for their dietary needs.
- Rudolph Wiley, PhD has divided people into acidic, alkalotic, or mixed

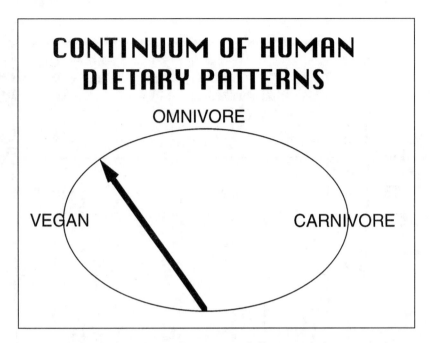

CONTINUUM OF HUMAN DIETARY PATTERNS

OMNIVORE

VEGAN   CARNIVORE

type, depending on the predisposition of their metabolism toward extreme pH.

■ Peter D'Adamo, ND has categorized human dietary needs by their blood types, which are representative of their ancestor's native regions.

■ and many others

What these bright people all agree is: Humans are different and require different diets to thrive. To quote Lucretius, a poet from ancient Rome, "What is meat to one is to others bitter poison." Parry of Bath, an English physician quipped: "More important to know what sort of patient has a disease than to know the sort of disease the patient has".

Most useful therapies evolved from bright clinicians. When a doctor meticulously and conscientiously treats thousands of patients over the course of many decades, his or her observations are worth a great deal. Patterns develop that provide predictability in patient outcome. One such pattern has come from Elliott Abravanel, MD, whose extensive medical practice found categories of patients. Based upon a dominant organ, a person develops a set of tendencies—both weaknesses and strengths. By understanding these pecularities, we can better manage the cancer patient. For instance, knowing a person is fair skinned should provide fair warning that this person should not over-indulge in exposure to the sun. Knowing that a thyroid dominant individual is very susceptible to stimulants, this person needs to avoid caffeine and sugar. Knowing that an

METABOLIC TYPE

	Shape	Exercise	Eat	Don't eat	Characteristics	Vulnerabilities
Gonadal	smaller above waist, lbs on rear	dance, gymnastics, jog w. heavy hands, tai-chi, nautilus	Pituitary stim: low fat, fr & veg, wh grains, yogurt, poultry, fish, light dairy	creamy & spicy foods; red meat, sour cr, ice cr., butter, rich desserts	mothering instincts can smother, frustration is stress, good at advertising	lumpy breasts, competition, interruptions, disorder, change in routine, assertiveness, risks
Thyroid	tall, long limbs, fine bones, fat on midriff, i.e. Victoria Principle, Jeremy Jones	swim, row, packback, nautilus, aerobic, no biking	Adrenal stim: eggs, poultry, veg & fr, fish, cheese, yogurt, wh grain, decaf, butter, veg oil	starches & sweets, refined carb, pasta, coffee, tea	solve all w bursts of flighty ideas, nervous, irritable, good at communication, the arts, entrepreneur	colds, flu, colitis, allergies, repetition, continuing demands, details, rejection, pain, lack of stim.
Adrenal	solid, muscular, beer belly, fat across back & neck, i.e. Mr. T, Nick Nolte, Linda Evans, Carroll O'Connor	handball, squash, tennis, b-ball, ping pong, Nordic track, no weight	Pituitary stim: lowfat dairy, fish, fr & veg, wh grain, poultry, coffee, tea, desserts	meat & potatoes, salty food, hi fat cheese, red meat, butter	stubborn, inflexible, impatient, good at business, sports, sales	CAD, DB, needs control, emotional, vacations stressful, children, creativity
Pituitary	child's body, slightly big head, baby fat all over, only 10% of US	aerobic dancing, karate, tai chi, martial arts, no wt lift, long distance running	Adrenal stim: beef, lamb, pork, organ meat, fr & veg, poultry, fish, skim milk, eggs, decaf, tea	regular dairy, coffee	try to use more intellect when emotions needed, good at computer design, architect	allergies (milk esp), emotions, sex, food, unresolved conflicts, animals, sickness

adrenal dominant person is susceptible to coronary artery disease (CAD) and diabetes (DB), he or she needs to plan their lifestyle accordingly. The following Metabolic Type chart comes from DR. ABRAVANEL'S BODY TYPE PROGRAM (Bantam, 1985). Use it as another instrument to help you create your own nutrition support program.

While none of these methods of categorizing humans for their specific dietary needs has withstood the rigors of scientific scrutiny, I have found a system that seems to help—follow your ancestral heritage. Figure out what your ancestors ate prior to the advent of agriculture, 5000 years ago, and follow that food pattern. Anthropologists tell us that mankind evolved some 2-3 million years ago, while agriculture and a high grain diet was introduced 5000 years ago, and nutrient-depleted junk food became our dietary staples in the past 50 years. Humans, like all other animals on earth, must pay homage to our origins. The momentum of 2 million years of adapting to and eventually depending on a certain diet cannot be overcome in a few decades. We must eat our "factory specification" diet. Trying to run a diesel truck on gasoline would ruin the engine. Many people are trying to run their body on the wrong fuel.

Our ancestors of 5000 years ago were mostly hunters and gathers. In colder climates, such as northern Europe, plant food was only available throughout the summer and fall. Lean wild game and fish provided the bulk of food intake throughout winter. In warmer climates, like central Africa and India, the inhabitants relied on a year round diet of mostly fresh plant food. There are many shades of dietary needs in between these extremes. The take home lesson here is: "eat what you are supposed to eat from your ancient heritage." As ethnic groups blend in marriage, this "ancestral diet" becomes a more complex issue with our mixed racial backgrounds.

Along the same line of logic, Dr. Roger Williams, professor emeritus at the University of Texas and one of the most productive nutrition scientists of all time, discovered the incredible biological diversity within any animal species. Dr. Williams inbred guinea pigs for 3 generations, which should have produced a very homogenous offspring. Yet he found a 20 fold variance in the vitamin C requirements of these genetically similar creatures. Armadillos commonly give birth to identical quadruplets which develop from one egg. Hence, these baby armadillos are as identical as they can get. Yet Dr. Williams found a two-fold variance in the size of key organs and a three-fold variance in the blood levels of hormones and amino acids. Williams book, NUTRITION AGAINST DISEASE, still stands as a cornerstone work in this century of nutrition science.

Biochemical individuality creates complications in nutrition therapy that defies "cookbook" therapy, or trying to follow some standard guidelines for all cancer patients. Our health care system is built on following protocols, which ignore the irrefutable presence of unique nutrient requirements and chemical sensitivities. I can give you guidelines in this book which will dramatically improve your chances of recovering from cancer, but only you can become sensitive to your individual requirements so that you can "fine tune" your program.

TRIAXIAL IINTERVENTION

As with all other areas of life, there are some systems in the body that are more important than others. This three dimensional graph, developed by Russell Jaffe, MD, PhD, is a brilliant way to assess your health. The three most important biochemical parameters in the human body are:

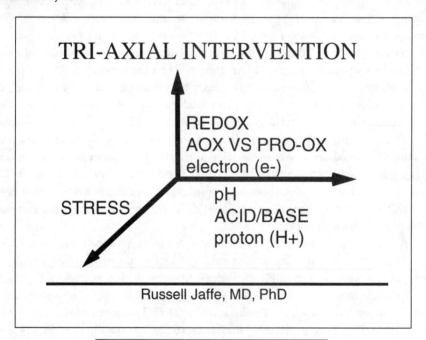

TRI-AXIAL INTERVENTION

REDOX
AOX VS PRO-OX
electron (e-)

pH
ACID/BASE
proton (H+)

STRESS

Russell Jaffe, MD, PhD

- pH, or acid to base balance
- Redox potential, or the dynamic balance between oxidation & reduction which arises from free radicals (by-products of immune functions and energy metabolism) and antioxidants (like vitamins C, E and beta-carotene)
- Stress from both physical and mental sources. Distress is negative while eustress is positive.

If these factors are off kilter, then nothing else in the body matters until these conditions are rectified. For instance, a cancer patient may have a selenium deficiency and mercury overload, but if their serum pH is abnormal, then adjusting pH takes precedence in the efforts to help the patient.

YIN-YANG BALANCE

I n Oriental philosophy, there are two opposing forces which create the dynamic way of the universe. In the human body there are two opposing forces that create a dynamic equilibrium of health. Too much serotonin in the brain may create a dull mind while not enough serotonin may lead to depression, schizophrenia or compulsive habits. Too much dopamine can create an anxious mind while not enough can cause hyperactivity or mental lethary. Balance the two forces of excitatory and inhibitory chemicals in the brain and you have a person who is alert yet relaxed. Antioxidants are crucial to slow down the corrosive effects of pro-oxidants, like oxygen. Yet insufficient oxygen in the cells may be at the root of some cancers, since cancer is primarily an anaerobic organism.

Yin-Yang

In Chinese philosophy, two cosmic energy modes comprising the Tao or the eternal dynamic way of the universe.

Dynamic equilibrium: active state in which the rates of chemical synthesis and degradation are in the balance. *(Human Physiology, Vander)*

Fiber is a valuable nutrient, but too much fiber will create diarrhea and a loss of certain minerals from the intestines. Sodium is essential for life, but too much sodium in the body may create cancer or heart disease. If glucose levels in the blood are low, then the brain starves for fuel. Yet, too much glucose in the blood can fuel cancer growth while suppressing the immune system. The cancer victor needs to re-establish that delicate balance of opposing forces which constitutes optimal health. Too much or too little of most substances, from sunlight to oxygen to selenium, will be harmful. True health is a yin-yang balancing act.

NUTRIENTS AS BIOLOGICAL RESPONSE MODIFIERS (BRM)

Most Americans choose their food for reasons of taste, cost, convenience and psychological gratification. All those reasons are okay, as long as we do not forget the real reason that we eat: to nourish the cells of the body with essential ingredients from the diet. Everytime you eat, picture the cavalry from the old west delivering the long-awaited supplies to the fort—you better have the right stuff with you. While humans can survive on many different bad diets for years, we can only thrive on a narrowly defined set of nutrition principles.

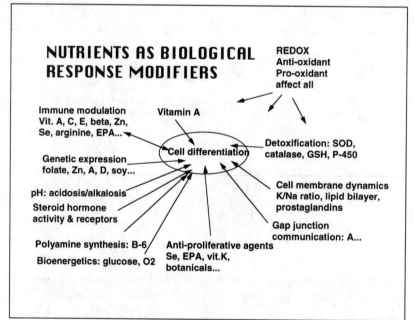

Know this rule: Everything that you put in your mouth is a BRM. Brilliant scientists at the National Cancer Institute have labored for years trying to produce something from the laboratory that will rectify human cancer. These researchers have developed the field of BRM, in which potent drugs and extracts from the immune system will hopefully improve health. Results in this area have been very disappointing.

But every time you eat a meal high in carbohydrates and get a little sleepy afterward, you have used food as a BRM to alter brain chemicals. A high salt diet changes the critical sodium to potassium ratio in the blood and cell membranes, which can affect many hormones and the permeability of cell membranes. Respect the incredible impact of food, water and air on the mind and body.

ALL LIFESTYLE FACTORS ARE HEALTH VECTORS

Vectors are forces, which vary in strength and direction. For instance, a small plane flying at 100 miles per hour north into a head wind at 120 mph has a ground speed of -20 mph. Progress is seriously impaired by the opposing force of the wind.

All lifestyle factors are vectors which either move you toward illness or wellness. Consider the person who is smoking (-80 mph), eats a low fat diet (+60 mph), takes vitamin supplements (+40 mph), has a stressful attitude (-100 mph), and eats a high sugar diet (-80). The overwhelming direction for this person is toward illness, even though he or she is doing some things right. Health is a sum total of vectors. The cancer patient is in need of all vectors being favorable.

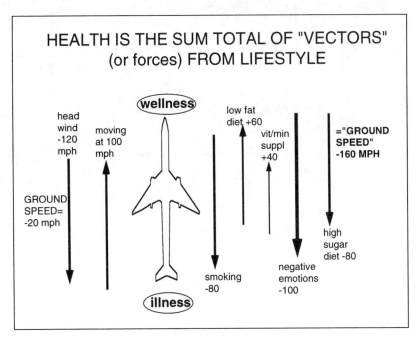

HEALTH IS THE SUM TOTAL OF "VECTORS" (or forces) FROM LIFESTYLE

HUMANS ARE A COMPLEX INTERPLAY BETWEEN PHYSICAL & METAPHYSICAL FORCES

There is documented evidence that humans can walk on firey coals without burning the skin, voluntarily alter heart rate, go into suspended animation and spontaneously heal from dramatic disease. All of these truths fly into the face of good science. Yet humans are intellectual and spiritual creatures who can defy some of the laws of physical science.

No doubt, we have only begun to tap into the vast potential of the human mind. Call it whatever you want: religion, psychology, philosophy, paranormal, metaphysics (beyond physical laws), or the catch phrase of today, psychoneuroimmunology. Humans do not always live by the rules of physical science. The more spiritual a person becomes, the less he or she is subject to physical laws.

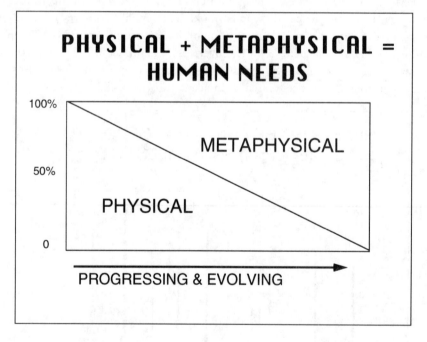

LIFE IS A CONTINUUM OF FLEXIBILITY, FROM BIRTH TO DEATH

A t conception, we are a tiny gelatinous egg. At birth, we are the amorphous "Houdini" that can contort our flexible bodies down the narrow birth passage. Babies' skeletons are composed primarily of flexible cartilage. As we mature, calcium is laid down in this bone matrix to solidify the skeleton. Some older adults develop brittleness in body, as in arthritis and osteoporosis, and mind, as in the curmudgeon unable to accept inevitable change.

Death is the ultimate rigid state of rigor mortis in which all unsaturated fats in the body turn to saturated fat, like lard. While aging is unavoidable, aging and disease are accelerated by rigidity of mind and body. To avoid disease and retard aging, stay flexibile in body, through exercises and stretching, and in mind, through openness to new ideas and tolerance of people.

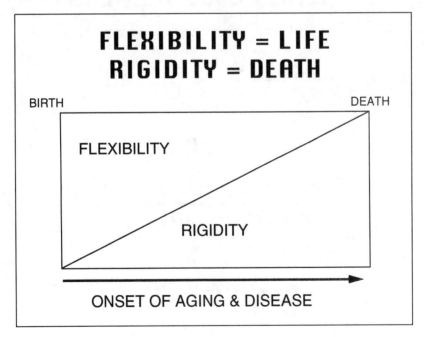

**FLEXIBILITY = LIFE
RIGIDITY = DEATH**

BIRTH   DEATH

FLEXIBILITY

RIGIDITY

ONSET OF AGING & DISEASE

THE MORE WELLNESS YOU HAVE, THE LESS ILLNESS YOU CAN HAVE

J ust like darkness is the absence of light, disease is the absence of wellness. Wellness is a state of optimal functioning of body, mind and spirit. A well person may have 90% wellness and 10% illness. A sick person may have 10% wellness and 90% illness. A body region cannot be well and ill at the same time. Therefore, curing illness is a matter of replacing it with wellness. The same unhealthy lifestyle may create heart disease in 30% of the people, cancer in 25%, arthritis in 10%, and mental illness in 5%. As per Dr. Charles Farr, in a very important step toward removing illness, simply allow wellness to infiltrate the body and mind.

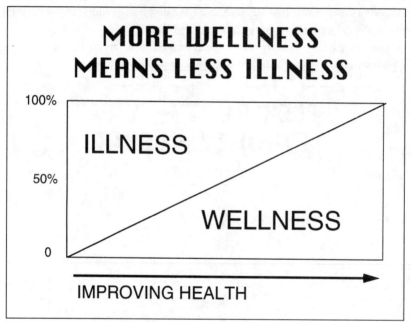

THERE WILL BE MORE LAWS

Nutrition is in its infancy. While the above laws apply in all humans, there will no doubt be more laws, since we are only beginning to understand the majesty of the human mind and body.

PATIENT PROFILE

Billie Sue Loveless, female, 56 years. I was admitted to Cancer Treatment Center of Tulsa in October, 1992 with a diagnosis of breast cancer, stage IV with pleural effusions (liquid in the lungs). I was in an extremely malnourished state. My prognosis was not favorable. Because eating was very difficult for me, I was placed on 24 hour total parenteral nutrition with oral vitamins. After three weeks, I had improved sufficiently to return home. For the next three months, I continued TPN therapy. At that time my weight had increased to an acceptable level and my TPN was stopped. Five months have passed and my weight holds steady. I have been eating lots of fresh fruits and vegetables, high protein shakes, and taking my vitamins, minerals and enzymes. I have been receiving chemo and radiation for the past 18 months with minimal side effects, largely due to the nutrition program I have followed. I am doing very well.

Chapter 7

The Strategy,
Why the Plan Works

Most cancer therapies merely deal with the cancer burden, not with the underlying causes that led to the abnormal growth. In this chapter, I will show you how to change the conditions that spawn cancer. This means bolstering the built-in mechanisms that protect us from cancer. As mentioned before, these protective mechanisms are ranked in order of importance, like a defensive football line trying to stop the runner from getting a touchdown.

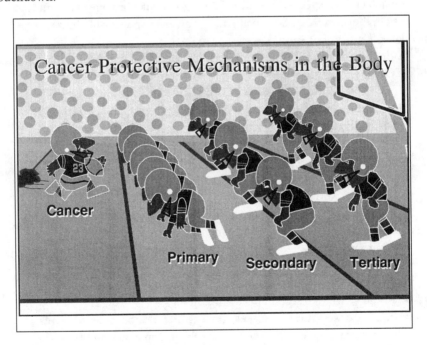

Cancer Protective Mechanisms in the Body

Cancer

Primary   Secondary   Tertiary

BOLSTERING THE BODY'S ANTI-CANCER MECHANISMS

THE FRONT LINE OF TACKLES & GUARDS—PRIMARY DEFENSE

IMMUNE SYSTEM.

We have an extensive network of protective factors that circulate throughout our bodies to kill any bacteria, virus, yeast or cancer cells. Think of these 20 trillion immune cells as both your Department of Defense and your waste disposal company.

Most experts now agree to the "surveillance" theory of cancer. Cells in your body are duplicating all day every day at a blinding pace. This process of growth is fraught with peril. When cells are not copied exactly as they should be, then an emergency call goes out to the immune system to find and destroy this abnormal saboteur cell. This process occurs frequently in most people throughout their lives. Fortunately, only one in three people will actually develop detectable cancer, yet most experts agree that everyone gets cancer about 6 times per lifetime. It is the surveillance of an alert and capable immune system that defends most of us from cancer.

In the cancer patient, for a variety of reasons, the immune system has not done its work.

The immune system can be *shut down* by:
- toxic metals, like lead, cadmium and mercury
- volatile organic chemicals, from agriculture and industry
- sugar
- omega-6 fats, like soy and corn oil
- stress and worry
- and more.

The immune system can also be *enhanced* by:
- vitamins, like A, beta-carotene, C, E, and B-6
- quasi-vitamins, like Coenzyme Q-10, EPA and GLA (special fats)
- minerals, like zinc, chromium, and selenium
- amino acids, like arginine and glutathione
- herbal extracts, like echinecea, ginseng, Pau D'arco, and astragalus
- nutrient factors, like yogurt, garlic, cabbage, enzymes and fresh green leafy vegetables.
- positive emotions, like love, forgiveness and creative visualization

---

We are going to bolster your immune army with improved:

■ **QUANTITY** by producing more Natural Killers cells, lymphocytes, interleukin and interferon.

■ **QUALITY** by:

1. Reducing the ability of cancer cells to hide from the immune system. A healthy immune system will attack and destroy any cells that do not have the "secret pass code" of host DNA. Both the fetus and cancer are able to survive by creating a hormone, HCG, which allows the fetus to hide from the immune system. Tumor necrosis factor (TNF), which is specifically made by the immune system to kill cancer cells, is like a sword. TNF-inhibitor is produced in the presence of HCG and is like putting a sheath on the sword. Digestive enzymes and vitamins E and A help to clear away the deceiving "Stealth" coating on the tumor and improve tumor recognition by the immune system.

2. Providing anti-oxidants. We can put special shielding on the immune soldiers so that when they douse a cancer cell with deadly chemicals, the immune soldier is protected and can go on to kill other cancer cells. Otherwise, you seriously restrict the "bag limit" of any given immune soldier.

■ **Enzymes** are organic catalysts that speed up the rate of a biochemical reaction. Enzymes either put things together, called conjugases, or take things apart, called hydrolases. There are literally millions of enzymes produced by your body each second. Without hydrolase enzymes in your gut, the digestion of food could not occur. Our body makes digestive enzymes to break down large food particles into usable molecules:

- proteins are digested into amino acids by the action of proteases, including trypsin and chymotrypsin
- starches are digested into simple sugars by the action of amylase
- fats are digested into fatty acids and glycerol by the action of lipase.

Our ancestors ate a diet high in uncooked foods. Cooking food denatures enzymes, like changing the white on an egg from waxey to white when it is cooked. All living tissue contains an abundance of hydrolase enzymes as part of the lysosomes, or "suicide bags", which are there to mop up cellular debris and destroy invading organisms. When our ancestors ate this diet high in uncooked food, they were receiving a regular infusion of "enzyme therapy" as a lucky by-product. These hydrolytic enzymes would help to digest the food, and about 10% of the unused enzymes would end up crossing through the intestinal wall into the blood stream.

It is clear that people who are undernourished without being malnourished live a longer and healthier life. Why this occurs is less obvious. Many good European studies support the use of digestive enzymes as a critical component of cancer treatment. Your mouth, stomach and intestines will make a certain amount of enzymes to digest your food into smaller molecules for absorption through the intestinal wall into the bloodstream. Enzymes absorbed into the bloodstream help to break up immune complexes, expose tumors to immune attack and assist in cell differentiation. People who eat less food may live longer because they are able to absorb a certain percentage of their unused digestive enzymes, which then have many therapeutic benefits. Indeed, as far back as 1934, an Austrian researcher, Dr. E. Freund found that cancer patients do not have the "solubilizing" tumor-destroying enzymes in their blood that normal healthy people have.

One of the founders of alternative cancer treatment, Donald Kelley, DDS, felt that cancer was caused by a deficiency of digestive enzyme production, just as diabetes is caused by a deficiency of insulin production. Both the diabetic and cancer patient have some genetic predisposition that makes he or she vulnerable to the disease. The symptoms of diabetes and cancer may be controlled with proper lifestyle, but the underlying genetic vulnerability will never go away. This enzyme theory may help to explain why the vast majority of cancer patients are older people, who have demonstrated a reduced output of digestive enzymes; and also explains why raw foods, which are high in hydrolytic enzymes, may sometimes help cancer patients.

There is twenty years of good research from Europe showing that enzyme therapy helps many types of cancer patients. Digestive enzymes can:

- reduce tumor growth and metastasis in experimental animals.[1]
- prevent radon-induced lung cancer in miners.[2]
- improve 5 year survival in breast cancer patients. Stage I at 91%, stage II at 75% and stage III at 50%.[3]
- bromelain (enzyme from pineapple) inhibited leukemic cell growth and induced human leukemia cells in culture to revert back to normal (cytodifferentiation).[4]
- reduce the complications of cancer, such as cachexia (weight loss), pain in joints, and depression.
- reduced the secondary infections that result from certain chemo and radiation methods, especially bleomycin-induced pneumotoxicity.[5]

Enzymes help the cancer patient by:
1. breaking up immune complexes, thus improving the efficiency of the immune system
2. chemically altering a by-product of the tumor to reduce cancer side effects
3. changing the surface of the tumor to make it more recognizable to the host immune system.

Enzymes are an important aspect of my program. Beyond the scientific evidence, I have personally seen enzymes help many cancer patients. While other enzyme products may work equally well against cancer, Wobenzym is one of the few enzyme products that has been clinically tested on cancer patients. Wobenzym (800-899-4499) is a unique product from Germany with a proprietary blend of various plant and animal-derived digestive enzymes, coupled with rutin (a bioflavonoid) all packaged in an enterically coated pill to survive the acid bath of the stomach and move into the intestines for absorption.

PROTECT AND REPAIR DNA

Your 60 trillion cells possess a thread of material that holds all the "blue print" information to make another you. This thread, called DNA, is truly the essence of life itself. DNA looks like a spiral staircase that is so long and flexible, it begins to wind around and wrap into "X" shapes. Stored on 23 pairs of chromosomes are 50,000 to 100,000 genes, collectively called the human genome. If you could unravel and place end to end the DNA in one adult body, it would reach to the moon and back—8,000 times![6]

This long spiral staircase is constantly under attack. As mentioned, each cell in the human body takes an average of 1,000 to 10,000 "hits" or DNA breaks each day. Imagine sitting on your roof in the middle of a hurricane while shingles are constantly being ripped off and you have to continuously repair this damage. Make a mistake, and cancer could be the consequence. Geneticists have estimated that each DNA molecule contains about the same amount of information as would be typed on 500,000 pages of manuscript. Imagine if trillions of times daily, you had to type a half million pages error-free. A mistake can lead to cancer.

Fortunately, the body is well prepared to keep the inevitable DNA errors from turning into cancer. DNA polymerase is a repair enzyme system that moves along this spiral staircase, like a railcar on railroad tracks, finding and fixing broken rail ties, or base pairs. This crucial repair system is fueled by folacin, zinc and other nutrients. A low intake of folacin increases the likelihood that cancer will become metastatic. One of the earlier drugs used against cancer, methotrexate, is a folacin inhibitor that limits new cell growth. Giving folacin to a patient on methotrexate does not inhibit the effectiveness of the drug, since it is folinic acid, a more metabolically active form of folacin, that is required to rescue a patient from methotrexate therapy.

Certain ethnic groups in the Middle East who eat extremely hot or abrasive foods have a higher incidence of cancer of the esophagus. Mechanical injury, especially when repeated, means that the repair process has accelerated beyond the normal hurricane into something much wilder. During these vulnerable phases, the body needs to be free of contaminants and have an adequate supply of growth nutrients—lest cancer surface.

I worked with a young patient who developed a cancerous growth in the exact same area where he had experienced a mechanical injury. This 32 year old male had been in a snow skiing accident, in which he fell and accidentally stabbed himself in his thigh muscle with his ski pole. He was a smoker and ate a typical American diet, which is low in zinc and folacin. His wound seemed to heal well within the expected few months; then one year later he developed a massive metastatic lesion exactly where he had injured himself and died soon thereafter. The injury created the stress, the tobacco provided generous amounts of a carcinogen to interrupt the repair process and his typical American diet lacked the growth nutrients required for accurate DNA synthesis.

There are food components in soybeans that shut down the cancer process at the DNA level. Twenty years of work by Dr. Ann Kennedy has shown that something in soybeans, coined the Bowman Birk Inhibitor, will both prevent and reverse the cancer process in numerous animal studies. You don't need to wait for this BBI to become an FDA-approved drug. By eating a 1/2 cup serving of soybeans daily, you can provide your body with this vital DNA-protector. Could it be that the successes from the macrobiotic diet are primarily due to this soybean factor?

Vitamin D inhibits the production of DNA fragments from cancer cells, hence helping to shut down the metastatic process. Residents of sunnier climates have a much lower incidence of breast cancer. Sunlight is essential for the production of vitamin D, which then prevents the "seeds" of cancer cells from being spread throughout the body.

We all contain oncogenes, or "oncology genes" on the DNA that are like a dormant saboteur waiting to be awakened to cause cancer. DNA has receptors for certain nutrients, just like immune soldiers have receptors for brain chemicals. Nearly seven decades of research shows that humans and animals have a higher cancer rate as vitamin A intake goes down. Molecular biologists have shown that vitamin A "plugs in" to the DNA to regulate growth. Studies in Europe with lung cancer patients show a higher survival rate and lower incidence of cancer recurrence with patients taking high dose vitamin A along with conventional therapy. Vitamin A may help shut down the cancer process by down-regulating oncogenes.

This continuous repair process of DNA is like a high speed bullet train that is easily derailed. Cancer is the resulting train wreck. We need to get these DNA repair mechanisms working properly in the cancer patient.

INFLUENCE CELL DIFFERENTIATION

Somehow, an invisible fertilized human egg cell will become a complex adult with millions of categories of specialized cells. Cell differentiation involves the process of one undifferentiated cell splitting and becoming a kidney cell and a liver cell. This miraculous process is one of the more bewildering aspects of human development. A cancer cell has differentiated into a rebellious saboteur. There are nutrients, including vitamins A, D and digestive enzymes that improve the accuracy of the cell differentiation process.

LINEBACKERS—SECONDARY DEFENSE

OXYGENATE YOUR BODY.

One of the most prominent differences between healthy cells and cancer cells is that cancer is an anaerobic cell, fermenting rather than metabolizing food and living in the absence of oxygen. Professor Otto Warburg received two Nobel prizes, in 1931 and 1944 for his work on cell bioenergetics, or how the cell extracts energy from food. In 1966, Professor Warburg spoke to a group of Nobel laureates regarding his work on cancer cells: "...the prime cause of cancer is the replacement of the respiration of oxygen in normal body cells by a fermentation of sugar." Cancer cells are more like primitive yeast cells, extracting only a fraction of the potential energy from sugar by fermenting food substrates down to lactic acid.

This singular difference is both the strength and weakness of cancer. Cancer slowly destroys its host by using up fuel inefficiently and thus causing lean tissue wasting, in which the patient begins to convert protein to sugar in order to maintain a certain level of blood sugar. Cancer also hides in its oxygen deficit pockets. The denser and more anaerobic the tumor mass, the more resistant the tumor is to radiation therapy.

■ **Aerobic-enhancing nutrients**. Yet, by oxygenating the tissue, you can exploit the "Achilles heel" of cancer. Cancer shrinks from oxygen like a vampire shrinking from daylight. Fuel is burned in the cellular furnaces, called mitochondria. As long as the mitochondrial membrane is fluid and permeable, oxygen flows in and carbon dioxide flows out and the cell stays aerobic. With a diet high in fat, saturated fat and cholesterol; the mitochondrial membrane becomes more rigid and less permeable to the flow of gases and electrons, which are essential to aerobic metabolism.

Nutrient factors that heavily influence aerobic metabolism include the B-vitamins, including biotin, B-1 thiamin, B-2 riboflavin and B-3 niacin. Numerous herbal extracts, including ginseng and ginkgo biloba, can enhance the aerobic capacity of the cell. Coenzyme Q-10 is a nutrient that is the rate-limiting step in aerobic metabolism, not unlike the bridge that ties up traffic going into the city during rush hour. Most people are low in their levels of CoQ. In an unpublished study of our cancer patients, we found that serum levels of CoQ were roughly half that of the average American, which is still well below optimal. Karl

Folkers, PhD of the University of Texas finds that 90% of Americans have serum CoQ levels that are indicative of a deficiency. CoQ:

- is a potent fat soluble anti-oxidant.[7]
- has been shown to prevent cancer and reduce the size and metastasis of induced cancers.[8]
- supplements taken orally usually elevate serum CoQ levels and improve aerobic metabolism.[9]
- improves cardiac ejection, or how much blood that the heart can pump.[10]
- improves immune functions overall.[11]
- improves the ratio of T-4 to T-8 lymphocytes.[12]

■ **Exercise**. Humans evolved as active creatures. Our biochemical processes depend on regular exercise to maintain homeostasis. A well respected Stanford physician, Dr. William Bortz, published a review of the scientific literature on exercise and concluded: "our dis-eases may be from dis-use of the body."[13] Cancer patients who exercise have fewer side effects from oncology therapy. Exercise oxygenates the tissue, which slows the anaerobic cancer cell progress. Exercise stabilizes blood sugar levels, which selectively deprives cancer cells of their favorite fuel. Even if exercise is not a possibility for the cancer patient, deep breathing would be invaluable. The most essential nutrient in the human body is oxygen. Sheldon Hendler, MD, PhD has written an excellent book on the need for oxygenation of tissue in THE OXYGEN BREAKTHROUGH.[14] Westerners typically are sedentary and breath shallowly, which deprives the body of oxygen, which is a perfect environment for cancer.

■ **Breathing** is a lost art in our modern world. Ancient scholars and spiritual teachers taught us that breath as the essence of life. Modern Americans breath shallowly, or try the military breathing stance with chest thrust out and stomach sucked in—all of which leaves the tissue oxygen-starved. Proper breathing should include stomach and diaphragm deep breathing. Lay flat on your back on the floor. Place a book on your stomach. Begin inhaling through the nose and push out the stomach. Raise the book as high as you can, then complete inhalation by filling the chest with air. Exhale through the mouth slowly. This is diaphragm breathing, which more thoroughly oxygenates tissue and can be done by the most bed-ridden patient.

In another effort to oxygenate tissue, some physicians have been using hydrogen peroxide therapy given intravenously for cancer, AIDS, chronic fatigue and allergy patients. For more information on physicians in your area who can administer this safe and potentially helpful therapy, contact the International Bio-Oxidative Medical Society in Oklahoma City at 405-478-4266.

CELL MEMBRANE DYNAMICS—THE GATEKEEPER

Each cell in your body is like a miniature water balloon with a semi-permeable outside membrane. This membrane becomes the "gatekeeper" that allows nutrients to flow in and toxins to flow out. The more flexible and selectively porous this membrane, the better. Many substances in the diet alter cell membrane dynamics.

While the protein and carbohydrates that make up the structure of our body cells are largely influenced by genetics, the structural fats in our cells are entirely based on our diet. You cannot make a silk purse out of a sow's ear. And you cannot make an essential fatty acid from a saturated or hydrogenated fat. The fats in the cell membrane are a perfect reflection of the diet.

Long ago, food manufacturers in America recognized the merits of saturated and hydrogenated fats: they have a long shelf life, they do not ooze out of the food product because they are solid at room temperature and they are cheap to produce. Unfortunately, these same fats create a rigid gatekeeper in the cell membrane. One third of fat intake in America is saturated and much of the remaining two thirds is at least partially hydrogenated. Hydrogenation involves adding a hydrogen atom to a fat to increase saturation and change three dimensional structure. If you want a flexible and cooperative gatekeeper, then you need to eat more complex carbohydrate foods and less overall fat. Of the fat that you do eat, consume more valuable fats like EPA from fish oil, GLA from black current seed, borage or evening primrose oil and ALA from flaxseed oil.

The fats that we eat do more than become an integral structural part of cell membranes, these fats also become part of prostaglandins, which are potent hormone-like substances that dramatically influence bodily processes. The same valuable oils mentioned above will also help create a prostaglandin series 1 and 3, which elevates immune function, reduces the stickiness of cells to deter metastasis, improves blood flow by vasodilation and reduces inflammation. Stickiness of blood components is another critical topic for the cancer patient. Rarely does any cancer patient die of one tumor. It usually takes massive spreading, or metastasis, of the tumor to cause death. Tumor cells spread by sending out "sticky" cancer cells to adhere to the walls of blood vessels, burrow through the vascular wall, then start a fresh tumor in another area of the body. By reducing stickiness, we can dramatically slow down the ability of the tumor to spread.

The sodium to potassium ratio in the diet also influences the cell gatekeepers. Potassium is found primarily in unprocessed plant food, like vegetables, fruit, whole grains and legumes. There is some sodium in all foods, with higher concentrations in animal foods, and much more of it in processed foods. Americans eat 10 times the sodium that our ancestors consumed. An ideal ratio of sodium to potassium would be 1 to 4, but ours is 4 to 1. By drastically changing this ratio, we have changed the "electrolyte soup" that bathes all cells and creates the electrical battery of life. This electrical charge influences the gatekeeper. High sodium diets increase both cancer incidence and metastasis. To improve the gatekeeper's functions, return to our "factory specification" diet of lots of potassium and little sodium. Consume a diet in which the calorie breakdown is about 1/3 each low fat animal food (like fish, turkey, chicken, lean ham), 1/3 unprocessed cooked plant food (like potatoes, garlic, squash, whole grains, legumes), and 1/3 unprocessed uncooked plant food (like fresh green leafy vegetables and fruit). That's the calorie breakdown. Since lean meat is very dense in calories compared to plant food, the volume breakdown is somewhat different:

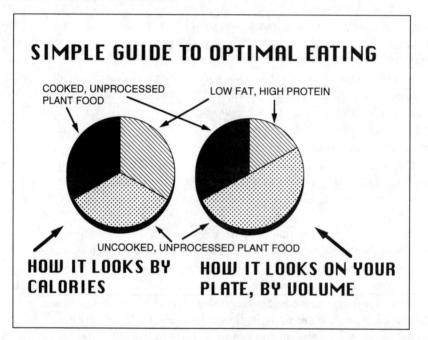

GET RID OF THE GARBAGE

Everyone is detoxifying their bodies all day throughout their lives—or they would die. But some people don't detox fast enough, and the toxins build up to encumber their bodily processes. One of the favored theories of aging says that eventually the accumulation of these cellular waste products overwhelms the cells and they begin to die. Similarly, fermenting yeast creates alcohol to a certain point and then dies in its own toxins. Cell cultures of living tissue that are kept in a fresh nutrient solution and changed daily to eliminate toxin buildup will experience slowed aging.

If I was forced to summarize the essence of good health into one simple sentence, it would be: "bring in the right groceries (nutrients) and take out the trash (toxins)." Each of the 60 trillion cells in your body is like a house in your neighborhood. You must bring in the right collection of essential groceries and remove the garbage often. Many cancer patients have erred at both ends of this equation: not enough essential nutrients coupled with an accumulation of poisons.

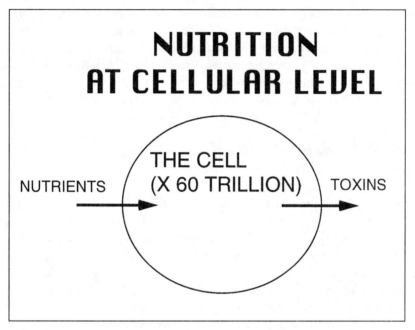

Fortunately, humans are not "virgins" at exposure to poisons. The human body, when properly nourished, has an enormous capacity to either excrete or neutralize poisons. Yet 20th century pollution has stretched the limits of our elaborate detoxification systems. We have physical means of eliminating waste products through urine, feces, exhaled air, sweat and tears. We also possess an enviable system of chemical detoxification that is mostly concentrated in the liver, where a complex array of enzymes serve to neutralize poisons. Cytochrome P-450, catalase, mixed function oxidase, conjugase and other enzymes are constantly at work neutralizing and excreting poisons from the body. That is why the liver is often the secondary organ affected after some other part of the body becomes cancerous—like trying to break up a fight and, instead, getting beat up.

Not only do many people voluntarily consume poisons, such as tobacco, alcohol, prescription and "recreational" drugs; but we are also exposed to an alarming amount of involuntary poisons in our air, food, and water supply. Annually, America alone dumps 90 billion pounds of toxic waste into our 55,000 toxic waste sites, sprays 1.2 billion pounds of pesticides on our food crops[15], and spews forth 600 pounds of air pollutants for every person in America. Scientists have found residues of the lethal industrial solvent PCB (polychlorinated biphenyls) and the pesticide DDT in every human on earth, including mother's milk. And on it goes.

After looking at the toxic burden carried by the average American adult, the question is not: "Why do 1/3 of us get cancer?", but a more appropriate question might be: "Why do *only* 1/3 of us get cancer?" Dr. Sam Epstein has profound evidence showing that regardless of other measures taken, our cancer epidemic will not be abated until we get our environmental disaster cleaned up. By increasing the body's ability to purge poisons, detoxification may help the cancer recovery process for some individuals. Toxic burden blunts the immune system, erodes the delicate DNA, changes cellular functions and encourages cancer growth.

A word on coffee enemas. Enemas are one of the oldest healing modalities in human literature. Milk enemas are still used by noted surgeons and gastroenterologists to stem diarrhea that does not respond to medication. Coffee enemas have been in the Merck Medical Manual for decades, until 1977, when editors of the manual claimed that this revered therapy was eliminated for "lack of space" in the new manuscript. The reality is that coffee enemas became the focal point in criticizing alternative cancer therapies. Coffee enemas help to purge the colon and liver of accumulated toxins and dead tissue. Coffee enemas are prepared by brewing regular organic caffeinated coffee, let cool to body temperature, then use enema bag as per instructions with 4 to 8 ounces of the coffee solution. Proponents of this therapy use it daily for very sick cancer patients, or weekly for recovering cancer patients.

As a by-product of living, we create our own waste products, which must be eliminated or we die in our own biological sewage. Urine contains a collection of worn out parts, filtered out toxins and potentially lethal ammonia. The intestines can become a distillation device like the old moonshiner "still", loaded with strange by-products as bacteria ferment food matter into an incredible array of chemicals and gases. Feces contains unabsorbed food matter, about 100 billion bacteria per gram and many toxins that could cause cancer if allowed to contact the intestinal wall long enough.

Detoxification includes:

■ **Urine**. Increasing urinary output and dilution of urine poisons by drinking more clean water, 8-10 cups of fluid daily, which is enough to have urine that is light yellow in color and inoffensive in odor. Drink filtered water, preferably from reverse osmosis. Chelation therapy helps the body to gather up toxic minerals and excrete them via the urine.

■ **Feces**. Improve fiber intake until feces are soft in consistency. Also, fix digestive problems, such as low output of hydrochloric acid or digestive enzymes. Take mild herbal purgatives, such as Perfect 7. Some people use enemas and colonic irrigation. The typical American diet is low in fiber and loaded with poisons. Colon cleansing, through a variety of methods, is crucial for whole body detoxification.

■ **Sweat.** Encourage purging of toxins through sweat glands by taking hot baths or steam baths, then scrubbing the skin with a natural sponge to scrape off the excreted poisons.

■ **Mercury.** With more than 90% of the American population sporting at least a few mercury fillings in their teeth, the subject of mercury poisoning has become a hot topic. Lewis Carroll's classic book, Alice in Wonderland, showcased the "mad hatter" as representative of an industry that whimsically used mercury to give stiffness to formal felt hats. Mercury is a deadly poison, and putting it in the mouth to erode over the years and eventually be swallowed is just plain ridiculous. About 1% of the population, or 2 million people, are very sensitive to any exposure to mercury while most other people would be better off without any mercury in their mouth. Some people have found relief from a wide assortment of diseases, including cancer, by having their mercury fillings replaced with non-toxic ceramic or gold material.[16]

■ **Chelation of heavy metals.** Lead poisoning is much more common than mercury poisoning. Though our use of lead is starting to be reduced, lead is a clearcut immune poison and has been targeted by the Environmental Protection Agency as a "top priority" cleanup item. Chelation therapy involves injecting chemicals (like EDTA) that put the heavy metal in a molecular "cage" and carry it out of the body in the urine. Chelation therapy may help to reduce heavy metal toxicity, which is assessed by mineral excretion in the urine or by hair/nail analysis.

■ **Reduce intake of poisons.** Over a century after the evidence clearly pointed toward the harmful effects of smoking, 25% of Americans and up to 90% of males in other countries still smoke. In my work with hundreds of cancer patients, I have never seen a smoker get better. Ironically, smoking may have a minor benefit for some people, since smoking elevates basal metabolism, which is particularly noticeable in hypothyroid individuals. My hunch is that people who find smoking such an addiction are using nicotine to elevate basal metabolism as a crutch to support their sagging thyroid output. A way to ease the withdrawal for these people is to normalize thyroid output. See the "action" plan for more details on thyroid help.

According to the National Academy of Sciences, pesticide residues on food crops causes 14,000 new cases of cancer each year out of 1.3 million total cases. Which means that about 1% of our cancer comes from pesticide use and abuse. That 1% is fairly insignificant, unless you are one of those 14,000 people. For those people who do not have easy access to organic produce, which is grown without pesticide use, peeling or washing produce is mandatory. For produce that you consume entirely, like broccoli and apples, soak it in a solution of one gallon of warm water per 2 tablespoons of vinegar for 5 minutes, then rinse and brush.

From tainted water, food and air; to exposure to carcinogens in the home and work place; to voluntary intake of poisons in drugs, alcohol and tobacco to showers of electromagnetic radiation falling on us—Americans are constantly pushing the outer envelope for toxin tolerance. Too many of these common toxins both assault the fragile DNA and blunt immune functions. We need to be more responsible in dealing with our 20th century waste products. Cancer patients need to do everything possible to eliminate accumulated wastes and minimize intake of new toxins.

BALANCING pH

Cancer is acidic (low pH) tissue.[17] It is clear from all human physiology textbooks that pH in the blood, saliva, urine and other areas is a critical factor for health. Blood pH is usually 7.35-7.45 with 7.41 thought to be ideal. Acceptable pH for saliva is 6.0-7.5, stomach 1.0-3.5, colon 5.0-8.4 and urine 4.5-8.4. Most foods influence pH—pushing toward either acid or alkaline. Clinicians will spend much time adjusting parenteral feedings to achieve a proper pH in the blood. Meanwhile, there have been many alternative health books that attempt to treat various diseases by adjusting the body pH via the diet.

Potential hydrogens, or pH, refers to the acid or alkaline nature of a chemical. If you mix a mild acid, like vinegar, with a mild alkaline substance, like baking soda, then the resulting reaction produces a salt—they neutralize one another by exchanging hydrogens. Just about everything that goes in your mouth can alter pH, including oxygen. The acidic pH of cancer cells also decreases the oxygen-carrying capacity of the surrounding blood so that tissue can become somewhat anaerobic—which are perfect conditions for cancer to thrive. Deep breathing has an alkalizing effect on the blood. An alkalizing diet of lots of plant food also helps to encourage removal of toxic heavy metals.

The macrobiotic book claims that pH adjustment is one of the more crucial objectives of their diet.[18] Yet, I have worked with a few cancer patients who got worse on the macrobiotic program. Remember our discussion of biochemical individuality—not everyone will thrive on the same diet. Nick Gonzales, MD sometimes uses a diet high in red meat to adjust the cancer patient's pH into a normal range. It appears that some people are prone toward extreme acid or alkaline metabolism. For these people on the edge of acceptable biological pH, diet provides a counterbalance to bring serum pH back toward normal. Think of sailing a small boat where you may have to use your body as a counterbalance to prevent the boat from being tipped over by the wind. If your metabolism is in jeopardy of "tipping over" toward extreme pH, then diet and breathing become your counterbalances that keep metabolism upright.

While this area may be absolutely essential for some cancer patients, a trial and error method may be the only way to find out which direction your pH needs adjusting. If your condition improves on the macrobiotic program, then you are pushing your pH in the right direction. If your condition worsens on the macrobiotic program, then you must push your pH in the opposite direction.

The following chart is a composite of many works, including Russell Jaffe, MD, PhD, the USDA food data base, FOOD & NUTRITION ENCYCLOPEDIA, NUTRITION APPLIED PERSONALLY, and ACID/ALKALINE. Use this chart as a guidepost to adjust your pH. About 8% of the population must have acid forming foods to counterbalance their extremely alkalotic pH. Some people can eat anything they want and their internal mechanisms compensate to find an acceptable pH. For many people, an alkalizing diet (toward the left) will help to neutralize their acidifying tendencies, which can invite cancer.

Venous pH is the most accurate indicator of your overall body pH. Yet blood tests are invasive, expensive and not practical for regular use. A rough indicator of your body pH is your saliva and urinary pH. You can purchase Nitrazine paper from your local druggist and follow the directions for measuring saliva or urine pH. Test your saliva at least one hour after any food or drink. If your saliva is strongly acidic, then you may need to emphasize this part of my program.

THE TELEGRAPH BETWEEN CELLS

Cells communicate with one another in an intricate system using ions that move in and out of the gap cell junctions. This system works like a telegraph to keep nearby cells relating on DNA content. Studies have shown that vitamin A, and probably other nutrients, encourage this healthy communication of cells which slows metastasis and improves the chances for a cancer cell reverting back to a normal healthy cell.

DECREASE THE "STICKINESS" OF THE SPREADING CANCER CELLS

Even tiny cancer growths are constantly sending out cells for "colonizing" other areas of the body. This metastatic process is the real problem in cancer. Prostaglandins are potent hormone-like substances that influence, among other things, the stickiness of cells. We all make prostaglandins all the time. The question is whether you are making "emergency" prostaglandins that are counterproductive for anything more than a few minutes a month, or healthy prostaglandins which can dramatically reverse disease.

Not long ago there was a toy fad involving a "wacky wall walker" in which some clever entrepreneur promoted a small piece of very flexible rubber that was

pH INFLUENCE OF FOODS

MOST ALKALINE ← | NEUTRAL | → MOST ACIDIC

Category	MOST ALKALINE				aspartame	vanilla	psychotropics	cocoa (MOST ACIDIC)
THERAPEUTICS	salt	mineral water	sake	algae	aspartame	vanilla	psychotropics	cocoa
SWEETENERS		molasses	rice syrup	sucanat	honey	tapioca	saccharin	sugar
OTHERS		sea salt	green tea		maple syrup	black tea	antibiotics	fried foods
VINEGAR		soy sauce	apple cider	umeboshi	rice	balsamic		white
DAIRY				human milk	cream/yogurt	milk/aged chez	casein, soymilk	ice cream, chez
MEAT, EGGS					eggs, organs	lamb	pork, veal	beef
FOWL, GAME					duck, venison	goose, turkey	chicken	pheasant
FISH, & SHELL					fish, crab	shell f., mollusk	eel, crustacea	lobster, oyster
NUTS, OILS	pumpkin, lotus	poppy, chestnut	primrose, sprout, sesame	avocado, flax, coconut	grape, sunflower, pine	almond, cashew	pistachio, chestnut, lard	cottonseed, hazel, walnut
GRAINS				oats, quinoa, wild rice	millet, kashi, amaranth	buckwheat, wheat, spelt	maize, corn, rye	barley
BEANS, VEGETABLES	lentil, yam, sea vegetables, onion	parsnip, garlic, kale, endive	potato, bell pepper, mushroom, cauliflower, egg plant	beet, brussel sprout, chive, okra, turnip gr.	spinach, fava, kidney, string bean	tofu, pinto, white, navy beans	green pea, peanut, carrot, garbanzo	soybean, carob
FRUIT	nectarine, watermelon, raspberry, tangerine	citrus, cantaloupe, honeydew, mango	pear, pineapple, apple, blackberry, cherry, peach, papaya	apricot, banana, blueberry, grape, strawberry	guava, pineapple, figs, persimmon, date	plum, prune, tomato	cranberry, pomegranate	

coated with a sticky material. You throw the toy at a window and it sticks, then slowly starts to move down the window. Cancer spreads in similar fashion. The initial tumor flings out colonizing cells that try to stick to the surface of blood vessel walls and start a new tumor. By reducing the stickiness of cells, we are coating the "wacky wall walker" of cancer with a layer of salad oil to reduce metastasis. If you can slow down the spreading of cancer, then you are winning an important battle in the war on cancer.

The stickiness of cells, or platelet aggregation, can be varied by:

- anti-coagulants, like coumadin derived from the rat poison Warfarin, have been shown to reduce metastasis and improve cancer outcome
- aspirin works by affecting prostaglandin metabolism and cell stickiness, hence some studies have shown a reduced risk for cancer with regular aspirin intake
- vitamin E works by protecting the prostaglandin that reduces the stickiness of cells
- enzymes, like Wobenzym, reduce the stickiness of cells and change the coating on cancer cells
- EPA (eicosapentaenoic acid) from fish oil feeds the prostaglandin pathway that makes cells more slippery
- the least toxic and most effective of these anti-metastatic efforts is to use food and supplements to direct healthy prostaglandin synthesis.

Drug companies have spent billions of dollars researching prostaglandins and trying to develop some "magic bullet" that could cure diseases. But prostaglandins taken orally do not survive the acid bath of the stomach, and prostaglandins injected are removed from the system long before they make one pass through the vascular network. Hence, if you want to create a favorable flow of prostaglandins, then you are going to have to do it with your diet: stabilize blood sugar levels while consuming a low sugar diet, while taking generous amounts of vitamin E, EPA and GLA.

ADJUST STEROID HORMONE ACTIVITY

Steroid hormones, particularly estrogen in breast cancer, can cause or worsen cancer. Some physicians and researchers have misinterpreted this information to recommend that women have wholesale preventive surgery to remove the breast and ovaries, which are main sources of estrogen production. You will notice that none of these predominantly male experts have recommended wholesale castration of males, which would follow a parallel path in preventing prostate cancer. Humans are not defective and universal removal of sexual organs is not the answer to cancer. There are numerous biological mechanisms that keep

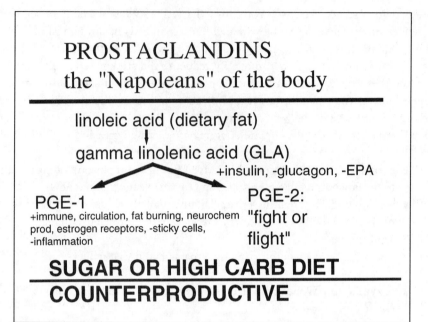

PROSTAGLANDINS
the "Napoleans" of the body

linoleic acid (dietary fat)

gamma linolenic acid (GLA)

+insulin, -glucagon, -EPA

PGE-1
+immune, circulation, fat burning, neurochem
prod, estrogen receptors, -sticky cells,
-inflammation

PGE-2:
"fight or
flight"

SUGAR OR HIGH CARB DIET
COUNTERPRODUCTIVE

these potentially lethal hormones under control.

Since estrogen is produced in adipose storage cells, the total amount of body fat dramatically influences estrogen metabolism.[19] Therefore, controlling obesity can reduce free circulating estrogen levels and help to control breast cancer. Also, the body makes its own estrogen binders as a by-product of healthy prostaglandin metabolism. Once again, high blood sugar levels can cripple these built-in mechanisms for controlling estrogen. Also, there are phyto-estrogens, or estrogen-like compounds found in plants (especially cabbage family and soybeans) that bind to estrogen receptors to inhibit estrogen-driven cancer. There are certain lignans in plant food that provide estrogen analogs (similar in structure) that can slow estrogen-related cancers.

The upshot of this area is: 1. avoid or reduce obesity, 2. eat more fresh vegetables, including broccoli, cabbage, brussel sprouts, cauliflower, and soybean foods, 3. control prostaglandin flow with more fish oil or flaxseed oil and very low controlled blood glucose levels.

BIOENERGETICS

Tumors have abnormal energy metabolism that more resembles a primitive yeast organism in fermenting sugar. We can capitalize on this difference to selectively starve tumors. Tumor growth can be controlled by minimizing rises in blood sugar. Thus, your strategy here includes aerobic exercise, with therapeutic levels of nutrients to encourage efficient aerobic metabolism:

Coenzyme Q-10, niacin, riboflavin, thiamin and perhaps germanium sesquioxide. Also, vitamin C selectively interferes with energy production in the tumor mitochondria.

PRO & ANTIOXIDANTS

Life is a continuous balancing act between oxidative forces (pro-oxidants) and protective forces (anti-oxidants). We want to fully oxygenate the tissue, which generates pro-oxidants, but we also want to protect healthy tissue from excess oxidative destruction, using anti-oxidants. Anti-oxidants are a sacrificial substance, to be destroyed in lieu of body tissue.

Salt water boaters know about the sacrificial plate that is mounted near the propeller of the boat. Salt water corrodes (pro-oxidant) all metals, including an expensive brass propeller. But we can slow down that corrosion by bolting a zinc plate near the brass propeller. The salt water then corrodes the sacrifical zinc plate in preference over the nearby brass propeller. Anti-oxidants act similarly, by being destroyed to protect something more valuable. Anti-oxidants include beta-carotene, C, E, selenium, zinc, riboflavin, manganese, cysteine, methionine, N-acetylcysteine, and many herbal extracts (i.e. green tea, pycnogenols, curcumin).

Tumor tissue does not absorb anti-oxidants as effectively as healthy host tissue. Hence loading the patient with therapeutic levels of anti-oxidants is like giving the good cells bullet proof vests before you go in with a SWAT unit that opens fire (chemo and radiation), thus killing more cancer cells than healthy cells. Some recent research shows that the destruction of tumor tissue that occurs with administration of EPA fish oil is because the tumor cells do not have normal protection against the oxidation of fats. These highly polyunsaturated fats are like grenades going off in cancer cells, but have minimum impact on healthy cells which are able to protect themselves with fat soluble anti-oxidants, like vitamin E and CoQ.

DEFENSIVE BACKS—TERTIARY DEFENSE

SELECTIVE TOXINS AGAINST CANCER

There are a number of substances in the diet and supplements that have been identified as selective toxins against cancer—they kill cancer but not healthy tissue:

- Vitamin K is similar in chemical structure to a potent chemotherapy drug, doxorubicin; yet vitamin K is non-toxic in normal dietary intake and has demonstrated a "selective toxin" effect as a supplement in human studies.[20]

- Bioflavonoids, especially quercetin[21] and rutin. Elliott Middleton, MD and colleagues have found that bioflavonoids cannot only slow down cancer, but may reverse cancer cells back to normal healthy cells.[22]
- Vitamin C[23], especially in combination with the B-12 vitamin[24]
- Garlic[25]
- Phycocyanins, or green pigment substances found in algae and spirulina.
- Sodium selenite[26]
- Vitamin E succinate[27]

GROWTH CONTROL FACTORS

Nutritionists are well aware of the need for nutrients to fuel growth, but when growth continues unrestricted, it becomes cancer. For every system in the body, there is something to turn it on and something to turn it off. Selenium and EPA are proposed nutrients that control growth.

THE ROOT KILLER—SHUT OFF THE BLOOD SUPPLY TO THE TUMOR

If you tie a tourniquet around your arm, the tissue on the other side will eventually die (ischemia). If you close all of the transportation routes into a city, it will eventually die. In 1980, well respected researchers Judah Folkman, MD at Harvard University and Robert Langer, MD of the MIT published an intriguing paper showing that something in cartilage tissue could slow down the growth of new blood vessel extending from tumors.[28] They coined this "X" factor, the anti-angiogenesis (making blood vessels) substance. The aggressiveness of tumor growth is clearly related to the number of new blood vessels being extended from the tumor(s).[29]

I. William Lane, PhD, found that shark cartilage was effective against animal tumors. Dr. Lane received a use patent on the use of shark cartilage to inhibit angiogenesis, indicating that even the United States Patent Office agreed that shark cartilage was a unique and potent anti-angiogenesis factor. Shark cartilage has fabulous potential as a non-toxic therapeutic substance against diseases that rely on the infiltration of new blood vessels, including solid tumors, rhematoid arthritis and inflammatory diseases.

Studies in Mexico and Cuba on end-stage cancer patients given shark cartilage found success with 1.5 gram per kilogram body weight given daily as oral powder or retention enema. A consultant in the Cuban study, Charles Simone, MD, is an NCI-trained oncologist. More studies are now underway with potential funding from the Office of Alternative Medicine through the National Institute of Health. While shark cartilage may sound like a therapy invented by Woody Allen; it may become a primary focus of cancer treatment in the near future. For localized solid tumors, the risk to benefit to cost ratio is heavily in favor of using this therapy.

Shark cartilage probably does not harm the growth of healthy blood vessels. Sharks have this anti-angiogenesis factor in their young, who are able to grow quite well in spite of the substance that selectively squelches tumor growth. Tumors send out blood vessels that grow in cork-screw fashion, while healthy tissue creates blood vessels that grow more direct, like tree roots. This difference allows the active ingredient in cartilage to selectively inhibit tumor tissue angiogenesis while allowing healthy host tissue to grow necessary blood vessels.

FIX WHAT'S BROKE

I f you have a zinc deficiency, then a truckload of vitamin C will not be nearly as valuable as giving the body what it needs to end the zinc deficiency. If an accumulation of lead and mercury has crimped the immune system, then removing the toxic metals is more important than psychotherapy. If a low output of hydrochloric acid in the stomach creates poor digestion and malabsorption, then hydrochloric acid supplements are the answer. If a broken spirit brought on the cancer, then spiritual healing is necessary to eliminate the cancer.

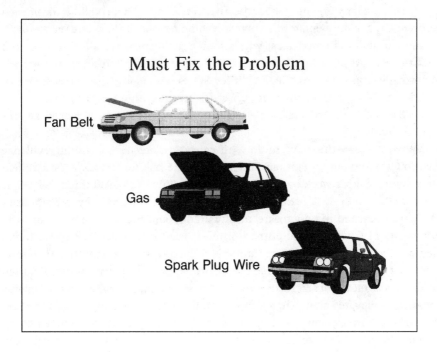

The need to "fix what's broke" is a prime limiting factor in studies that examine cancer therapies. In a given group of 100 cancer patients, based upon my experience, 10 may need grievance counselling, 10 may need high dose supplements to stimulate the immune system, 5 may need serious detoxification, and the remaining 75 have a complex combination of problems. This issue complicates cancer treatment tremendously and makes "cookbook" cancer treatment an exercise in futility. Our progress against cancer has been crippled not only by the complexity of cancer, but also by the need for Western science to isolate one variable. While it is easier to conduct and interpret research with one or two variables, cancer and the human body are far more complex than that. We will eventually help most cancer patients by fixing whatever bodily function needs repair. This is easier said than done. Finding the underlying problem requires a physician trained in comprehensive medicine.

THYROID CHECK

The second most common malnutritive condition in the world, after protein-calorie, is iodine deficiency, with about 400 million people suffering this condition. The mineral iodine feeds the thyroid gland, a small walnut-shaped gland in the throat region that produces a mere one teaspoon of thyroxin annually. But that thimble-full of thyroxin can make a huge difference in whether you will be bright or dull, fat or lean, healthy or sick, energetic or always tired. Like other organs, when the thyroid gland is deprived of its needed nutrients, it becomes enlarged. There are some regions of the world, particularly inland and mountainous areas, where iodine deficiency (goiter) is so common that the few people who do not have goiter are called "bottlenecks" for their abnormally slim necks. While the United States has made progress against goiter by adding iodine to salt, there are unsettling results from studies showing that about 33% of children consuming with seemingly adequate iodine intake still have goiter.[30]

What does all this have to do with cancer? There is compelling evidence that low thyroid output substantially elevates the risk for cancer.[31] Based upon the groundbreaking work by Broda Barnes, MD, PhD from 1930 through 1980, it is clear that about 40% of the population suffers from chronic hypothyroidism. Dr. Barnes earned his doctorate in physiology and medical degree from the University of Chicago. His primary interest was the thyroid gland. He found that people with a basal temperature of less than 97.8 F. were probably suffering from low thyroid. Symptoms include coldness; easy weight gain; constipation; sexual dysfunctions of infertility, frigidity, heavy periods, regular miscarriages or impotence; elevated serum lipids to induce heart disease; mental confusion and depression; hypoglycemia and diabetes; and cancer. This may sound like an improbable grocery list of diseases that can all stem from one simple cause. But realize that the thyroid gland regulates energy metabolism throughout the body, which is the basis for all other functions.

Work with your physician on this issue. Blood tests for thyroid function are not valid indicators of thyroid problems. Body temperature is the best way to detect hypothyroidism. Take your temperature first thing in the morning on several consecutive days before getting out of bed. If your temperature is below 97.8 F., then you may have a problem that can be easily resolved. Dessicated thyroid supplements are inexpensive and non-toxic. For some people, ginseng, kelp, chromium picolinate, L-carnitine and/or medium chain triglycerides (MCT) will slowly bring thyroid function up to normal. People who consume kelp, or sea vegetables, often have healthier thyroid functions, which indicates that sea vegetables or kelp tablets should be consumed by cancer patients. Here is another area of "simple solutions for major problems".

DEAL WITH YOUR ALLERGIES.

If nutrition itself is a controversial subject, then allergies represent controversy to the cubed power. From 25% to 50% of the population suffer from allergies, which can come from foods that we eat (ingestant), air particles that we breath (inhalant) or substances on our skin (contact). Allergies can cause an amazing array of diseases, including immune problems, arthritis, diabetes, heart disease, mental illness and more. The reason allergies are so complicated to detect and treat is the limitless combinations of chemicals in the human body. You might react to wheat products **only** if you consume citrus at the same meal **and** are under stress. Otherwise, wheat may not create any problems. Some people have transient food allergies, that come and go along with the pollen seasons. Because of this trend, some allergists subscribe to the "rain barrel" theory, in which you only have allergic reactions when the rain barrel is overflowing, such as combined allergies with stress.

Allergies are generated by an over-reactive immune system. What happens is that small undigested particles (polypeptides and peptides) of food pass through the intestinal wall into the blood stream and are recognized by the immune system as an invading bacteria (since its DNA is not yours). Now, you may be thinking that an over-reactive immune system should help to fight cancer, yet the immunoglobulins that instigate allergies will depress the production of cancer-killing immune factors, like natural killer cells and tumor necrosis factor. Allergies create an imbalanced immune system. Correct the allergies and you can re-establish a balanced immune attack.

Detecting and correcting allergies is a challenge at the Sherlock Holmes level. There are many methods designed to determine allergies, including radio-allergo-sorbent test (RAST), skin patch, dietary food challenge and sub-lingual testing. Probably the best tests are either the ELISA/ACT test from Serammune

Labs (800-553-5472) or ImmunoLaboratories Elisa test (800-231-9197).

Another way to relieve and/or detect allergic reactions is to use the Ultra-Clear program distributed by Metagenics (800-692-9400) This product is composed of rice protein (hypoallergenic) coupled with vitamins, minerals and amino acids to help the body eliminate toxins. For the full program, you consume this powdered protein drink as your only food for 21 days. Once you have allowed your allergic reactions to subside on this diet, then you can detect the offending substances by methodically re-introducing foods to your diet. Once you determine what foods or inhalants that you are allergic to, then it requires diligence to avoid that substance for at least 2 weeks while you reset the switch on the immune system. Allergic reactions can be:

■ Type 1. Immediate reaction of less than 2 hours. It is estimated that less than 15% of all food allergies are of this easily-detected   type.

■ Type 2. Delayed cytotoxic reaction which may require days to develop into subtle and internal symptoms. It is estimated that 75% of food allergies involve this category of cell destruction. The ELISA/ACT test detects type 2 delayed reactions.

■ Type 3. Immune complex mediated reactions. In this reaction, a "wrestling match" goes on between the antigen (offending factor) and antibody (immune factor trying to protect the body) which can easily slip through the permeable blood vessels due to large amounts of histamine release.

■ Type 4. T cell dependent reactions. Within 36-72 hours after exposure to the offending substance, inflammation is produced by stimulating T-cells.

Allergies are common, complex to diagnose, difficult to treat and very related to a variety of diseases, including cancer. A primitive and not terribly accurate way to find allergies involves the hypoallergenic diet. For 4 days, eat nothing but rice, apples, carrots, pears, lamb, turkey, olive and black tea. If you find relief from any particular symptoms, then add back a new food every four days and record the results. The most common allergenic foods are milk, wheat, beef, eggs, corn, peanut, soybeans, chicken, fish, nuts, mollusks and shellfish. Outside of humans, no other creature on earth consumes milk after weaning. Only 11-20% of Americans breast feed, which helps explain why the most allergenic food in the world is cow's milk.

Detecting and treating food allergies is a real challenge. I have found that any or all of the following can blunt allergic reactions: alfalfa (3-6 tablets daily), bee pollen (2-4 tablets daily), L-histidine (1000-1500 mg) and vitamin C (2-20 grams) .

IMPROVE DIGESTION

As many people mature, they can lose their ability to produce hydrochloric acid in the stomach (hypochlorhydria), or digestive enzymes in the intestines (pancreatic insufficiency), or their intestines become inhabited by hostile bacteria (dysbiosis), or their intestines become more permeable to food particles which causes allergies to surface.

Charles Farr, MD, PhD has been a pioneer in many areas of comprehensive health care, including nutrition and computer diet analysis. Dr. Farr has noticed that humans seem to slide into an "involutional malnutrition", meaning a retrograde or degenerative change in health. The beginning of the problems may stem from low output of stomach acid or pancreatic enzymes, which leads to poor digestion. Also, pathogens can now survive the less hostile GI tract for absorption into the bloodstream. Since the cancer patient has a compromised immune system that is not firing on all cylinders, this problem leaves the patient open to infections, called opportunistic infections, which can only gain a foothold in that person when their host defenses are down. Among the key host defense mechanisms against infections are mucous, saliva, acid and enzymes that guard the GI tract.

To determine the health of the digestive tract, you will probably need the help of a holistically oriented physician. There are diagnostic companies that are skilled at detecting the problem in a compromised GI tract. If you cannot find professional help, then here are some tips to help you determine if you have a problem with digestion. If your GI tract is working well, then you should have:

- a sensation of stomach emptying about 30-60 minutes after a meal.
- no excessive gas or discomfort.
- daily soft bowel movements that do not have greasy appearance or terribly offensive odor.
- bowel movements that do not have undigested food matter within.

If you do not have this "ideal" GI tract, then read on.

1. Hypochlorhydria. If you have a sense of stomach fullness for more than 30 minutes after eating, then you may be suffering from insufficient hydrochloric acid flow. To test this hypothesis, take 2 capsules of betaine hydrochloride (derived from beets), available at most health food stores, with your meal. If this therapy improves symptoms, then hypochlorhydria was indeed your problem. If this does not improve symptoms, then add 1 more pill with each meal until you get to five pills. If you have heartburn, then decrease dosage next time. If you find no relief, then discontinue altogether.

2. Pancreatic insufficiency. If you have cramps, heart burn or your food appears relatively undigested or greasy in the stools, then you may not be making enough digestive enzymes to break down your food. For enzyme replacement therapy, use digestive enzymes from Enzymatic Therapy (800-558-7372), called BioZyme. You may need 2-3 pills with each meal. If symptoms improve, then you may need to continue this therapy for the foreseeable future.

3. Parasites. Most of us have intestinal parasites. In some of us, these worms and bacteria are causing serious harm to the lining of the intestinal tract, such as a permeable gut which allows allergies to form. Our ancestors developed many de-worming techniques that they used seasonally, such as fasting while consuming purgative herbs or regular flushing out with garlic. In order to confirm if you have a problem, you must send a stool sample to a lab capable of detecting the myriad of microorganisms that inhabit the GI tract.

Change Your Diet

■ *Eat your ancestral diet.* There has been an endless parade of diets that were hailed as "the perfect diet". But there is no one perfect diet. Behold the fascinating spectrum of 5 billion people on the planet earth. We are all different. While macrobiotics may be helpful for some, it seems counterproductive for a few. In order to have a decent grasp on the core diet for humans, we need to take a ride in our time machine back 5000 years, to our hunter and gatherer ancestors who roamed the earth before the dawn of agriculture. By examining the diet of primitive hunter gatherer societies plus archeological findings, a trio of modern day "Indiana Jones" researchers turned up some of the most important nutrition data of the 20th century.[32]

Our ancestors ate a diet consisting of about 1/3 lean animal tissue with the remaining 2/3 of the diet unprocessed plant food; mostly vegetables, some grains, some fruit, nuts, seeds and legumes. If the creature runs, flies, or swims, then it may be about 4% body fat, with obvious exceptions including duck and salmon. Cows, the staple meat of America, do none of the above and are about 30-40% body fat. While there are certainly variations on this theme, this is the basic diet of our ancestors and a good starting point for our cancer-fighting diet. Both studies and my clinical experience show that a low fat diet with lots of fresh vegetables will improve cancer outcome. Take a look at the following graphic illustration of the contrast between the modern American diet and our "factory specification" diet. Notice how far we have strayed from our ancestral diet.

Keep in mind that you may have to "fine tune" this diet to suit your ethnic background. The macrobiotic diet was developed by a Japanese physician who

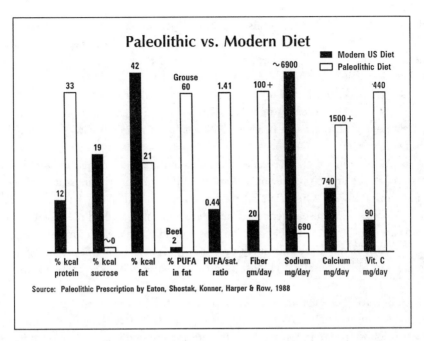

cured himself of cancer in the 19th century. The macrobiotic diet tends to encourage anything Oriental (even soy sauce and pickles) and discourage anything Western, including chicken, turkey, fish and fruit. Macrobiotics may be

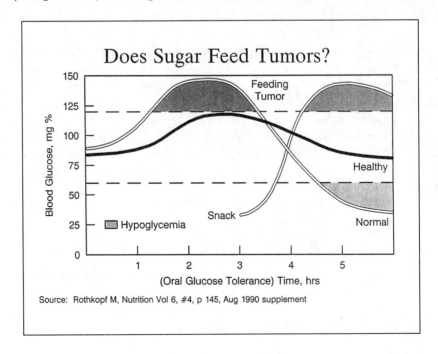

ideally suited for many Orientals, and has helped some Caucasians because it is such a vast improvement over the nutritional quality of the typical American diet. I encourage people to determine the diet of their ancestors 5000 years ago and use that food pattern as a starting point.

■ *Stabilize your blood sugar levels.* Cancer is a sugar-feeder.

The literature clearly points toward a substantial increase in glucose metabolism with the onset of cancer. Sugar has a number of ways in which it promotes cancer:

1. Rises in blood glucose generate corresponding rises of insulin, which then pushes prostaglandin production toward the immune-suppressing and stickiness-enhancing PGE-2. While fish oil (EPA) and borage oil (GLA) have a favorable impact on cancer, these potent fatty acids are neutralized when the blood glucose levels are kept high. Refer back to the prostaglandin chart earlier in this chapter.

2. Cancer cells feed directly on blood glucose, like a fermenting yeast organism. Elevating blood glucose in a cancer patient is like throwing gasoline on a smoldering fire.

3. Elevating blood glucose levels suppresses the immune system

■ *Normalize your sodium to potassium ratio.* Notice the very low intake of sodium found in our ancestors diet. By altering our sodium to potassium intake from a healthy 1:4 to a very unhealthy 4:1, we have literally changed the battery of life. Each cell in your body has an electrical charge that is generated by the difference in concentration between lots of potassium on the inside of the cell and lots of sodium on the outside of the cell. This electrical potential drives the cell membrane fluidity which allows oxygen and nutrients to flow into the cell and toxins to flow out. Slight changes in the electrolyte balance between sodium and potassium will create havoc on cell membrane dynamics. The cell begins to "secede from the union" and develop its own "country" of fermenting anaerobic rapidly growing cancerous cells.

Birger Jansson, PhD of the University of Texas has conducted studies of diets around the world showing a clear link between high sodium and low potassium intake and the elevated risk for cancer.[33] Other studies have found that you can turn on and off metastasis by altering the sodium to potassium ratio in the animal's diet.

Interestingly enough, many people have tried to explain why Black Americans have a higher cancer incidence than Caucasians. Blacks also have a higher incidence of hypertension. Blacks adapted to a warm equatorial climate where potassium intake was plentiful from fresh fruit and vegetables and sodium intake was sparse due to limited access to salt. Blacks have probably developed a sodium-sparing mechanism and higher need for potassium. Which makes the typical high sodium American diet even more disastrous in African Americans. Back to the issue: "eat what you are supposed to eat."

■ *Eat more vegetables.* Too many of our cancer patients have told me that the only green vegetable they ever ate were pickle relish on their hamburgers and olives in their martinis. Vegetables are low in glucose, high in fiber and Nature's richest repositories of cancer-fighting agents. Remember our discussion of the elegant tapestry of minor dietary constituents in food and how they fight cancer. Which might explain why scientists at the University of Hawaii found a direct relationship between vegetable intake and longevity in lung cancer patients.[34] Eat lots of fresh vegetables, some of which should be uncooked, especially green and orange fruits and vegetables.

Some of the earlier efforts at treating cancer with nutrition involved diets high in vegetables with regular fruit and vegetable juices offered throughout the day. Juicing has its advantages, because one glass of carrot juice is equal to about a pound of carrots, which few of us could eat. Unfortunately, much of the valuable anti-cancer nutrients in the vegetables get tossed out with the pulp that is discarded. That is why I recommend a complete liquification of the vegetable or fruit rather than just extracting juice from it. Vitamix (800-848-2649) is a unique blender device which keeps all the valuable nutrients in while allowing you to consume more vegetables in a liquid form. There are 10 times more cancer fighting agents in pureed whole vegetables than in juice extracted from vegetable pulp.

■ *Eat less fat.* A low fat diet enhances the outcome of cancer therapy. One of the few characteristics that the many seemingly different anti-cancer diets have in common is low fat. In both animals and humans, a low fat diet will improve cell membrane fluidity for better oxygenation of tissue and provide less opportunity for fat-rusting that can worsen the symptoms of chemo and radiation therapy. Of the fat that you do consume, make most of it olive or canola oil, with liberal amounts of fish, borage, flax and medium chain triglycerides (MCT) added in. MCT is the latest rage for body builders since this unique fat has been demonstrated in Harvard studies to prevent lean tissue wasting and elevate basal metabolism. More importantly for cancer patients, MCT helps to reduce lean tissue wasting in critically ill patients.[35]

■ *Slowly, safely, & nutritiously lose excess body fat.* Percent body fat is a major risk factor toward cancer, especially breast cancer. Losing weight properly will help improve the odds of beating cancer. Meanwhile, be certain that you are not loosing weight too rapidly, which can debilitate the immune fight against cancer.

CREATE A NEW WAY OF THINKING (CRISIS=OPPORTUNITY OR DANGER)

It was Hans Selye, MD who first scientifically showed that animals subjected to stress undergo thymic atrophy (immune suppression), elevations in blood pressure and serum lipids, and erosion of the stomach lining (ulcers).[36] Since then, literally thousands of human studies have demonstrated that an angry, stressed, or depressed mind can lead to a suppressed immune system, which allows cancer and infections to take over. Drs. Locke and Horning-Rohan have published a textbook consisting of over 1300 scientific articles written since 1976 that prove the link between the mind and the immune system.

We are finally beginning to accept what philosophers and spiritual leaders have been telling us for thousands of years: the mind has a major impact on the body and health. Proverbs 17:22 tells us "A joyful heart is good medicine, but a broken spirit dries up the bones." Over 100 years ago, observant physicians claimed that significant life events might increase the risk for developing cancer.[37] In the 1800s, emotional factors were related to breast cancer, and cervical cancer was related to sensitive and frustrated women. Loss of a loved one has long been known to increase the risk for breast and cervical cancer. When 2000 men were assessed and then followed for 17 years, it was found that depression doubled the risk for cancer.

Researchers at the National Institute of Health, spearheaded by Candice Pert, PhD, have investigated the link between catecholamines, endorphins and other chemicals from the brain as they influence cancer. A reknowned researcher, Jean Achterberg, PhD, has demonstrated a clear link between the attitude of the cancer patient and their quality and quantity of life.[38] In my years of experience, about 90% of the cancer patients I deal with have encountered a major traumatic event 1-2 years prior to the onset of cancer. This is especially true of breast cancer patients. There is even a medical textbook on the subject of "STRESS AND BREAST CANCER".[39]

Not only can mental depression lead to immune suppression and then cancer, but there may be a metaphorical significance to the location of the cancer. Divorced women may lose a breast as they feel a loss of their feminity. One of my patients developed cancer of the larynx a year after his wife left him. He tried to get her to talk about it, but she said there was "nothing left to say".

There is a "good news bad news" contrast here. Like the pilot who comes on over the intercom system with "Ladies and gentlemen, this is your captain speaking. I have good news and bad news. The bad news is that we are lost. But the good news is, we are making good time." Similarly, the bad news is: your mind is probably the "lifeguard" that keeps cancer at bay, hence major stress is literally inviting cancer into the body. The good news is that the mind can be a powerful instrument at eliminating cancer. This is a frightening or empowering concept, depending on how you choose to perceive it. The cancer patient who knows that he or she can do something about getting well is more likely to beat the disease. Helplessness and hopelessness are just as lethal as cigarettes and bullets.

Norman Cousins cured himself of a painful collagen disease by using laughter and attitude adjustment, along with high doses of vitamin C. Bernie Siegel, MD, a Yale surgeon, noticed that certain mental characteristics in his cancer patients were indicators of someone who would beat the odds: live each moment, express yourself, value your dreams and maintain an assertive fighting spirit against the disease. Carl Simonton, MD, a radiation oncologist, found that mental imagery and other mind techniques vastly improved the results in his cancer patients. In a National Cancer Institute study conducted at the University of Texas, researchers were able to predict with 100% accuracy which cancer patients would die or deteriorate within a two month period—strictly based upon the patient's attitude.[40] While tobacco products contain carcinogenic substances, mentally handicapped people, many of whom smoke, experience a 4% death rate from cancer, compared to 22% for the population at large.[41] Indeed, there may be a certain amount of bliss in ignorance.

Enkephalins and endorphins, also called "the mind's rivers of pleasure", are brain chemicals that are secreted when the mind is happy. Endorphins improve the production of T cells, which improves the effectiveness of the immune system against cancer and infections. Enkephalins increase the vigor of T-cells attacking cancer cells as well as increasing the percentage of active T-cells. Essentially, your immune system is a well orchestrated army within to protect you against cancer and infections. And your mind is the four star general directing the battle. Depending on your attitude, your mind either encourages or discourages disease in your body.

The take-home lesson here is: You can take a soup bowl full of potent nutrients to fight cancer while you are being treated by the world's best oncologist; but if your mind is not happy and focused on the immune battle that must occur, then the following program of nutrition will not be nearly as effective as it should be.

We are all going to experience certain setbacks, losses and injustices in our lives. How we react to these life stresses will play a major role in our health and longevity. We all have to drive over the "bumps in the highway of life". Your "shock absorber system" is your coping ability that makes stressful events less damaging to your well being.

PATIENT PROFILE

C.H., female, 32 years. In May of 1989, C.H. underwent surgery, chemo, radiation and Tamoxifen therapy for her breast cancer. By July, 1991, her cancer had returned. In 1991, C.H. was treated for two 3 week sessions in Mexico. By July, 1992 CT scan showed advanced metastatic lesions in the lungs, liver and bones. C.H. was admitted on September 1, 1992 with stage IV (last stage) breast cancer. In her assessment, the physicians had doubts that this mother of 3 young children would get to see Christmas 1992. As of July, 1993, C.H. has had considerable shrinkage of her metastatic and primary tumors. Her intense bone pain is gone. She has been reasonably compliant in her food and supplement program and has enjoyed a dramatic improvement in quality and quantity of life.

REFERENCES

1. Ransberger, K, et al., Medizinische Enzymforschungsgesellschaft, International Cancer Congress, Houston 1970
2. Miraslav, H., et al., Advances in Antimicrobial and Antineoplastic Chemotherapy, proceedings from 7th international congress of chemotherapy, Urban & Schwarzenberg, Munchen, 1972
3. Rokitansky, O., Dr. Med., no.1, vol.80, p.16ff, Austria Maurer, HR, et al., Planta Medica, vol.54, no.5, p.377, 1988
5. Schedler, M., et al., 15th International Cancer Congress, Hamburg, Germany, Aug.1990
6. Naisbitt, J., et al., MEGATRENDS 2000, p.257, Morrow, NY, 1990
7. Frei, B., et al., Proceedings National Academy of Science, vol.87, p.4879, June 1990
8. Bliznakov, EG, Proceedings National Academy of Science, vol.70, no.2, p.390, Feb.1973
9. Folkers, K., Medicinal Chemistry Research, vol.2, p.48, 1992
10. Langsjoen, PH, American Journal Cardiology, vol.65, p.521, Feb.1990
11. Folkers, K., et al., in VITAMINS AND CANCER PREVENTION, p.103, Wiley-Liss, NY 1991
12. Folkers, K., et al., Biochemical and Biophysical Research Communications, vol.176, no.2, p.786, 1991
13. Bortz, WM, Journal American Medical Association, vol.248, no.10, p.1203, Sept.10, 1982
14. Hendler, SS, THE OXYGEN BREAKTHROUGH, Simon & Schuster, NY, 1989
15. Quillin, P, SAFE EATING, M. Evans, NY, 1990
16. Huggins, HA, IT'S ALL IN YOUR HEAD, Life Sciences Press, Colorado Springs, 1989
17. Newell, K, et al., Proceedings of National Academy of Sciences, vol.90, no.3, p.1127, Feb.1993
18. Aihara, H., ACID & ALKALINE, Macrobiotic Foundation, Oroville, CA, 1971
19. Rose, DP, et al., Medical Oncology and Tumor Pharmacotherapy, vol.7, no.2, p.121, 1990
20. Chlebowski, RT, et al., Cancer Treatment Reviews, vol.12, p.49, 1985
21. Castillo, MH, et al., American Journal of Surgery, vol.158, p.351, Oct.1989
22. Quillin, P (ed.), ADJUVANT NUTRITION IN CANCER TREATMENT, Cancer Treatment Research Foundation, 1993 (in press)
23. Chen, LH, et al., Anticancer Research, vol.8, p.739, 1988
24. Poydock, ME, et al., Experimental Cell Biology, vol.47, p.210, 1979
25. Xiyu, P., Chung Hua Chung Liu Tsa Chih, vol.7, no.2, p.103, 1985

26. Greeder, GA, et al., Science, vol.209, p.825, Aug.1980
27. Kline, K, et al., Nutrition and Cancer, vol.14, p.27, 1990
28. Langer, R, et al., Proceedings National Academy of Science, vol.77, no.7, p.4331, July 1980
29. Weidner, N., et al., New England Journal of Medicine, vol. 324, no.1, p.1, 1991
30. Ziporyn, T., Journal American Medical Association, vol.253, p.1846, Apr.1985
31. Langer, SE, et al., SOLVED: THE RIDDLE OF ILLNESS, Keats, New Canaan, 1984
32. Eaton, SB, et al., New England Journal of Medicine, vol.312, no.5, p.283, Jan.1985
33. Jansson, B., Cancer Detection and Prevention, vol.14, no.5, p.563, 1990
34. Goodman, MT, et al., European Journal of Cancer, vol.28, no.2, p.495, 1992
35. Jensen, GL, et al., Journal of Parenteral and Enteral Nutrition, vol.14, p.467, 1990
36. Selye, H, STRESS WITHOUT DISTRESS, JB Lippincott, NY, 1974
37. Newell, GR, Primary Care in Cancer, p.29, May 1991
38. Achterberg, J., IMAGERY IN HEALING, New Science, Boston, 1985
39. Cooper, CL (ed.), STRESS AND BREAST CANCER, John Wiley, NY, 1988
40. National Cancer Institute, NCI# NO1-CN-45133, National Institute of Health, Washington, DC 1977
41. Achterberg, J, IMAGERY IN HEALING, New Science Library, Boston, 1985, p. 177

CHAPTER 8

MAKING IT NUTRITIOUS & DELICIOUS

by Noreen Quillin and Patrick Quillin

"Let your food be your medicine and your medicine be your food."
Hippocrates, father of modern medicine, circa 400 B.C.

Nutrition and health. It makes so much sense: "You are what you eat." Veterinarians know the irreplacable link between nutrient intake and health. Actually, most of our pets eat better than most Americans. Your dog or cat probably gets a balanced formula of protein, carbohydrate, fat, fiber, vitamins and minerals. Yet, most of us eat for taste, cost, and convenience. The most commonly eaten food in America is heavily refined and nutritionally bankrupt white flour. Meanwhile, our livestock eat the more nutritious wheat germ and bran that we discard. When our crops are not doing well, we examine the soil for nutrients, fluid and pH content. Our gardens prosper when we water, fertilize, and add a little broad spectrum mineral supplement, such as Miracle Gro.

A sign posted near the junk food vending machines in a major city zoo warns: "Do not feed this food to the animals or they may get sick and die." Think about it. The food that might kill a 400 pound ape is okay for a 40 pound child who is biologically very similar? If our gardens, field crops, pets, exotic zoo creatures and every other form of life on earth are all heavily dependent on their diet for health, then what makes us think that humans have transcended this dependence?

FOOD

Food is a rich tapestry of various chemicals. For some advanced cancer patients, TPN is often the only route which can provide adequate nutrient intake. However, for other patients, food can be an integral part of their recovery. Food contains anti-cancer agents that we are only beginning to understand. One third of all prescription drugs in America originated as plant products. It is food that provides macronutrients, like carbohydrate, fat and protein, that drive extremely influential hormones and prostaglandins in your body. It is food that establishes your pH balance and electrolyte "soup" that bathes every cell in your body. While supplements are valuable, they cannot replace the fundamental importance of a wholesome diet.

This chapter can make or break your cancer-fighting program. The food discussed in this chapter has been fine tuned over the years to be tasty, nutritious, inexpensive and easy to prepare. Our eating habits are all acquired. We base our current diet on what mother cooked when we were younger; what our society, ethnic and religious groups prefer; what is advertised in print and electronic media, and what is available in the local grocery store. People in the Phillipines or the Amazon are born with structurally identical taste buds to Americans, yet they eat entirely different foods.

It takes about 3 weeks to acquire new eating habits. Try this program for 3 weeks, at which time it will become easier to stay with and you may just find that the nutrient-depleted junk food of yesterday really doesn't satisfy your taste buds like the following whole foods outlined by Noreen Quillin.

TRUE CONFESSIONS

P atrick Quillin has not always eaten as he does now. I now talk the talk and walk the walk. But I was raised in middle America, with roast beef, potatoes and gravy every Sunday afternoon; Captain Crunch for breakfast and a soda pop if you were good. White bread and bologna were the standard fare at home. My parents provided what they felt were lavish and well balanced meals to the best of their knowledge, as millions of other American families.

As I began studying nutrition in college, my eating habits improved, but were still far from enviable. I remember one semester in college while taking 19 units, 3 labs and working part time, I had no spare time to cook or even eat, so I kept a large box of Twinkies in the back of my van to provide "sustenance" when needed. For many months those Twinkies baked in the hot southern California sun and were always as fresh as the day they were bought. I began to question the shelf life of this food: "If bacteria is not interested in this food, then what makes me think that my body cells are interested in it!"

At that point in my life, my lovely and talented wife Noreen began exploring alternative cooking styles. While I was studying the lofty sciences of nutritional biochemistry, Noreen was busy making nutritious taste delicious. It was a true turning point in my life. I started eating properly, felt better, got fewer colds, and could sincerely lecture on the subject to others. Noreen got books on everything that you can do with soybeans, crockpots, pressure cookers, whole grains and vegetarian lifestyles. She bravely and diligently tried everything. We sometimes would come home with bags of food from some ethnic grocery store that we later had to re-identify in order to try some recipe. Some of it was good. Some was edible. Some we had to throw out. But we learned. And for the past 3 years, Noreen has taught cooking classes to our cancer patients. And we have all learned. What you have in this chapter is a time-tested approach to making your anti-cancer diet practical and tasty. Bon appetit!

SYNERGISTIC FORCES IN FOODS

A lthough 1000 mg daily of vitamin C has been shown to reduce the risk for stomach cancer, a small glass of orange juice containing only 37 mg of vitamin C is twice as likely to lower the chances for stomach cancer. *Something* in oranges is even more chemo-protective than vitamin C. Although most people only absorb 20-50% of their ingested calcium, the remaining calcium binds up potentially damaging fats in the intestines to provide protection against colon cancer.

In 1963, a major "player" in the American drug business, Merck, tried to patent a single antibiotic substance that was originally isolated from yogurt. But this substance did not work alone. Since then, researchers have found no less than 7 natural antibiotics that all contribute to yogurt's unique ability to protect the body from infections. There are many anti-cancer agents in plant food, including beta-carotene, chlorophyll, over 500 mixed carotenoids, over 600 various bioflavonoids, lutein, lycopenes and canthaxanthin. The point is: we can isolate and concentrate certain factors in foods for use as therapeutic supplements in cancer therapy, but we must always rely heavily on the mysterious and elegant symphony of ingredients found in wholesome food.

HOW DO FOODS PROTECT US FROM TOXINS AND CANCER ?

■ By spurring on the body to produce more toxin scavengers, like glutathione peroxidase from indoles in cabbage.

■ By bolstering the immune system. Once the external therapies of chemo, radiation and surgery have eliminated the visible tumor, then the real and final cancer battle is totally dependent on the immune factors. Many foods and individual nutrients are influential here.

■ By stimulating certain detoxifying enzyme systems, like the liver's cytochrome P450.[1] Selenium, vitamin C and milk thistle help here.

■ By shutting down the oncogene in human cells, that acts like a traitor to participate in cancer growth. Soybeans, vitamin A and D help here.

■ By directly killing tumor cells. The bioflavonoid quercetin, vitamin C, B-12, K, and garlic help here.

■ By directly killing bacteria or viruses that may cause cancer.

■ By binding up substances, like bile acids, that can decay into a carcinogenic substance. Fiber is a champion here.

■ By caging carcinogenic heavy metals, in a process called chelation (say 'key-lay-shun'), and carrying these toxic minerals out of the body. Bioflavonoids, vitamin C and garlic help this way.

■ By attaching to fats, to stop the carcinogenic fat "rusting" process. Calcium, vitamin E and fiber use this method.

■ By providing the known essential and unknown important nutrients that the body needs to better defend itself against pollutants.[2] A well-nourished body is better able to detoxify, neutralize and excrete the ubiquitous poisons of the 20th century.

USING GUIDELINES THAT ARE UNIVERSAL

T here have been a number of diets developed for the cancer patient: Drs. Moerman[3], Livingston[4], Gerson[5], and the macrobiotic[6] diets to mention a few. Each of these visionaries was a physician who spent at least several decades ministering to cancer patients. While there are some differences in these diets, there is also some common ground. Peculariarities about each program include:

■ Dr. Moerman recommends supplements of iron for cancer patients, yet other data shows that elemental iron may accelerate cancer growth. He allows the yolk of the egg, but not the white part.

■ Macrobiotics allow liberal amounts of soy sauce and pickles, yet restrict intake of fruit and fish.

■ Dr. Gerson used to encourage raw pureed calf's liver, which can contain a number of dangerous bacteria.

■ Dr. Livingston prohibits any chicken intake, since a cancer-causing organism thrives in chicken.

The points just mentioned are the oddities about each program which lack a good explanation. Yet, we don't want to throw out the "baby with the bath water". Each of these programs embraces a common thread, which includes a number of explanable nutrition principles. They all provide a diet that:

■ uses only unprocessed foods, nothing in a package with a label
■ uses high amounts of fresh vegetables
■ employs a low fat diet
■ emphasizes the importance of regularity
■ uses little or no dairy products, with yogurt as the preferred dairy selection
■ stabilizes blood sugar levels with no sweets and never eat something sweet by itself
■ increases potassium and reduces sodium intake

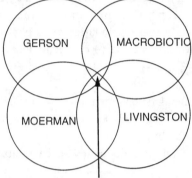

USING THE COMMON AREA

GERSON

MACROBIOTIC

MOERMAN

LIVINGSTON

DIET: high plant food, more vegetables, no sugar, low fat, low/no dairy,unprocessed & unrefined, some protein

SUPERFOODS

Though there are many nourishing foods, there are only a few superfoods that contain such a potent collection of protective factors that they deserve regular inclusion in most diets.

■ *Yogurt*. While dairy products are the world's most common allergenic food, for 1/2 to 2/3 of the population, yogurt can provide some dramatic immune stimulation. On the surface, yogurt appears to be nothing more than a fermented dairy product. Yet, modern scientists find that the active culture of bacteria in yogurt (Lactobacillus) can fortify the immune system. Yogurt is an impressive immune stimulant.[7] In both humans and animals, yogurt in the diet tripled the internal production of interferon (a powerful weapon of the immune system against tumor cells) while also raising the level of natural killer cells. Yogurt has been shown to slow down the growth of tumor cells in the GI tract while improving the ability of the immune system to destroy active tumor cells.[8] Yogurt can block the production of carcinogenic agents in the colon. When scientists looked at the diet of 1010 women with breast cancer and compared them to an equally matched group without breast cancer, they found an inverse dose-dependent relationship: the more yogurt consumed, the lower the risk for breast cancer.[9]

In several European studies, yogurt in animal studies was able to reverse tumor progress. A 1962 study found that 59 percent of 258 mice implanted with sarcoma cells were cured through yogurt. A more recent American study found a

30 percent cure rate through yogurt.[10] While it is doubtful that yogurt is going to cure advanced human cancer, it is likely that yogurt can better fortify the cancer patient's immune system.

■ *Garlic*. This stinky little vegetable has been used for 5000 years in various healing formulas. Pasteur noted that garlic killed all of the bacteria in his petri dishes. More importantly, garlic has been found to stimulate natural protection against tumor cells. Tarig Abdullah, MD of Florida found that white blood cells from garlic-fed people were able to kill 139% more tumor cells than white cells from non-garlic eaters.[11] Garlic and onions fed to lab animals helped to decrease the number of skin tumors.[12] Researchers found that onions provided major protection against expected tumors from DMBA in test animals.[13] Mice with a genetic weakness toward cancer were fed raw garlic with a lower-than-expected tumor incidence.[14]

The most common form of cancer worldwide is stomach cancer. Chinese researchers find that a high intake of garlic and onions cuts the risk for stomach cancer in half.[15] Garlic provides the liver with a certain amount of protection against carcinogenic chemicals. Scientists find that garlic is deadly to invading pathogens or tumor cells, but is harmless to normal healthy body cells; thus offering the hope of the truly selective toxin against cancer that is being sought worldwide.

■ *Carotenoids*. Green plants create sugars by capturing the sun's energy in a process called photosynthesis. The electrons that must be corralled in this process can be highly destructive. Hence, nature has evolved an impressive system of free radical protectors, including carotenoids and bioflavonoids, that act like the lead lining in a nuclear reactor to absorb dangerous unpaired electrons. Both of these substances have potential in stimulating the immune system while there is preliminary evidence that carotenoids may be directly toxic to tumor cells.

Carotenoids are found in green and orange fruits and vegetables. Bioflavonoids are found in citrus, whole grains, honey, and other plant foods.

■ *Cruciferous vegetables*. Broccoli, brussel sprouts, cabbage, and cauliflower were involved in the "ground floor" discovery that nutrition is linked to cancer. Lee Wattenberg, PhD of the University of Minnesota found in the 1970s that animals fed cruciferous vegetables had markedly lower cancer rates than matched controls. Since then, the active ingredient "indoles" have been isolated from cruciferous vegetables and found to be very protective against cancer. Scientists at Johns Hopkins University found that lab animals fed cruciferous vegetables and then exposed to the deadly carcinogen aflatoxin had a 90 percent reduction in their cancer rate.[16]

Cruciferous vegetables are able to increase the body's production of glutathione peroxidase, which is one of the more important protective enzyme systems in the body.

■ *Mushrooms*. Gourmet chefs have long prized various mushrooms for their subtle and exotic flavors. Now there is an abundance of scientific evidence showing that Rei-shi, Shiitake, and Maitake mushrooms are potent anti-cancer foods.[17] Actually, Maitake literally means "dancing mushroom" since people would dance with joy when finding these delicate mushrooms on a country hillside. Oral extract of Maitake provided complete elimination of tumors in 40% of animals tested, while the remaining 60% of animals had a 90% elimination of tumors. Maitake contains a polysaccharide, called beta-glucan, which stimulates the immune system and even lowers blood pressure.

■ *Legumes*. Seed foods (like soybeans) have a substance that can partially protect the seed from digestion, called protease inhibitors (PI). For many years, these substances were thought to be harmful. New evidence finds that PIs may squelch tumor growth.[18] Researchers at the National Cancer Institute find a collection of substances in soybeans, including isoflavones and phytoestrogens, appear to have potent anti-cancer properties.[19] Dr. Ann Kennedy has spent 20 years researching a compound in soybeans that:

- prevents cancer in most animals exposed to a variety of carcinogens
- retards cancer in some studies
- lowers the toxic side effects of chemo and radiation therapy
- reverts a cancer cell back to a normal healthy cell.[20]

■ *Others*. There are numerous foods that show an ability to slow tumor growth in some way. Apples, apricots, barley, citrus fruit, cranberries, fiber, figs, fish oil, fish, ginger, green tea, spinach, seaweed and other foods are among the reasons that I heavily favor the use of a mixed highly nutritious diet as the foundation for nutrition in cancer therapy.

Food treats malnutrition. Food contains known essential nutrients that stimulate the immune system and provide valuable protection against carcinogens. Foods also contain poorly understood factors that may add measurably to the recovery of the cancer patient. Many foods have tremendous therapeutic value in helping the patient to internally fight cancer.

HOW TO USE THIS SECTION

T his cookbook chapter was written with the cancer patient in mind and can also be helpful to people who want to eat properly but have little time to spend in the kitchen. Remember: the more wellness you have, the less illness you can have. One full week of menus is vegetarian style with no dairy products, but eggs are allowed. Another week's menu includes low fat poultry and fish. This will show you how to prepare meals that can be tasty and nutritious. The recipes are just a guide to show you the possibilities in creative cooking.

There is a section of tips to stimulate the appetite or lose weight rationally. Also included is the concept of bulk cooking, which is a great way to have a freezer full of ready-made meals at 1/4 the cost. "Fast food" at our house usually means microwaving some frozen beans, adding leftover bits of chicken or fish, and rolling this tasty collection into whole wheat tortillas with fresh salsa. The seasonings of Spike and Gayelords powdered vegetable broth may be purchased at your local heath food store.

Realize that there is no one perfect diet. Laying out a weekly menu of "nutritious" food is frought with peril, since another nutritionist could have their own valid criticisms of this program. Life is not perfect, nor are our eating habits. The most nourishing meal in the world is useless unless eaten. This chapter demonstrates healthy eating habits within the context of practical and tasty recipes. There are some noteworthy spartan cancer diets that only an extremely dedicated cancer patient can follow.

Given the choice between an unpalatable and labor-intensive eating program or returning to their old destructive eating habits, many cancer patients chose the later. Gleaning from dozens of good cookbooks and years of experience, the menus provided in this chapter make precious few compromises in nutritional quality while emphasizing taste, cost and practical preparation.

TO GAIN WEIGHT

■ Don't drink fluids or have soup or salad before the meal. It will fill you up on foods that are low in calorie density.

■ Eat on a large plate, thus avoiding food portions that appear overwhelming. Have small portions, knowing you can always have more.

■ People eat more when dining in groups than by themselves. Go to buffets. Eat with friends or other patients if possible. At our hospital, we were constantly battling the problem of patients not wanting to eat, no matter how appetizing the food looked and smelled. One Fourth of July, we set up a family picnic, with broiled chicken, baked beans, watermelon, corn on the cob and more. People who had not eaten well all week suddenly developed a ferocious appetite. We have been serving buffet family style meals ever since.

■ Distract your mind. Rent a good video and have your meal in front of the TV. Have you ever sat down with a bowl of popcorn and realized you had eaten the whole batch and didn't even realize it?

TO LOSE WEIGHT

■ Eat 6 times a day. That doesn't mean 6 Big Macs. It means a light breakfast upon rising; a piece of fruit later in the midmorning; a salad and half a sandwich at lunch; and the other 1/2 of the sandwich at mid-afternoon. Even if you over-indulge at one meal, make sure you eat on schedule. This concept, called periodicity, trains the mind and body that food is constantly coming into the system and there is no need to overindulge or become exceedingly efficient at storing calories.

■ Have warm fluids, like tea or soup, about 20 minutes before mealtime.

■ Use a smaller plate. It gives the illusion that you're eating more.

■ Drink plenty of purified water. It's good for both weight loss, constipation and wrinkles.

■ Adjust your bathroom scale to the exact weight you want to be. As you lose weight, you can readjust it closer to the zero, but always see your weight as you want it to be. This way when you think about having that huge piece of cake, you will think to yourself, "A person of my weight won't eat that."

■ Exercise within your own ability. Make sure you enjoy it.

■ Eat more high-fiber foods, such as fruits, vegetables, beans and whole-grain cereals.

■ Plan your meals and snacks instead of waiting until you are hungry.

DINING TIPS FOR THE CANCER PATIENT

■ You eat with your eyes first, so make sure that your plate looks appetizing. Have different colors. No matter how tasty the food might be, if it is all the same color (i.e. turkey, mash potatoes, and cauliflower), then you won't enjoy the meal as much.

■ Crock pot cooking is a great idea. It is a relatively inexpensive kitchen tool which cures the 5 o'clock dilemma of haphazard meal preparation. There are many advantages to making your dinner in the morning. You prepare the food early which means that the kitchen will be clean and the urge to order out at 5 pm has been eliminated. Also, the aromas of cooking food wafting throughout the house can help stimulate a sagging appetite.

■ Cook up more food than is needed. Freeze leftovers in baggies in individual servings. This way you will have a freezer full of ready-to-eat nutritious meals.

■ Pressure cooking is wonderful. Your cooking time for whole grains and beans will be cut by 75%.

■ Instead of soda pop, try diluted apple juice or ginger tea with 1/4 tsp of vitamin C per cup.

■ Ginger helps to relieve nausea. You can take tablets, or drink ginger tea cold or hot.

■ Acupressure wrist bands, available at your pharmacy or health food store, also help to relieve nausea.

■ Avoid frying foods. Make sure that you have foods like carrot sticks or baked whole wheat tortilla chips to satisfy that need for crunchy food.

EATING OUT

■ Iceberg lettuce is the most common salad bar offering, but is "junk food" relative to most other vegetables. Skip the iceberg lettuce and enjoy the healthier fruits, vegetables and whole-grain foods from the salad bar. A good rule of thumb: the deeper the color of the vegetable, the more nourishing it is. Dark greens are better than pale greens, dark orange squash is better than pale squash, and so on. In nature, cauliflower is a dark green vegetable, until human intervention ties the leaves around the developing flower to deprive it of sunlight.

■ Many restaurants offer low-calorie or light meals with gourmet versions.

■ Instead of accepting that "fried" meal from a restaurant menu, most places will steam or broil your food.

■ Airlines can be very accommodating in having a special meal ready for you. Give them at least 1 week advance notice.

■ Ask for the salad dressing to be served on the side.

■ Have the rich sauces or gravies left out.

■ Avoid sauteed and deep-fried food.

FOODS TO HIGHLIGHT IN YOUR DIET

■ yogurt
■ sprouts
■ onions
■ garlic

- ginger
- cabbage, broccoli, Brussel sprouts, cauliflower
- carrots
- soybeans, garbanzo beans and other legumes
- rice, barley and other whole grains
- sea vegetables, a.k.a. seaweed
- dark green and dark orange fruits & vegetables
- apples, berries
- eggs
- figs
- fish
- honey

BEVERAGES TO HIGHLIGHT

- Purified water
- Cafix
- Roma
- Herb tea
- Vitamin C powder & honey in hot water
- Ginger tea
- Hot natural apple juice with vitamin C
- Fresh orange juice
- Postum
- Chickory
- Japanese Green tea
- Roasted rice or barley tea
- Vinegar, honey & water

DRAGON-SLAYER SHAKE

I hate taking pills, even when I know the value of using supplements to improve my health. That's why I developed this "shake". While most of us are familiar with milkshakes, there are many variations on that theme which can provide nutrient-dense foods in a convenient format. I have found that many cancer patients would avoid taking their supplements of vitamins, minerals and botanicals because they didn't like swallowing pills. To solve that problem, I have developed this shake, which can incorporate many nutrients in powder form, thus eliminating taking pills at all, and the remaining pills are easier to swallow with the lubricating ability of this smooth shake.

Shakes can be a quick and easy breakfast. Depending on your calorie requirements, use this shake in addition to or instead of the breakfast suggestions listed later. My typical breakfast consists of this Dragon-Slayer shake, whole grain rolls, bagles, muffins or Pita bread, along with a large serving of fresh fruit in season.

Take up to half of your pills with the "Dragon-Slayer shake" and save the remaining pills for later in the day. Taking supplements in small divided dosages helps to maintain sustained levels of nutrients in the bloodstream.

Ingredients:

4-8 ounces of dilute fruit juice, including apple, cranberry, orange, fresh squeezed, juice extracted, etc. I add twice the specified water to a can of frozen unsweetened concentrated apple juice from your grocery store.

10-15 grams of powdered protein from (listed in order of preference): whey, rice, soy, alfalfa, egg white, non-fat yogurt solids, spirulina. Do not use powdered proteins that are based upon non-fat milk solids. Too many people are allergic to this product. Your health food store should have a dozen different products to select from. ProMod is a name brand pure whey protein product.

1/2 tablespoon of Perfect 7. This is an excellent product to maintain regularity and encourage proper detoxification. It includes fiber, an herbal laxative, proper bacteria for colonizing the intestines and botanicals for detoxification. You may be surprised at the fecal matter eliminated in the first few weeks on this program.

One sliced ripe banana or less, depending on how thick you like your shakes. Banana adds texture via pectin to make this shake have true milk shake viscosity.

2-4 grams of buffered vitamin C powder from Emergen-C or Seraphim. Both products have an effervescent action that brings a "soda pop" like flavor to this drink, along with high doses of vitamin C that won't upset even the most delicate stomach.

1 tablespoon of OmegaSyn 1 fatty acids (a blend of EPA and GLA) from BioSyn (800-346-2703)

1/2 tablespoon of pure, cold pressed flaxseed oil (optional)

1/2 tablespoon of wheat germ oil (optional)

For those who need to slow down weight loss or gain weight, add 2 tablespoons of MCT (medium chain triglyceride) oil

Directions:

Use a large blender or a small hand held blender, like the ones originally developed to mix diet drinks. First add the oils (EPA, wheat germ and flax) to coat the bottom of the container for easy mixing and cleaning. Add the powdered ingredients and cut up fruit next. Blend until smooth, or about 15 seconds.

BULK COOKING

Yogurt

Scald (foaming but not yet at boiling) 8 cups of milk with one cup of added powdered milk.

Turn heat down and simmer for at least 5 minutes; the longer you simmer (up to 25 minutes) the thicker your yogurt will be.

While the milk is simmering, place 2 tablespoons of live cultured good-tasting yogurt in each of two quart-glass peanut butter jars and stir briefly with a plastic spoon until creamy.

After simmering milk, let the temperature drop to 49 degrees C. (112 F.). You don't want to kill the yogurt bacteria with milk that is too hot.

Add about a half cup of the warm milk to the yogurt starter in each of two jars and stir gently but thoroughly. Then add the rest of the milk to the glass jars.

Place the jars (uncovered) in a picnic thermos (the size that holds a six pack of beer). Close the thermos lid and leave for 6-10 hours. The longer it sits, the thicker it gets. Do not open container and peek while the fermentation is occurring.

This recipe allows you to cut the cost of yogurt from $14.00 per gallon to $2.10 per gallon (cost of milk).

Growing Your Own Sprouts

You will need a glass jar (quart size or larger), a soft plastic screen for the top, and a rubber band to hold the screen in place. There are also commercial sprouting kits available in most health food stores. Place about one heaping tablespoon of seeds in your glass container with the screen doubled on the top. The seeds will expand about tenfold as they sprout, so allow enough room for their expansion. Fill the container half full of purified water and let stand overnight. Next morning drain and rinse the seeds. Let stand inverted over the sink for proper drainage. Rinse and drain twice each day for the next 6-7 days. Keep the jar in a dimly lit area.

Larger seeds, like peas, beans, and lentils take a shorter time to grow and should not be allowed to grow more than a half inch long, since they will develop a bitter flavor. Mung bean sprouts can get up to two inches in length without bitter flavor. Wheat, barley, oats, and other grass plants make terrific sprouts. Smaller seeds, like alfalfa, can grow to an inch in length without any bitter flavor. For some extra vitamin A, let the alfalfa sprouts sit in a sunny window for the last day before eating. The green color indicates the welcome addition of chlorophyll, folacin and beta-carotene.

In excess quantities, sprouts may blunt the immune system in humans. Do not eat more than two cups of sprouts daily.

Homemade Mayonnaise
1 egg
1 tsp. prepared mustard
1/2 tsp. salt
3 tbs apple cider
1 cup sunflower or canola oil

Put the egg, mustard, salt, and 1/2 cup of the oil in the container of an electric blender or food processor. Blend until smooth. Continue blending or processing while adding the remaining oil very slowly in a steady stream into the center of the egg mixture. Use a small rubber spatula to scrape the mayonnaise into a jar. Store covered in the refrigerator. Yields about 2 cups.
Note: If the mayonnaise curdles, blend or process 1 egg in the container of a clean electric blender or food processor and gradually pour the curdled mayonnaise back in while blending or processing at high speed.

Spicy Beans
3 cups of pinto beans
1 large onion cut up
3-4 garlic cloves minced
2-3 dry red peppers cut up fine
1 tablespoon chili powder
1 tsp cumin powder
1/3 cup olive oil
Lite salt

Sort and wash beans in a colander. Soak the beans overnight in about 8 cups of water in a heavy saucepan. Drain, then fill with another 8 cups of clean water. Add rest of the ingredients. Cover and simmer for 90-120 minutes or until beans are tender. Blend with an egg beater. Add a bit of salt to taste.

If you need the beans sooner:

Rinse beans. Then fill pot with beans and 8 cups of water Allow to boil for 2 minutes. Let sit in a covered pot for 1 hour. Proceed to next step.
(For best results, use a pressure cooker)

Place the soaked and rinsed beans in 5 cups of water in pot. Add ingredients. Bring lid weight to a gentle rocking motion, then pressure cook for 25 minutes. Let cool down. Beat with a mixer to desired consistency.

Barley

Rinse barley and cook for 35-45 minutes in a large volume of boiling water. Barley increases its bulk by four fold when cooked. Drain excess water. Store extra barley in baggies and place in freezer for later use. Season the barley with spices that go with the entree. Spike, Mrs. Dash and other herbal seasonings go with anything.

If using a pressure cooker, use twice the amount of barley measurement for the water. Bring to a rock, then immediately remove from stove burner. Follow rest of the directions.

Better Butter

Blend equal parts of olive oil and softened butter.

Whole Wheat Piecrust

1 cup whole wheat pastry flour
1/2 teaspoon salt
3 tablespoons oil
1/4 cup water

Stir dry ingredients together. Mix in oil. Add enough of the water to make the dough form a ball. Roll flat between sheets of waxed paper and lift into pan. Make edge.

Roasted Brown Rice or Barley Tea

Dry roast uncooked grain over medium flame for 10 minutes or until a fragrant aroma develops. Stir and shake pan occasionally. Add 2 to 3 tablespoons of the grain to 1 1/2 quarts of purified water. Bring to a boil, simmer 10 to 15 minutes.

The following recipes are not carved in stone. If you do not like a certain spice or seasoning, leave it out. Also, some days you might feel like cooking more than others. These menus were based more on giving maximum variety with different foods than offering no-effort cooking. Feel free to mix the ideas to your pleasure.

Also, it is a good idea to have leftovers to freeze in serving sizes so you can just pull out easy-to-serve dinners on days you want to relax.

ONE WEEK OF ONCOLOGY DIET

	MONDAY	TUESDAY	WEDNESDAY	THURSDAY	FRIDAY	SATURDAY	SUNDAY
Breakfast	instant pudding with yogurt in pita bread, fruit in season	whole wheat english muffin, sesame spread, fruit	Dragon Slayer drink, toast	Apple bran muffin, yogurt	Shredded wheat cereal with apple juice, yogurt and fruit	Mexican omelete, fruit	eggs fried in pam or a bit of butter, Anner's blender pancakes, fruit
Lunch	chicken sandwich with fruit salad	linguini, cabbage salad	pita bread sandwich, onion soup	Cottage cheese sandwich, fresh piece of fruit	turkey bacon, tomato and onion sandwich, spinach bean sprout salad with sesame dressing	tofu steak, fruit, tomato juice	humus in pita bread, candy carrots with nuts
Dinner	Baked or broiled salmon with herbs, fast vegetable soup, evening oats, chocolate cake	Baked chicken, yams, California spinach salad, frozen yogurt pie	Turkey loaf, homemade applesauce, sprout salad with peaches and almonds, pita bread, miso dessert balls	Pressure cooked stew, rye bread, carob cookies	crab dinner, fruited bulgur pilaf, cold Italian veggies, banana pudding	Turkey sausage pizza, banana waldorf, Chinese chews	turkey, seasoned bulgur, orange and onion salad, yogurt pudding

ONCOLOGY DIET

Monday

Yogurt Pudding
Use 1 box of instant pudding with 2 cups of yogurt. Stir until well blended. Refrigerate.

Chicken Salad Sandwich
Finely diced chicken
plain yogurt
pickle relish
chopped red or spring onion to taste
salt and pepper (optional)
diced celery (optional)
Spike to taste.

    Mix chicken, relish, onion, celery and Spike. Add enough yogurt to make it the consistency you enjoy. Spread on whole wheat bread.

Fruit Salad
Any fruit in season chopped into bite size pieces. Pour vanilla yogurt over the top.

Baked Salmon
1 whole salmon or piece about 2 1/2 pounds
1/2 cup chopped fresh parsley
2 tablespoons combination of chopped fresh herbs: dill,
chives, chervil, basil, sage
1 teaspoon Spike (optional)
1 tablespoon water
1 tablespoon lemon juice

    Place salmon on foil. Sprinkle herbs to taste inside cavity. Mix water with lemon juice and sprinkle over outside of salmon. Fold foil over and seal.

    Place wrapped salmon on baking sheet and bake in 450 degree oven for 10 minutes for every 1 inch thickness of fish, plus an additional 10 minutes cooking time because it's wrapped in foil (35 to 40 minutes total cooking time), or until salmon is opaque. Unwrap and discard skin; most of it should stick to foil. Place salmon on warmed platter. Garnish with parsley, dill, or watercress if you'd like.

Fast Vegetable Soup

2 cups skim milk (or a milk substitute from soy or rice)

1 tablespoon butter or "better butter"

2 tablespoon whole wheat flour

2 teaspoons Gayelord's all natural vegetable broth

1 teaspoon Spike

1/4 teaspoon pepper (optional)

2 cups cooked vegetables

Put all ingredients in blender in order listed. Cover and blend until smooth. Pour into a saucepan. Cook, stirring occasionally, over low heat until hot.

Evening Oats

1 small to medium apple chopped

1 tbs. butter

1 1/2 cup uncooked oats

1 egg beaten

1/2 cup water

1-2 tbs. honey

1 tsp. cinnamon

1/4 tsp. salt

1/2 tsp. vanilla

Saute the apple bits in butter in a skillet. Combine oats and egg in a bowl. Mix. Add oats to apples. Cook over medium heat 3 to 5 minutes, stirring until oats are dry and lightly brown. Add remaining ingredients. Continue cooking, stirring occasionally until liquid evaporates–about 3 minutes. Makes 2 cups.

Chocolate Cake

Whole Wheat Cake bottom:

1/3 cup honey

1/4 cup butter softened

1 egg

2/3 cup yogurt

1-2 tsp. vanilla

1/2 tsp. almond extract (optional)

1 cup whole wheat flour

1 1/2 tsp. baking powder

1/4 tsp. Lite salt

Cream together honey and butter; add egg, yogurt, and vanilla. Stir. Add remaining ingredients stirring until smooth. Pour batter into greased 8 or 9 inch round baking dish. Heat 10 minutes on power level 7 or medium in microwave.

Let stand, covered, 10 minutes. Store covered until cool.

Chocolate Frosting

1/4 cup butter softened

1/4 cup honey

1-2 teaspoon vanilla

1/2 cup yogurt

3 tablespoons cocoa powder

3 tablespoons carob powder (or a total of 6 tablespoons cocoa powder if you don't want to use carob)

dash of salt (optional)

1/4 cup chopped nuts (optional)

About 1 1/2 cups dry non-fat milk powder (or whey milk substitute)

dry pectin or powdered sugar (optional) for thickener

Mix first 4 ingredients until smooth. Stir in cocoa and carob. Sift or stir in the powder milk. Will be slightly lumpy if just stirred. Mix until slightly runny. Taste to see if mixture needs to be sweeter. Can add powder sugar. The frosting tends to thicken up, so wait a few minutes before frosting the cake for the right consistency. Sprinkle with nuts. Keep in refrigerator. Frosts 2 single layer cakes.

Tuesday

Sesame Spread

3/4 cup sesame seeds

1 tablespoon honey

1/4 cup apple juice or water

1/8 teaspoon salt

Toast sesame seeds and grind into a meal in a blender. Remove to a bowl and add honey, water, and salt. The mixture will thicken as it cools, so you may want to thin it by adding more juice.

Linguini

1/2 pound linguini

1 tablespoon olive oil

1 clove garlic, minced

1/2 cup finely diced mushrooms

1/3 cup minced fresh parsley

1/4 cup grated soy cheese

Lite Salt or salt substitute to taste

Bring 2 quarts of water to a boil in a medium size saucepan. Add the noodles and cook for about 5 minutes. Drain thoroughly. Immediately return the pot to the stove and add the olive oil, garlic, and mushrooms. Cook for 3 minutes over medium heat. Add the drained noodles and parsley, and toss. Add the cheese and salt to taste and toss again.

Cabbage Salad

1/4 of a head of a medium cabbage
2 carrots
1 diced onion (small)
raisins
sunflower seeds
Italian dressing

Grate cabbage and carrots. Add onion, raisins and sunflower seeds to taste. Sprinkle with Italian dressing.
Variation: Add any of the following: diced prunes, diced apples, walnuts, pecans, bell peppers, any other vegetables or dried fruit.

Baked Chicken and Yams

4 pieces of chicken
4 baking yams (medium size)

Wash chicken and place in oven-proof pan with enough room so the pieces aren't crowded. Scrub yams and poke with a knife several times. Place chicken and yams in oven and cook at 375 F. for 45 to 50 minutes.

California Spinach Salad

4 cups torn spinach leaves
1-2 cups alfalfa sprouts
1/4 pound mushrooms, sliced
1 large tomato, cut in chunks
2 spring onions, chopped

Toss ingredients together. Serve with Avocado dressing or your favorite.

Avocado Dressing

1/2 large ripe avocado
1 tablespoon lemon juice
1/8 teaspoon Lite salt
1/8 teaspoon chili powder
squeezed garlic
1/4 cup buttermilk (or milk substitute)

Mix all ingredients well. Serve over salad.

Frozen Yogurt Pie
4 cups of your favorite flavor of frozen yogurt (we like Yarnell's)
8 ounces of Cool whip
9 inch baked whole wheat pie crust

Thaw Cool whip for 4 hours in the refrigerator. Thaw the frozen yogurt just to where you can stir in Cool whip. Don't let it get too soft. Place mixture into the pie crust. Freeze.

Wednesday

Pita Bread Sandwich
You can create your own with: cheese, tomato, sprouts, garbanzo beans, grated carrot, sunflower seeds with Italian dressing

Onion Soup
1/2 to 1 tablespoon canola or sesame oil
2 lb. onions, thinly sliced
2 cloves garlic crushed
1/2-1 qt. stock (Gayelord's vegetable broth)
1-2 tablespoon miso
1/4 cup chopped celery leaves (optional)
2 teaspoons molasses
1-2 teaspoons Spike

Saute onions and garlic in butter over medium heat in a large saucepan for about 10 minutes. Add the rest of the ingredients and bring to a boil. Reduce heat and simmer for 5 to 10 minutes. Can serve with croutons.

Turkey Meat Loaf
1 pound extra lean ground turkey
1 large onion, finely chopped
1/4 cup natural bran
1 slice whole wheat bread, crumbled (or 1/2 cup Rice crispies)
1/2 teaspoon thyme
1 teaspoon Spike
dash of Worcestershire sauce
1 cup tomato juice or tomato sauce
1 egg, lightly beaten
1 tablespoon chopped fresh herbs-thyme, rosemary, savory, sage, parsley (optional)

In a mixing bowl, combine all ingredients. Turn into 9x5-inch loaf pan or baking dish. Bake in 350 degree oven for 45 minutes, or until brown and firm to the touch.

Homemade Applesauce

6 apples
handful raisins
1/2 cup water or apple juice
honey to taste
1/2 teaspoon cinnamon
1/4 teaspoon nutmeg
1/4 teaspoon allspice
1/4 teaspoon cloves

Core apples and cut into chunks. Add remaining ingredients including enough honey to sweeten to taste. Bring to a boil and then simmer until tender. Mash with a fork or potato masher. Lemon lends a nice bit of zip to the flavor.

Sprout Salad with Peaches

sprouts
peaches
almond slices

On a bed of sprouts, add some peaches with their juice. Sprinkle a few almond slices on top.

Miso Dessert Balls

1/2 cup peanut butter
1/2 cup honey
1/4 cup carob powder
1/4 cup milk powder (or milk substitute whey powder)
1/4 cup wheat germ
1/4 cup chopped almonds
1/4 cup sunflower seeds
1 1/2 teaspoon miso
1/2 teaspoon cinnamon

Combine all ingredients and mix throughly. Roll into bite size balls. Refrigerate.

Thursday

Apple Bran Muffin

1 cup whole wheat flour
3/4 cup wheat bran
1/4 teaspoon salt
1/2 teaspoon baking soda
1/4 teaspoon nutmeg
1/4 teaspoon cinnamon
1/2 cup finely chopped apple
1/4 cup raisins
1/4 cup chopped nuts
1 cup buttermilk
1 beaten egg
1/4 cup molasses
1 tablespoon oil
1/2 teaspoon maple flavor

Preheat oven to 350 degrees. Grease a 12-cup muffin pan. Toss flour, bran, salt, soda, nutmeg cinnamon together with a fork.

Stir in apples, raisins, and nuts. Combine the liquid ingredients. Stir the liquid ingredients into the dry with a few swift strokes. Pour into greased muffin cups, filling them at least 2/3 full, and bake for 25 minutes. Makes 12.

Cottage Cheese Sandwich

1/2 cup creamed cottage cheese
1/6 cup wheat germ
1/2 tbs. green chillies
1/8 tsp. oregano leaves
1/8 tsp. basil leaves
2 tsp. finely chopped onion
dash salt
dash tabasco (optional)
tomato slices
alfalfa sprouts

Mix first 8 ingredients together well. Put mound of mixture on a slice of whole wheat bread or toast. Top with a tomato slice and sprouts. Can have an open face sandwich or closed.

Pressure Cooked Stew

1 pound lean chicken, turkey, fish or ham, cut into 1-inch cubes

1 tablespoon olive oil

3 cups water with vegetable broth added

1 large diced potato

2 medium diced carrots

1 onion diced

3 cloves garlic crushed

1 bay leaf

1 tsp. soy sauce

1/4 tsp. Worcestershire

2 tablespoons whole wheat flour

1/2 cup cold water

Shake the 1/2 cup cold water and flour in tightly covered container. Set aside.

Cook and stir meat in olive oil in a pressure cooker until meat is browned, about 15 minutes. Add the water. Pressure cook by bringing it to a rock and let it gently rock for 30 minutes. Take off heat. Let off steam properly. Add the rest of the ingredients and let it get back to a rock for 7 minutes. Remove from heat. Let off steam properly. Stir in the flour mixture. You can use a strainer to remove any lumps. Bring to a boil. Serves 5 or 6.

Cookies

1/2 cup better butter

1 cup brown sugar

1 egg

1-2 teaspoons vanilla

1 cup whole wheat flour

1 cup oat flour (add one cup whole oats to a blender)

1 1/2 teaspoon baking powder

Beat first 4 ingredients until creamy. Add rest of the ingredients and mix well. Place about a teaspoon full of dough for each cookie on a cookie sheet. Bake at 350 degrees for about 8 minutes or until cookies puff up light brown.

Cookie Flavor Options:

- 1/4 cup peanut butter. Might need to add 1 teaspoon of flour extra.
- 1/2 cup chocolate chips or carob chips
- 1/4 cup chopped almonds, walnuts, or pecans
- 1/4 cup chopped dates, prunes, or raisins

Friday

Turkey Bacon Sandwich
4 strips turkey bacon cooked (we use Louis Rich)
tomato slices
red onion slice
alfalfa sprouts
2 pieces whole wheat bread
Spread: equal parts yogurt and mayonaise

Spinach & Bean Sprout Salad
8 ounces spinach
16 ounces bean sprouts or alfalfa sprouts
croutons (optional)

Sesame Dressing
1/4 cup soy sauce
2 tablespoons toasted sesame seeds
2 tablespoon finely chopped onion
1/2 teaspoon honey
1/4 teaspoon pepper
Mix all ingredients.

Variations:
- grated carrots
- grated cheese
- cooked noodles
- diced egg
- chopped apples
- cut up dried fruit
- avocado
- nuts
- onions
- crushed bacon
- tomatoes
- any vegetables

Crab Dinner
Fry in a small amount of olive oil and butter: imitation crab (pollock fish), diced onions, garlic, sliced mushrooms, bell pepper, ginger. Sprinkle sunflower seeds or crushed almonds on top before serving.
Variations: bamboo shoots, olives, green chillies, Spike seasoning

Fruited Bulgur Pilaf
1 tablespoon "better butter"
1 medium onion chopped
1 cup bulgur uncooked
1/4 teaspoon dill weed
1/4 teaspoon oregano
1/2 teaspoon salt (optional)
1/4 teaspoon pepper
1 tablespoon parsley chopped
chopped apricots, dates and raisins to taste
2 cups water with 1 tablespoon miso mixed in it

Melt butter in large skillet. Add bulgur and vegetables. Stir constantly until vegetables are tender and bulgur is golden. Add the rest of the ingredients. Bring to a boil. Stir. Reduce heat and simmer 15 minutes.

Italian Cold Vegetables
Using up leftover vegetables (i.e. broccoli, cauliflower, Chile peppers, mushrooms, carrots, zuccini, all beans). Just make sure they haven't been overcooked.
Sprinkle with small amount of marinade from:
1/2 cup olive oil
1/2 cup apple cider vinegar
1/2 tsp. basil
1/2 tsp. oregano leaves
1/2 chopped onion
1 chopped clove garlic
1/4 tsp. sea salt
1/2 tsp dry mustard
1 tsp. paprika
1 tbs. honey

Banana Pudding
5 ripe bananas
4 oz. low fat cream cheese
3/4 cup yogurt

1 tsp. vanilla
2 tbs. lemon juice
   Blend all ingredients. Chill.

Saturday

Mexican Omelet
3 eggs scrambled
salsa
grated cheese (optional)
   Spray Pam in a frying pan. Add the scrambled eggs. Cover and cook over medium low heat until almost set. Flip. Add salsa to top of eggs and spread. Can add a bit of grated cheese. Put cover back on. Finish cooking. Remove lid. Fold the omelet in half.

Textured Tofu
(The day before, slice firm tofu and pat dry. Freeze separately.) Drop frozen tofu into boiling water. Take out when it's been defrosted. When cool enough to touch, ring out and pat dry. Set aside.

Tofu Steak
In a baggie, add:
1/4 cup water
1 tsp. vegetable broth
dash Spike
dash poultry seasoning
   Add tofu to baggie and marinade. Dip tofu in a beaten egg. Then bread in equal parts of whole wheat flour and corn meal. Fry in small amount of olive oil.

Turkey Sausage Pizza
1 cup cooked ground turkey sausage
1 pound ripe tomatoes, blanched, seeded, chopped, and drained as much as possible
Lite Salt & pepper
4 ounces soy cheese, thinly sliced
1 tsp. dried basil
1/2 tsp. oregano
1/2 tsp. parsley
1 onion sliced fine

mushrooms sliced fine (optional)

4 tablespoons Parmesan cheese

1 tablespoon olive oil

Prepare the pizza dough. Spread the tomatoes almost to the edge, and season well. Cover with the thinly sliced mozzarella; onions, mushrooms, then top with the basil, parsley, oregano, sausage and cheese. Sprinkle a little olive oil over the top, and place in a preheated hot oven (450 degrees) for 20 minutes, or until the dough has cooked through and the cheese has melted. Serve.

Pizza Dough

1/2 tablespoon dried yeast

1/2 teaspoon sucanat (sugar cane)

2/3 cup warm water

2 cups whole wheat flour

1 teaspoon Lite Salt

2 tablespoons olive oil

Dissolve yeast with the sugar in 3 to 4 tablespoons of warm water. Leave for 5 to 10 minutes in a warm place (until frothy). Put the flour and salt into a warm bowl; make a well in the center, and pour in the yeast mixture, water, and oil. Mix until it forms a soft dough, adding a bit of warm water if necessary. Turn out onto a floured surface, and knead well for about 5 minutes. Place dough in a floured bowl and cover with a damp cloth. Leave in a warm place until it doubles–about 1 1/2 to 2 hours. Knead lightly. Roll out or press into a pizza pan or baking tray. Pat gently so it fits,with the edges a bit higher.

Banana Waldorf

2 cups diced banana

1 1/2 cups diced apple

1 cup diced celery

1/2 cup chopped walnuts

1/2 cup raisins

1/2 cup yogurt

1 tablespoon lemon juice

Use well-chilled fruit. Combine all ingredients. Mix well and serve on top of fresh spinach leaves or alfalfa sprouts. Yields 6 small servings.

Chinese Chews

1/4 cup butter

1 1/2 cups hulled sesame seeds (or: 3/4 cup sesame seeds, 1/4 crushed almonds, 1/4 cup coconut)

3/4 cup dry milk (or whey milk substitute)

1/6 cup wheat germ

1/2 cup honey
1 to 2 tsp. vanilla
2 tsp. brewers yeast (optional)

Melt butter in skillet. Add sesame seeds and lightly toast, stirring often. Stir in powder milk and wheat germ. Add honey and vanilla mixing well. Continue to cook for about 7 to 8 minutes, stiring constantly. Scoop and press lightly into a greased cookie sheet. Cool and cut into squares.

Sunday

Anner's Blender Pancakes
1 ripe banana
1 egg
1/2 cup flour (wheat, oat, buckwheat)
2 teaspoon baking powder (without alum as an ingredient)
1/2 teaspoon maple flavoring (optional)

Blend the banana, egg, and flavoring in a blender. Add the dry ingredients. Fry as normal in Pam; covering the pan while cooking on the first side.

Humus
1/2 onion, chopped
1 clove garlic crushed
1 tablespoon olive oil
dash cumin
1 teaspoon basil
1/2 teaspoon oregano
2 tablespoon parsley, chopped fine
juice of 1 lemon
1/4 cup sesame seed butter tahini (optional)
3 cups cooked garbanzo beans, mashed
salt to taste

Saute onion and garlic in oil until onion is transparent. Add cumin and cook until fragrant. Add herbs at the last moment, cooking just enough to soften parsley. Mix with the lemon and mashed beans and tahini, stirring together thoroughly. Makes about 3 cups.

Candy Carrots

1/2 pound fresh carrots

honey

chopped almonds

Cut carrots into 2 1/2x1/4 -inch strips. Place carrots in a microwave bowl. Drizzle honey over top. Sprinkle almonds. Cook on high for about 6 minutes in the microwave.

No Fuss Turkey

Clean turkey. Place in a turkey pan. Spread a bit of canola oil over the top and cover tightly with lid or foil. Cook turkey for the amount of time needed based upon the weight of the bird.

Seasoned Bulgur

To 3 cups cooked bulgur, add:

1 1/2 tablespoon vegetable broth

raisins

sunflower seeds

2 teaspoons Spike

Mix together and warm in the microwave.

Orange and Onion Salad

2 oranges

1 diced avocado (optional)

1 grapefruit

1 small red onion, thinly sliced and separated into rings

1/3 cup yogurt

2 tablespoons chopped walnuts (optional)

salad greens or spinach leaves

salt and pepper to taste

Peel and section the fruit. Cut each section into two or three pieces and put in a salad bowl. Add all the juices from the oranges and grapefruit to the onion. Add avocado. Pour yogurt over mixture, toss and chill. Sprinkle with nuts, salt and pepper and serve on salad greens.

	MONDAY	TUESDAY	WEDNESDAY	THURSDAY	FRIDAY	SATURDAY	SUNDAY
VEGETARIAN WEEK	**Breakfast:** Bagel w/ peanut butter spread, honey, fruit	**Breakfast:** Homemade granola w/ juice, banana, whole wheat toast	**Breakfast:** Health bar, fruit	**Breakfast:** Vegetable scrambled eggs, banana bread	**Breakfast:** Dragon-slayer drink, oatmeal cereal with banana	**Breakfast:** Anner's blender pancakes, fruit bowl	**Breakfast:** mushroom omelet, rye toast, fruit
	Lunch: Tabouli w/ chickpeas, steamed vegetables, dates	**Lunch:** Hummus w/ pita bread, sliced carrots,	**Lunch:** Avocado filled pita bread, banana nut salad	**Lunch:** Bean taco, Mexican rice, dried papaya	**Lunch:** egg sandwich, minestrone soup, dried apple chips w/ pecans	**Lunch:** tangy tomato soup, sesame spread on whole wheat buns, collard greens with eggs	**Lunch:** Dragon-slayer drink, tofu surprise, ginger bananas
	Dinner: Spicy Tofu with Cashews, crisp vegetable salad with lemon dressing, banana pudding	**Dinner:** Baked lentil loaf, miso rice, healthy gelatin, spicy carrot bars	**Dinner:** Tofu burger, whole wheat chips, tomato & onion salad, cherries jubilee	**Dinner:** Barley stew, whole wheat crackers, grapes, oatmeal cookies	**Dinner:** Nutty lentil loaf, pineapple rice, molasses cookies	**Dinner:** Tempeh a la orange, steamed broccoli, pecan cookies	**Dinner:** Bean burrito, carrot & raisin salad, apple crisp

VEGETARIAN WEEK

Monday

Peanut Butter Spread

1 cup peanut butter
1/3 cup milk powder (or whey milk substitute)
1 tbs. soft butter
2-3 tbsp honey (optional)
   Mix all ingredients together.

Tabouli with Chickpeas

1 cup bulgar (cracked wheat)
1-1/3 cups water
1/4 to 1/3 cup olive oil
1/3 cup lemon juice
1 cup finely chopped green onion
1 cup chopped fresh parsley
1/4 cup chopped fresh mint
2 tomatoes, diced
1/2 cup cooked chickpeas
1 cup chopped cucumber (optional)
2 tsp. soy sauce
dash of cayenne
ground pepper to taste
   To cook, combine water and cracked wheat and bring to a boil, then cover and simmer until done. Cool completely Drain off any excess water. Mix the rest of the ingredients with the bulgur. Refrigerate.

Spicy Tofu with Cashews

3 tbs. soy sauce
2 tsp. cornstarch
2 tbs dry wine (optional)
1 tsp. honey
1 tsp. grated fresh ginger root
1/2 tsp. crushed red pepper or 1/4 tsp chili powder
14 ounces tofu
1 tbs. olive oil
4 green onions
1 cup cashews

one 11 ounce can mandarin orange sections, drained
2 cups hot cooked brown rice or noodles.

Mix soy and cornstarch; stir in 1/3 cup water, wine, honey, red pepper and ginger root. Set aside. Press moisture from tofu with paper towels or towel. Cube tofu. In wok, stir-fry tofu in hot oil 3 to 4 minutes. Remove tofu. Stir fry nuts & onions for 1 to 2 minutes. Stir soy mixture into nuts. Cook and stir till bubbly; about 2 minutes. Add tofu to wok. Cover and cook 1 minute. Stir in oranges. Heat. Serve over rice. Serves 4. Can use texturized tofu for this recipe.

Crisp Vegetable Salad with Lemon Dressing
1 cup julienne strips of carrot
1 cup julienne strips of zucchini
1 cup green beans, in 1 1/2-inch lengths
1/2 cup sliced mushrooms
salt and ground pepper to taste

In a bowl, combine vegetables.

Lemon Dressing
1 tbs. olive oil
1/4 cup lemon juice
2 tbs. chopped fresh parsley
2 tbs. chopped spring onions
1 clove garlic, finely chopped

In a small bowl, combine oil, lemon juice, parsley, spring onions, and garlic. Mix thoroughly. Pour over vegetables and toss to mix. Add salt and pepper to taste. Cover and refrigerate.

Tuesday

Homemade Granola
1 cup whole wheat flour
1 cup rye flour
1 cup yellow cornmeal
1 cup soy flour
1/2 cup wheat germ, toasted
1 cup unsweetened coconut, toasted
1/4 cup sesame seeds, toasted
1 cup sunflower seeds, toasted
1/2 cup chopped dates
2/3 cups raisins

oil
2 cups rolled oats
3/4 cup chopped roasted peanuts
1 tsp. salt
1 cup honey
1/2 cup canola oil

Stir the flours together. Toast them over medium heat in a frying pan. No oil is needed. Toast them until they are well browned, but not too dark. Watch carefully because once the flour gets hot it browns fast. Stir often.

Put flours in a large mixing bowl and stir in the wheat germ, coconut, sesame, and sunflower seeds.

Oil the pan and brown the oats until they are golden. Add these to the mixing bowl with the roasted peanuts. Stir everything together thoroughly.

Heat the honey, oil, and salt in a small saucepan until the mixture is thin. Pour this over the cereal, blending carefully to spread it evenly. Let the cereal cool in the mixing bowl, where it will form large lumps. When cool, break it up and pour into storage jars.

For a change, serve granola with apple juice poured over it instead of milk.

Hummus
2 cups cooked garbanzo beans (drained)
2 tbs. tahini (sesame seed paste)
1 1/2 tbs. soy sauce
3/4 tsp. vit. C powder
5 tbs. olive oil
2 tsp. lemon juice
1 tbs. honey
1/4 tsp. dill weed
1/4 tsp. onion powder
1/4 tsp. garlic
1/2 tbs. mustard (not the dried type)
1 tsp. Lite salt
1 tbs. vinegar

Mix all ingredients in a blender or food processor till well blended. Use as a dip or sandwich spread.

Baked Lentil Loaf
1 onion, chopped fine
1 tbs. oil
2 cups cooked, drained lentils
1/4 cup wheat germ

1/4 cup whole wheat bread crumbs

1/2 cup toasted sunflower seeds

1/2 tsp. sage

1 tsp. Spike

1 tsp. dried parsley

2 tbs. whole wheat flour

2 eggs, beaten

1/2 cup vegetable broth

2 tsp. vinegar

2 tsp. soy sauce

1 tbs. toasted sesame seeds

Saute onion in oil until translucent and slightly browned. Mix ingredients, except sesame seeds, and place in greased loaf pan. Sprinkle top with the seeds. Bake for 30 minutes covered, then for 10 minutes uncovered.

Miso Rice

2 cups cooked brown rice

1 tbs. strong vegetable broth

1 tsp. Spike

1 tbs. finely chopped parsley

1 tsp minced spring onion

Mix all ingredients together. Heat in the microwave.

Healthy Gelatin

1 stick agar agar (can find in health food stores)

3 cups unfiltered apple juice

1-2 bananas, sliced

any other fresh fruit (optional)

Bring agar agar and juice to a boil, then simmer for 10-15 minutes until the stick has disolved. Add fruit and chill until firm.

Variation: Can use any other fruit juice flavoring. If it isn't sweet enough to your taste buds, can add a bit of honey.

Spicy Carrot Bars

1/3 cup butter

1/4 cup water

1/2 cup oat flour

1/2 cup whole wheat flour

1/4 cup wheat germ

1/2 cup honey

1 tsp. ground cinnamon
1/2 tsp. baking soda
1/4 tsp. salt
1/4 tsp. ground nutmeg
1/4 tsp. ground ginger
1 slightly beaten egg
1/4 cup apple juice
1/2 banana mashed
1/2 tsp. vanilla
1 cup shredded carrots
1/2 cup raisins

In a small saucepan, combine butter and water. Bring to boiling, stirring to melt butter. Remove pan from heat.

In a large mixing bowl, stir together the dry ingredients. Add the rest of the ingredients except the carrots and raisins, and mix. Fold in the carrots and raisins. Pour mixture into greased 9x9x2 inch baking pan. Bake at 375 degrees for 20 to 25 minutes or till a wooden tooth pick inserted in center comes out clean. Cool in pan on wire rack.

Wednesday

Avocado-Filled Pita Bread
1 large ripe avocado, peeled and diced
1 tbs. lemon juice
1/2 tsp. garlic salt
1/4 tsp. spike
1/2 tsp. Worcestershire sauce
homemade mayonnaise (optional)
4 whole wheat pita halves
1 tomato sliced
1 spring onion diced
salsa
alfalfa sprouts

Combine the first 5 ingredients. Lightly spread the mayonaise if you choose. Fill pita halves with the mixture. Sprinke the rest of the ingredients to taste. Four servings.

Banana Nut Salad
3 bananas
1 tbs. sesame tahini

1 tbs. honey
1 tbsp. soy protein powder
chopped dates
chopped almonds

Mix tahini, honey, and soy protein powder together and chop bananas into it. Mix in dates, and nuts. Chill.

Tofu Burger

1 pound tofu, drained and crumbled
1/2 cup finely grated carrot
1/4 cup chopped scallions
6 tbs. wheat germ
1 tbs. chopped parsley
4 ounce alfalfa sprouts
1 tbs. soy sauce
dash Tabasco sauce (optional)
1/2 tsp. Worcestershire sauce
1/4 cup whole wheat bread crumbs
canola oil

Put all ingredients, except wheat germ, in a bowl and mix well. Add just enough homemade mayonnaise to make the mixture hold together for shaping. Shape into 4 to 6 burger patties, coat with the reserved wheat germ, and pan-fry in a small amount of oil until browned and hot.

Whole Wheat Chips

Cut up whole wheat tortillas into strips and then bite size pieces. Lay sections flat on a ungreased cookie sheet and bake at 325 degrees on the top rack in the oven for about 7 to 8 minutes or until slightly browned. Let cool or serve warm

Tomato and Onion Salad

thin sliced red onions
sliced big red tomatoes
dash of dill
Italian dressing
sunflower seeds

Alternate slices of the onions and tomatoes. Sprinkle with dill. Add the dressing. Top with sunflower seeds. Chill.

Cherries Jubilee

1 qt. apple juice or cherry juice
1/3 cup agar flakes
1 lb. cherries, halved and pitted
1 tsp. vanilla
dash of cinnamon (optional)
pinch of salt

Pour apple juice into pot and add agar. Stir and bring to boil over medium flame. Lower flame and simmer 15 to 20 minutes until agar is completely dissolved. While sauce is cooking, halve and pit cherries. After 20 minutes, add vanilla and cherries. Simmer 5 minutes; remove from heat. Pour into baking dish or bowls. Cool and place in refrigerator.

Thursday

Vegetable Scrambled Eggs

4 eggs, beaten
1/2 tbs. water
2 tsp. olive oil (or Pam)
1/2 cup chopped mushrooms
1/2 cup chopped onions
1/4 cup chopped green peppers (optional)

Beat the water into the eggs and set aside. Saute in a frying pan, the mushrooms, onions and peppers in the oil for about 5 minutes. Add the rest of the ingredients and cook like plain scrambled eggs.

Banana Bread

1 cup oat flour
1 1/2 cup whole wheat flour
3/4 cup brown sugar
1/4 cup honey
3 1/2 tsp baking powder
1 tsp. salt
3 tbs. vegetable oil
1 1/4 cups mashed bananas
1/3 cup soy milk or apple juice
1 egg
1 cup chopped nuts

Heat oven to 350 degrees. Grease bottom only of loaf pan, 9x5x3 inches, or 2 loaf pans. Mix all ingredients, beat 30 seconds. Pour into pan(s). Bake until wooden toothpick inserted in center comes out clean. 9-inch loaf needs 55 to 65 minutes, 8-inch loaves 55 to 60 minutes. Cool slightly. Loosen side of loaf from pan; remove from pan. Cool completely before slicing. To store, wrap and refrigerate no longer than 1 week.

Bean Taco
1 cup cooked pinto beans
diced tomatoes
sliced olives
alfalfa sprouts
diced green chilies
salsa
corn or whole wheat tortillas
   Place warm beans in a hot tortilla. Add your favorite toppings.

Mexican Rice
2 cups cooked brown rice
1 tsp. green chillies
2 tbs. salsa
2 tbs. diced onions
2 cloves of garlic minced
1/4 tsp. cummin
1 tbs. olive oil
   Saute onion and garlic in the oil in a frying pan. Add the rest of the ingredients and heat.

Barley Stew
1 1/3 cups raw barley, cooked
1/2 cup dry beans, cooked
3 tbsp. oil
1 large onion, chopped
2 cloves garlic
1/4 cup chopped fresh parsley
1 cup sliced carrots
1 cup fresh peas (or frozen)
6 cups vegetable stock
3 tbsp. miso
1 tbsp. Gayelords vegetable broth powder
1 tsp. Spike
2 cups chopped tomatoes
pepper to taste
   Saute the onion and garlic. Stir in the stock, and seasonings. Dissolve the

miso in a small amount of hot stock. Add miso to the pot. When the mixture has begun to simmer, add the rest of the ingredients. Simmer the soup, covered, for about 1/2 hour, stirring occasionally.

Oatmeal Cookies (find under cookie recipe)

Friday

Oatmeal Cereal

Use the directions on the package of oatmeal and add any of the following ideas while cooking:

- raisins, 1/4 tsp. cinnamon
- 1/2 tsp. vanilla or maple flavor
- 1/2 tbs. honey or brown sugar
- dried apricots or any other type of dried fruit

Egg Sandwich

2 hard-cooked eggs, coarsely chopped
1/6 cup mayonnaise or yogurt
1/2 tsp. curry powder
1 tbs. spring onion diced
dash salt and red pepper to taste
1 tbs. chopped parsley
1/2 tbs. finely diced cucumber (optional)
1/2 tbs. pickle relish
1 whole wheat pita, cut in half
alfalfa sprouts

Combine first 8 ingredients. Fill the pita pockets with the mixture. Top with the sprouts.

Minestrone Soup

1/4 cup olive oil
1 cup diced celery
1/2 cup diced onion
2 cloves garlic
1 1/2 qts. water
1 to 2 tbs. flakey nutritional yeast (optional)
1 cup diced tomatoes
1/2 cup tomato paste
1 tsp. Spike

1/2 tbs. Gayelord's vegetable broth powder
1 cup diced carrots
1 cup diced potatoes
1/2 cup diced green beans
1/2 tsp. basil
1 tsp. oregano
1 tsp. Worcestershire sauce
1 cup whole wheat noodles, broken up
1 cup cooked pink beans

Saute first 4 ingredients together. Put the the rest of the ingredients, except the beans, in a pot and add the onion mixture. Blend the beans to a puree. Add the beans to the pot. Bring to a boil, then turn heat down and simmer for 20 minutes.

Nutty Lentil Loaf
1 onion chopped fine
1 tbs. olive oil
2 cups cooked, drained lentils
1/4 cup whole wheat bread crumbs
1/4 cup wheat germ
1/4 cup sunflower seeds
1/4 cup chopped walnuts
1/2 tsp. sage
2 tbs. whole wheat flour
2 eggs, beaten
1/2 cup vegetable broth
2 tsp. vinegar
2 tsp. soy sauce
1 tbs. sesame seeds
1 tsp. Spike

Preheat oven to 350 degrees. Saute onion in oil until slightly brown and translucent. Mix ingredients, except sesame seeds, and place in greased loaf pan. Sprinkle top with the seeds. Bake for 30 minutes covered, then for 10 minutes uncovered.

Pineapple Rice
To the Miso rice recipe, add 1 cup small diced pineapple, 1/2 cup raisins, 1/2 cup walnuts, 1 tsp. grated fresh ginger and 1 tsp. honey.

Molasses Ginger Cookies

1 egg

1/3 to 1/2 cup molasses (to taste)

1 cup brown sugar

2 1/4 cups whole wheat flour

1/2 cup oats

1/2 teaspoon salt

1/4 teaspoon baking soda

1/4 teaspoon baking powder (alum-free)

1 teaspoon ground cinnamon

1 teaspoon ground ginger

1/4 teaspoon ground cloves

1/4 teaspoon ground nutmeg

dash ground allspice

Preheat oven to 325 degrees. Mix molasses, shortening and brown sugar. Mix in remaining ingredients. Drop cookie dough by the teaspoon on a cookie sheet, preferably on pastry paper. Bake for 8 to 10 minutes until light brown.

Sucanat Variation:

■ Instead of 1/2 cup molasses, use 1/4 cup molasses.

■ Instead of 1 cup brown sugar, use 1 cup sucanat.

Other Variations:

■ add chopped nuts

■ add raisins or other dried fruit diced fine.

Saturday

Tangy Tomato Soup

2 tsp. oil

1 onion diced

2 cloves minced garlic

1 tbs. minced ginger

3 cups tomatoes

2 cups vegetable stock

1 tsp. soy sauce

1 tsp. Spike

1 tbs. whole wheat flour

pepper to taste

Saute onions and garlic in oil. Add the flour and toast it (don't burn) to remove the paste-like flavor. Add the rest of the ingredients and simmer until tomatoes are cooked. Makes about 5 cups.

Sesame Spread

3/4 cup sesame seeds
1 tbs. honey
1/4 cup apple juice
1/8 tsp. salt
1/4 tsp. vanilla or maple flavoring
1/2 tsp. molasses (optional)

Toast sesame seeds and grind into a meal in blender. Remove to a bowl and add the rest of the ingredients. The mixture will thicken as it cools, so you may want to thin it by adding more juice.

Collard Greens with Eggs

1 bunch collards, washed and sliced
2 tsp. sesame or olive oil
1 onion sliced
2 cloves garlic, minced
1 tsp. soy sauce
2 hard cooked eggs peeled and diced

Wash and slice collards. If stems are thick, slice thinly so they will cook faster. Microwave for 4-5 minutes or until done. Meanwhile, heat oil in skillet; add onions and garlic and saute 2 to 3 minutes. Mix together with the collards. Gently toss in the eggs and soy sauce.

Tempeh a l' Orange

8 ounces tempeh (fermented soybeans)
3-4 tbs. oil
1 large onion
1 stalk celery, chopped
1 carrot, grated
3 tbs. whole wheat flour
2 cups boiling water
1/2 cup orange juice
1 1/4 tsp. salt
1 1/2 tsp. honey
1 orange peeled & finely chopped with juice
dash red pepper
1/4 cup chopped fresh parsley
1/2 cup white wine (or more orange juice)

Cut tempeh in 1/2 inch chunks and saute in 2 tablespoons oil for about 5 minutes. Drain on paper towels. Tempeh will soak up all the oil you give it, so save half the oil to saute the second side.

Saute onion and celery in remaining oil until celery is tender. Stir in flour and keep stirring over medium heat just a minute or so; then add boiling water gradually.

Cook, stirring, while mixture thickens. Add orange juice, salt, carrot, honey, orange, pepper, parsley, and wine. Stir, bring to a boil, and simmer 4 to 5 minutes. Add tempeh chunks and simmer a few minutes longer to let flavors be absorbed. Serves 4, over brown rice, quinoa, or bulgur wheat.

Pecan Cookies (under cookie recipe)

Sunday

Mushroom Omelet
3 eggs
1 cup sliced fresh mushrooms
1/2 tbs. olive oil
1/2 tbs. water

Saute the mushrooms in oil in a frying pan. Scramble the eggs with the water. Add to the mushrooms. Cook over medium low heat covered. Flip over when the eggs are almost set. Cook the other side until done. Fold in half. Serve.

Tofu Surprise
1/4 onion, chopped
1 tsp. olive oil
1 clove garlic, minced
1/2 tsp. minced ginger
1/4 green pepper
1 tbs. peanut butter
1 tbs. soy sauce
1/2 cup water (or more)
2 tbs. celery leaves, chopped
1 tbs. wakame (sea vegetable), soaked, rinsed and drained and diced
1 tsp. honey
1/4 pound firm tofu, cubed
2 tbs. toasted cashew pieces

Saute onion in oil with the minced garlic. Add the ginger and pepper and cook a minute more. Stir in the peanut butter, soy sauce. Then add water, celery leaves, wakame, and honey. Stir and then simmer about 5 minutes. Add the tofu and cashews and heat through. Serve over steamed vegetables or noodles. Can use the texture tofu concept (see earlier in chapter) in this recipe.

Gingered Banana
4 bananas, sliced
juice of 2 lemons
2 tsp. grated ginger
1 tsp. honey
> *Toss ingredients together.*

Bean Burrito
1 tbs. canola oil
4 whole wheat tortillas
diced spring onions
spicy beans
salsa
> *Place about 3 tbs. or more of beans toward one end of a tortilla. Sprinkle on some spring onions. Roll up. Finish the other 3. Place oil in frying pan and put in the burritos. Brown on all sides. Remove and spread salsa on top.*

Carrot and Raisin Salad
2 cups grated carrots
2/3 cup raisins
1/3 cup sunflower seeds
Italian dressing
> *Mix the first 3 ingredients together. Moisten with the Italian dressing.*

Apple Crisp
2 lbs. apples, slices
1/2 tsp. cinnamon
1/6 cup apple juice
juice of one lemon
Crisp
2 cups rolled oats
1/2 cup whole wheat pastry flour
1/4 cup oil
2 tbs. maple syrup
pinch sea salt
1/ tsp. cinnamon
1/3 cup brown sugar
1/2 cup chopped pecans
> *Toss the apples, lemon juice, and apple juice. Place apples in a deep baking*

dish. Mix crisp ingredients and crumble over apples evenly. Press down gently; bake at 350 degrees for 30 to 45 minutes, or until crust is crunchy and golden, and apples are soft.

SUBSTITUTIONS

Instead of White Sugar try (listed in order of preference):
honey
barley malt
concentrated apple juice
fructose
molasses
sucanat
maltose
fruit juice
date sugar
rice syrup
dried dates
apricots
carob powder
apple butter

White flour:
whole wheat flour
barley
buckwheat
grind own flours
chickpeas
amaranth
soy

Oil/Fat:
olive oil
fat free foods
natural fats
canola oil
low-cal mayonnaise
lemon instead of Hollandaise sauce

Salt:
lite salt
salt substitute
soy sause
miso
extra seasonings

Dairy:
nonfat for whole milk
yogurt for sour cream
frozen yogurt for ice cream

Eggs:
boiled or poached for fried egg

Meat:
turkey bacon
turkey hot dogs
roast instead of fried chicken
tuna sandwich for hamburger

Desserts:
fruits
frozen yogurt instead of ice cream
angel food instead of chocolate cake

Snacks:
unbuttered popcorn instead of peanuts or chips
plain muffin instead of doughnut
baked potato instead of french fries
frozen yogurt popsicles
frozen orange juice bars
frozen orange sections
frozen bananas

TIPS:

- start off by using 2/3 of sugar called for in recipes, then decrease
- use honey and cut the amount called for in the recipe by 1/2
- use whole grain breads, rolls, crackers & pasta
- make whole wheat croutons

- use brown rice instead of white
- use more herbs and spices instead of salt and sugar
- start out changing your recipes by substituting 1/2 of the flour amount with whole wheat, then whole grain amounts
- serve fruit with a bit of yogurt for some of your desserts
- try to add one new healthy recipe into the menu per week
- don't skip meals
- try enjoying the taste of clean pure water

PATIENT PROFILE

L C, female 22 years old. In 1988, her diagnosis of breast cancer was treated elsewhere with surgery and chemotherapy. In December of 1990, she began noticing pain in the lower back region. In April of 1991, LC had another surgical removal of a breast tumor. By December of 1991, she had lost 25 pounds, was in considerable back pain, and told that she was terminal by her physician. LC was admitted in December of 1991 and given a regimen of fractionated chemo along with parenteral nutrition to reverse her weight loss and various nutritional supplements. She regained her lost weight and has experienced a high quality life. As of July 1993, LC is in very good condition.

REFERENCES

1. Boyd, JN, et al., *Food Chemistry and Toxicology*, vol.20, p.47, 1982
2. Quillin, P., SAFE EATING, p.129, M.Evans, NY, 1990
3. Jochems, R., DR. MOERMAN'S ANTI-CANCER DIET, Avery, Garden City, NY, 1990
4. Livingston-Wheeler, V., et al., THE CONQUEST OF CANCER, Waterside, San Diego, 1984
5. Gerson, M., A CANCER THERAPY, Gerson Institute, Bonita, CA 1958
6. Aihara, H., ACID & ALKALINE, George Ohsawa Foundation, Oroville, CA, 1986; see also Kushi, M., THE CANCER PREVENTION DIET, St. Martin Press, NY, 1983
7. Conge, G., et al., *Reproduction, Nutrition, Development* (French), vol. 20, p.929, 1980
8. Hitchins, AD, and McDonough, FE, *American Journal of Clinical Nutrition*, vol.49, p.675, 1989
9. Le, MG, et al., *Journal of the National Cancer Institute*, vol.77, p.633, 1986
10. Shahani, KM, et al., *Society of Applied Bacteriology Symposium Serial, vol.11, p.257, 1983*
11. Abdullah, TH, et al., *Journal of the National Medical Association*, vol.80, no.4, p.439, Apr.1988
12. Belman, S., *Carcinogenesis*, vol.4, no.8, p.1063, 1983
13. Kiukian, K., et al., *Nutrition and Cancer*, vol.9, p.171, 1987
14. Kroning, F., *Acta Unio Intern. Contra. Cancrum, vol.20, no.3, p.855, 1964*
15. You, WC, et al., *Journal of the National Cancer Institute*, vol.81, p.162, Jan.18, 1989
16. Ansher, SS, *Federation of Chemistry and Toxicology*, vol.24, p.405, 1986

17. Chihara, G., et al., Cancer Detection and Prevention, vol.1, p.423, 1987 suppl.

18. Kennedy, A., and Little, JB, *Cancer Research*, vol.41, p.2103, 1981

19. Messina, M., et al., *Journal National Cancer Institute*, vol.83, no.8, p.541, Apr.1991

20. Oreffo, VI, et al., *Toxicology*, vol.69, no.2, p.165, 1991; see also von Hofe, E, et al., *Carcinogenesis*, vol.12, no.11, p.2147, Nov.1991; see also Su, LN, et al., *Biochemical & Biophysical Research Communications*, vol.176, no.1, p.18, Apr.1991

Chapter 9

Action Plan Against Cancer— What to Do

The previous sections of this book were designed to prepare you for this chapter—the battle plan. Now that you know the strategy, or the "why" of the plan, you are ready for the "what to do". There are literally hundreds of nutritional products and programs that have at least anecdotal evidence of effectiveness against cancer. You cannot take all the pills and try all the diets. For many people there is the problem of convenience, or ability to swallow pills, or swallow anything when you are feeling nauseated. Then there is the obvious dilemma of cost. Insurance companies are still reluctant to reimburse for these relatively inexpensive and non-toxic nutritional supplements. Hence, the patient is left with some very tough decisions: "If I can't take them all, then which ones are most important?" For these people, I have rated the following supplements based upon the available scientific and clinical information.

1. **BEST (THREE STARS***)** are relatively inexpensive and easy to administer and are most likely to help all cancer patients.

2. **VERY GOOD (TWO STARS**)** may be very costly or inconvenient to administer, but may help many cancer patients. Use these if you have the money, inclination and time.

3. **GOOD (ONE STAR*)** means there is very limited data supporting the use of these products against cancer. Use them if you are willing to spend the money and time for what may constitute a "long shot" for most cancer patients.

DIET

★★★ WORLD CLASS GOURMET HEALTH FOOD CUISINE, delicious for most patients and acceptable for all. See the chapter with menu plan for examples. Calorie distribution:

20% fat (low in omega 6, saturated & hydrogenated; high in omega
3 from fish, canola, flaxseed oils and olive oil)
50-60% carbohydrate (low in sugar, high in fiber & vegetables)
20-30% protein (low in fat, beef & dairy; high in soy & whey)

■ **Food extracts**

★★★ Daily blending (use the Vitamix, 800-848-2649) for juicing of fresh carrots, cabbage, or other fruit and vegetables: 2 eight ounce glasses to be taken with meals to avoid elevations in blood glucose levels. Mix 4 ounces of pureed veggies with 4 ounces of purified water for a pleasant meal time beverage.

★★ Garlic: Kyolic 12 capsules, powder, or liquid equivalent. For a tasty and convenient way to eat more fresh garlic; place 6 garlic cloves unpeeled in 1/2 teaspoon of olive oil and cover. Microwave for 20-30 seconds. Cloves easily slide out of their peeling and taste somewhat like cashews. Eat garlic often or take garlic supplements.

★★ Shark cartilage (Cartilage Technology 914-939-9000). 60-80 grams powder (1-1.5 gm/kg body wt) either mixed in food or taken as retention enema. For those who would like to take orally, mix 20 grams of powdered shark cartilage in yogurt, apple sauce, pureed vegetable drink, or such. Do this 3 to 4 times daily, depending on your body weight and tumor size. For retention enema: mix 20 grams of shark cartilage powder in blender with 4 ounces of lukewarm water. Add to rectal syringe bottle (available at pharmacy). Lie on left side in bed with bed pan nearby. Follow directions from rectal syringe placing bottle higher and allowing gravity feed of solution into anus. The idea is to keep this solution in the colon for full absorption, which takes about 30 minutes. Try taking a nap. This procedure takes some adjusting, but the early data on shark cartilage is very encouraging.

★★ Shark oil (alkylglycerols) as Ecomer. 2 caps three times daily for patients undergoing radiation therapy. Provides protection against radiation damage. Begin 2 weeks before radiation therapy and continue throughout therapy.

★★ Greens: 2 tablespoons powder daily. The powdered essence of young green plants can be found in a number of products at your health food store. May be added as powder to your "Dragon-Slayer" shake in the morning or taken as pills. Chlorophyll, beta-carotene, potassium, glutathione and other nutrients are jammed into this wonder food.

★ Asparagus: 2 tablespoons powder

★★★ Mushroom extract: 6-12 capsules daily of Maitake (800-747-7418)

★★ Soybeans: 1/2 cup daily of soy products like tempeh, or Haelan Soy Product 851 (504-885-2776) or Lumen Soy Products (800-256-2253)

★★ Spirulina: 2 tablespoons powder, may be added to "Dragon-Slayer" shake in morning for protein component.

★ Royal bee jelly: 500 mg

★★★ Enzymes: Enzymes should be taken with a meal if the desire is to improve digestion, or on an empty stomach if the desire is to help fight cancer. For cancer support, take 15 Wobenzym (800-899-4499) first thing in the morning at least 1 hour before mealtime. Take 15 more Wobenzym last thing at night at least two hours after the last meal. Megazyme (5 pills in morning & 5 before bed) from Enzymatic Therapy is not enterically coated nor clinically tested on cancer patients, like Wobenzym, but is more concentrated. Bromelain is a vegetarian source of enzymes.

★★ Rice bran, pressure cooked (rich in tocotrienols), 2-3 tablespoons daily or as much as you can eat.

★★ Sea vegetables in soups and stews on a daily basis, or kelp tablets 6-12 daily depending on your thyroid function

★★ Aloe vera extract, contains active immune stimulant ace mannan. Drink as liquid. Can be used instead of fruit juice for "Dragon-Slayer" shake, 2-6 cups daily from Royal Body Care (800-722-0444), which is one of the few companies that has painstakingly preserved the active ingredient.

★★★ **Intestinal microflora**. If you use the Perfect 7 product as outlined for the "Dragon-Slayer" shake, then you may not need these other items. Options include:

Broad spectrum Kyodophilus (lactobacillus, bifidus, streptococcus faecium) from Tyson (800-367-7744)

Milk-free lactobacillus from Klaire Labs (800-533-7255)

Perque Product from Seraphim (800-525-7372)

★★★ **Intestinal cleansing/detoxification.** Many aspects of cancer therapy, including chemo and radiation therapy, pain killers and sedatives, will reduce muscular contractions in the intestines, which then cause constipation. These detox and herbal purgative formulas will help most patients, but for some people, there may be a need for physical assistance. Using the flat side of your fist, create a gentle but deep massaging rocking motion from top to bottom that moves laterally across your intestines, pushing in about 1-2 inches. This method helps many people who are losing the muscle tone of youth that moves food through the intestines. Sick and older people often have weak or sedated muscles throughout the body, including the intestines. This massaging technique really helps.

Perfect 7: combined herbal GI cleanser, 2 teaspoons in "Dragon-Slayer" shake; contains psyllium seed, alfalfa, cascara sagrada, rose hips, buckthorn bark, lactopriv/B (a special non-dairy lactobacillus), bentonite, garlic, golden seal, capsicum.

Homemade fiber combination. Sesame seeds ground with flax seeds to form a "nut butter". Use as a sandwich spread or to season soups.

High fiber supplement. Matol Fibre Sonic containing fiber from soy, gum arabic, cellulose gel, cellulose gum, apple, pea, corn bran, guar gum, locust bean gum, psyllium seed, rice bran, wheat bran, oat bran, rye, superbeet, xanthum bean gum, tofu (soybean), citrus pectin, prune, cellulose, barley, fig, beet, malted grain, pear, soy lecithin. 3 gm protein, 3 gm fat, 11 gm fiber per 8 ounce serving. From Matol, a network marketing group.

★★★ **Broad Spectrum Food Supplement**

For patients who cannot consume adequate calories via food, use 2-3 "Dragon-Slayer" shakes" per day as described in the recipe chapter.

SUPPLEMENTS

★★★ **Broad spectrum vitamin & mineral coverage.** This is critical, since so many cancer patients experience a wide array of nutrient deficiencies, it is impossible to take a separate pill for each vitamin and mineral. Hence, this product is the "core" of the vitamin and mineral program, with additional supplements providing therapeutic doses of other nutrients. Find a multiple vitamin and mineral that is in capsule form, for enhanced bioavailability. Tablets are often compressed under 200 pounds per square inch of pressure, with a resulting "rock" that dissolves poorly or not at all in the GI tract. Match the following formula as closely as possible, or use one of the following multiples:

Immuno Max from Optimal Nutrition Labs (800-795-9579)
VM-2000 or VM-75 from Solgar (800-645-2246)
Perque 2 from Seraphim (800-525-7372)

NUTRIENTS	AMOUNT
Vitamins	
A palmitate	5000 iu
A beta carotene	15,000 iu
D	400 iu
E succinate	300 iu
K	1000 mcg
C	250 mg
B-1 (thiamin)	25 mg
B-2 (riboflavin)	25 mg
B-3 (niacin)	100 mg
B-5 (pantothenate)	100 mg
B-6 (pyridoxine)	25 mg
B-6 (P-5-P)	5 mg
B-12	100 mcg
folic acid	800 mcg
biotin	300 mcg
bioflavonoids	100 mg
Minerals	
calcium (citrate)	250 mg
magnesium (citrate)	200 mg
iron (glycinate)	18 mg
zinc (picolinate)	30 mg
copper (gluconate)	3 mg
manganese (gluconate)	5 mg
molybdenum	100 mcg
iodine	150 mcg
chromium (picolinate)	200 mcg
selenium (methionine)	400 mcg
tin	10 mcg
silicon	10 mcg
vanadium	10 mcg
nickel	10 mcg

■ **Vitamins**

Fat soluble

★ A: retinyl palmitate 300,000 iu. While vitamin A can be valuable for many cancer patients, it is also one of the more potentially toxic nutrients. There are clinics in Europe and Mexico that use 1.5 million iu of vitamin A daily, though I do not recommend these levels without medical supervision. Dry skin, headache or weak hand shake is an early warning that vitamin A toxicity is being reached. There is some preliminary data showing that vitamin A toxicity can be reduced when taking high doses of vitamin E at the same time. The theory is that peroxides, or "rusted" versions of vitamin A create the toxicity, not normal vitamin A. Taking 3200 iu of vitamin E with the 300,000 iu of vitamin A would lower the risks for toxicity of A.

Nevertheless, it is important to emphasize the potential for toxicity in this nutrient and to have continuous medical monitoring if you are using it. Normal fat soluble vitamin A is quickly removed from lymphatic circulation and stored in the liver. Yet emulsified vitamin A will make several passes through the bloodstream in its water soluble form before being removed by the liver. Emulsified A (from Naturally 800-899-4499) is more likely to benefit the cancer patient.

★★★ Beta-carotene: 100,000 to 500,000 iu of liquid beta-carotene in soft gelatin capsule from Betatene of Australia. This product is based on a blue green ocean algae (Duneliela) and has been shown to be selectively toxic to tumor cells in animal studies.

★★★ E: Mixed natural tocopherols (to stimulate immune functions) at 400 iu per 40 pounds of body weight. Hence, a 160 pound person would need 1600 iu.

★★★ E succinate (to selectively kill cancer cells). Take 1600-3200 iu per day, based upon body size and aggressiveness of tumor. Total vitamin E intake should not exceed 5000 iu per day.

★★ K: 25-75 mg K-1 in liquid form from Scientific Botanicals (206-527-5521). This nutrient is particularly valuable when taken in conjunction with high dose vitamin C (10-20 grams) two weeks prior to beginning chemo or radiation therapy. K seems to potentiate the tumor kill rate from chemo and radiation.

★ D: 400-1000 iu orally. There is some encouraging evidence that topically applied vitamin D as 1,25 dihydroxycholecalciferol may soon become a potent cancer fighter. This product has shown promise, but must be used judiciously by experienced physicians due to possible toxicity.

★★★ Coenzyme Q-10: at 200 mg from Biotics (800-231-5777), Metabolic Maintenance (800-772-PURE), or Seraphim (800-525-7372). Cancer is clearly an anaerobic cell growth. CoQ augments aerobic metabolism and immune function. CoQ also blunts the toxicity on the heart from various chemo agents.

Water Soluble

★★★ C: 12-20 grams of potassium ascorbate as Emergen-C from Alacer (800-854-0249), or buffered C from Seraphim (800-525-7372), or C with bioflavonoids from Bronson (800-235-3200).

A special note on vitamin C, since this nutrient was one of the first nutrients suspected of altering cancer outcome. Below you will find a chart that neatly describes the functions, toxicity, deficiency symptoms and intake levels for C as part of cancer treatment.

ASCORBIC ACID

FUNCTIONS	TOXICITY
anti-oxidant regulate serum lipids collagen synthesis iron absorption immunity CNS neurochem. trans.	abnormal iron depos (genet.) diarrhea kidney stones (genet.) rebound scurvy-no!!
DEFICIENCY SYMP.	**INTAKE**
slow wound healing immune suppression pain in joints bleeding gums irritability inc. risk ca, CAD, glstn	RDA: 60 mg usual US: 114 mg-destruct. prophylactic: 500-2000 mg therapeutic: 500-100,000 mg toxic: ??1000-30,000 mg CTCA: 1000-12,000 mg

There is a great deal of confusion regarding the efficacy of vitamin C for cancer patients. Max Gerson, MD used high doses of vitamin C in the 1950s to treat cancer patients. Ewan Cameron, MD and Linus Pauling, PhD published several studies in the 1970s showing that therapeutic supplements of C provided improvement in the quality and quantity of life for cancer patients. Then Charles Moertel, MD of the Mayo Clinic conducted a study which found that vitamin C did not help cancer patients. Unfortunately, with all the prevailing evidence in favor of using C, this one study by Moertel sticks in the minds of physicians, who consider the case closed. Actually, the case is quite open and encouraging.

The chart below shows the bulk of data pointing toward C as both protective and therapeutic against cancer. This chart also summarizes the conflict between Drs. Pauling and Moertel. Moertel did not replicate Pauling's study. Pauling's cancer patients were on 10 grams of vitamin C for up to 12 years, while Moertel's

VITAMIN C & CANCER

>35 separate studies show increase vit.C diet, decrease cancer risk
>increase ther.value chemo., decrease toxicity on host (animals)
>inhibits tumor cell growth
>protects host against carcinogen-induced DNA damage
>immune potentiation: lymphocyte transformation, etc.
>reverses pre-malignant lesions, rectal polyps (animals)
>induces tumor encapsulation via collagen synthesis
>may selectively inhibit energy metab. in tumor mitochondria
>reversal of transformed cell back to normal phenotype (in vitro)
>interferon & IL-2 deplete vit. C reserves

PAULING vs. MOERTEL

12 yrs, 10 grams
decreased cachexia, anorexia
inc. muscle strength, qual. life
+257 days vs. 36 & 42; untreat.

2.5 months, 7.5 grams (2 gm control)
only died after vit.C stopped
end stage, heavily pre-treated

patients were on 7.5 grams of C for only 2.5 months, during which no cancer patient died until the C was stopped. The average intake of vitamin C in the "control" group for Moertel's study was 2.5 grams, since end-stage cancer patients were unwilling to be the placebo group. In Pauling's study, cancer patients on high dose C lived an average of 257 days beyond the point of being "untreatable". None of Moertel's patients, who were all heavily pre-treated with chemo and radiation and considered "end-stage, terminal", died while on the vitamin C therapy.

Since this controversy, Pauling and Hoffer have shown a dramatic improvement in quality and quantity of life with cancer patients who received a good diet coupled with therapeutic levels of various nutrients, including 12 grams of vitamin C. A 1990 symposium on vitamin C and cancer held at the National Institutes of Health further exonerates vitamin C as a true champion in the war on cancer.

★★ Bioflavonoids: 1 gram daily of quercetin (with bromelain for absorption) from Allergy Research (800-545-9960), or from Enzymatic Therapy (800-783-2286), or BioQuercetin from Seraphim (800-525-7372).

★★ Anti-oxidant formula from Enzymatic Therapy (800-783-2286), including 1 gram potassium ascorbate, 400 iu vit. E acetate, 20,000 iu beta-carotene, 400 mcg selenium (from selenomethionine), 30 mg zinc (from picolinate), 12 mg riboflavin, 30 mg manganese, 200 mg N-acetyl cysteine, 200 mg curcumin, 100 mg procyanolic oligomers (bioflavonoids), 200 mg green tea extracts, 200 mg cabbage extract, 200 mg deodorized garlic extract, 200 mg Klamath blue green algae, 200 mg ginger extract

★★★ B-3: niacin 2 grams from niacinamide, or inositol hexaniacinate from Enzymatic Therapy, KAL or Twin Labs

★★ B-6: pyridoxal with pyridoxal-5-pyrophosphate (P-5-P), total 250 mg. May be particularly helpful in reducing damage from radiation therapy and slowing cancer growth from polyamine synthesis of the tumor. Becomes a three star ★★★ for melanoma patients who need to apply a B-6 ointment to their surface tumor as well as consume 250-1000 mg orally.

★★★ B-12: 3-5 mg as sub-lingual tablets or nasal gel form at your health food store, or B-12 hydroxycobalamin from Seraphim (800-525-7372). B-12 dramatically augments the tumor kill of vitamin C.

■ **Minerals**

★★★ Potassium & magnesium. Potassium and magnesium are among the more crucial minerals for cancer recovery. Magnesium helps to stabilize cell membranes and elevate immune activity while potassium plays a critical role in membrane permeability.

Liquid K Plus with 99 mg potassium and 100 mg magnesium per teaspoon from Twin Labs (800-645-5626). Take one tablespoon per day.

Herbal K from Enzymatic Therapy with 718 mg potassium per 2 tablespoons. Take 2 tablespoons daily.

KM from Matol with 585 mg potassium per 2 tablespoons. Take 2 tbsp. daily.

★★★ Magnesium: get 400-800 mg daily as aspartate, citrate or orotate

★★★ Zinc: 30-100 mg zinc picolinate

★★★ Selenium intake should not exceed 2500 micrograms (2.5 milligrams) per day. Immuno Max contains 400 mcg. Take additional selenium as sodium selenite liquid from Allergy Research (800-545-9960) or selenomethionine from Metabolic (800-772-PURE)

Selenium merits a footnote since it helps beat cancer on many different fronts: bolsters immune function, improves detoxification, directly toxic to tumor cells and may be a valuable anti-proliferative factor. Below you will find the functions, toxicity symptoms, deficiency symptoms and intake levels for selenium along with a separate chart summarizing the many links between selenium and cancer, including 10 years of unpublished clinical work by R.C. Donaldsen, MD of the VA Hospital in St. Louis. Throughout the 1970s, Dr. Donaldsen used varying levels of oral selenium supplements to improve the outcome of most types of cancer. Selenium is on the "first assault team" in my cancer battle plan.

SELENIUM

FUNCTIONS:	TOXICITY
anti-oxidant detoxification (GSH) protects membranes & DNA prostaglandin synthesis immunity anti-proliferative nutrient?	garlic breath abnorm bone dev. abdominal pain paralysis "loco weed" inc. risk cancer ???
DEFICIENCY SYMPTOMS muscular dystrophy increased peroxidation suppressed immunity inc. risk ca. & CAD	INTAKE RDA: 55-70 mcg usual US: 83-129 mcg prophylactic: 200-600 mcg therapeutic: 400-7000 mcg toxic: 5000 mcg (hair/nails) CTCA: 800 mcg

SELENIUM & CANCER

>increase selenium content forage plants; decrease cancer mortality
>increase selenium intake; decrease ca. mort. (17 sites, 27 countries)
>increase selenium intake; decrease liver ca. China
>decrease plasma selenium; increase risk non-melanomous skin ca.
>increase serum selenium, decrease risk recurrence, localized, metastasis
>selenium supplements can inhibit chemically induced tumors in animals
>selenium supplemented animals inc. macrophage TNF-alpha tumor kill
>critical element in glutathione peroxidase (inhibit membrane lipid peroxidation)
>enhanced immune function: phagocytosis, complement, PMN, NK cytotox, etc.
>reduces thromboxane production, spares PGE-1
>spares chemo-induced rise in creatine kinase
>complete inhibition of tumor growth in mice inoculated with tumor cells
>protects against chem. carcinogenesis at initiation & promotion phase
>Donaldson, MD 10 yrs VA hospital St. Louis, selenium improves ca. outcome

★★★ Chromium as picolinate, an additional 400-800 mcg.

The other relevant essential minerals are already found in therapeutic doses in the multiple vitamin and mineral formula described above.

■ Fatty acids (as liquid or capsule)

★★★ Eicosapentaenoic acid (EPA) from fish oil has been well proven to slow metastasis. Take up to 6 grams in conjunction with GLA in a 5:1 EPA to GLA ratio. Make sure that you take adequate vitamin E (at least 1000 iu) to prevent the formation of "rusted fat" or lipid peroxides from the fish oil. Best form is OmegaSyn liquid as mentioned in the "Dragon-Slayer" shake, or Omega Syn capsules (6 per day) from BioSyn (800-346-2703). Remember the intricate "dance" between fatty acids and hormones. Control blood sugar and less of these fatty acids become far more potent against cancer.

★★ Gamma linolenic acid (GLA): up to 1.5 grams. Taken separately as oil from borage, evening primrose (plants native to cold climates) or black current seed.

★★ Alpha-linolenic acid (ALA) from flaxseed oil. Use cold-pressed flaxseed oil that is in the refrigerator section of your health food store. Take 1-2 tsp. daily.

★ Wheat germ oil. Use cold-pressed oil from refrigerator section of health food store. Take 1-2 tsp. daily.

■ Organ replacement

★ Natural dessicated thyroid, 2-5 grains as a prescription item, if morning basal temperature is below 97.8 F. If you need thyroid, then this is a crucial supplement and becomes ★★★. You may try "jump starting" your thyroid gland with non-prescription nutrition factors first: including 6 tablets of dried ocean kelp, or Liquid Kelp from Hickey Chemist (800-724-5566), or Thyroid Herbal Tonic from Natural Herbal Extracts (718-638-7889). Other nutrition factors that help to elevate basal metabolism include MCT oil, chromium picolinate (400-600 mcg), L-carnitine (200-1500 mg), certain herbal combinations (like Escalation from Enzymatic Therapy 800-558-7372), exercise and exposing skin surface.

★ Thymus 1-2 tablets from Enzymatic Therapy or Thymex from Standard Process Labs. The thymus organ is considered the master gland of the immune system and often atrophies with age. Thymic extract has been shown to help people with hepatitis viral infections through "jump starting" the immune system. Prevents leukopenia atrophy from chemo and radiation. Initially, you may need to take much larger (up to 20 tablets daily) amounts of thymus to get a therapeutic effect.

■ Amino acids

★★ L-Arginine as pill or powder (very bitter flavor) up to 12 grams daily. Patients who are subject to herpes simplex should note that arginine may accelerate cold sore growth.

★★ L-Glutamine: up to 5 grams. Most likely to help patients who have GI problems, like diarrhea or cramping.

★★ L-Carnitine: up to 1.5 grams. Most likely to help patients who are on a lipid-based parenteral formula to help prevent fatty build-up in the liver.

★★ N-acetylcysteine 1-2 grams or 200 mg glutathione to bolster glutathione peroxidase (GSH) activity. Most likely to help relieve the toxicity of chemo and radiation therapy when taken one week prior to and during therapy.

■ **Herbs** are best if used in standardized herbal concentration. Enzymatic Therapy (800-783-2286), Eclectic Institute (800-332-4372) or Min Tong (800-562-5777) are reputable manufacturers.

★★★ Astragalus (radix), ★★Echinecea (augustifolia), ★goldenseal (Hydrastis canadensis), and ★★liquorice (Glycyrrhiza glabra) are immune stimulants that can be taken as dried root in tea (1-2 grams/day), or freeze dried root (500-1000 mg), or tincture (4-6 ml or 1-1.5 tsp), or powdered solid extract 250-500 mg daily. Super-Immuno Comp from Enzymatic Therapy is a combination herbal product.

★★ Siberian Ginseng (Eleuterococcus senticosis) is an adaptogen, which helps to rectify abnormal cellular metabolism. Daily intake of 2-4 grams of dried root, or 10-20 ml (2.5-5 tsp) tincture, or 100-200 mg pills in greater than 1% concentration.

★★ Ginkgo biloba at 120 mg daily has been shown to dramatically improve peripheral circulation, and hence may slow cancer through oxygenation.

★ Milk thistle (silybum marianum) is a potent liver protector and detoxifier. Take 70-210 mg silymarin concentrate as pills 2-3 times daily.

★★★ Pau D'Arco (LaPacho or Tabebuia Avellanedae) is a likely cancer fighter with initial favorable studies from the National Cancer Institute. LaPacho has an ingredient, a quinone, that is similar in structure to vitamin K and may well attack the tumor in a similar fashion to K. Take as 1 cup of bark boiled into decoction and taken 2-8 times daily, or more precise lapachol content (active ingredient) at 1.5-2.0 grams daily from pills or powder.

★★ Australian tea tree oil (Leptaspermum and Melaleuca) is showing early promise as an anti-fungal agent for the common fungal infections that coat the mouth, teeth and probably other areas of cancer patients. Remember that half of all fatal infections in cancer patients are caused by fungus. Take 1-2 drops of concentrated oil in a small glass of apple juice, rinse around the mouth and swallow.

★ Japanese Green Tea from Tyson (800-367-7744).

★★★ **Topical application of herbal combination**. Use as an escharotic, or corrosive ointment to burn away unwanted skin, as in basal cell, or squamous cell carcinoma or melanoma. Use Cansema from Applied Botanical Research (800-256-2253)

ENTERAL FORMULAS

When the GI tract is working but the patient is not voluntarily eating, then enteral formulas may solve the riddle of getting adequate nourishment into the patient. Patient tolerance varies widely when nasogastric tubes are inserted into the nose and down the esophagus. Impact, available from your pharmacist, is the best formula, but has an awful taste that must be disguised (see suggestions below) and is very expensive.

★★ Impact is fortified with fish oil, arginine, and nucleic acids for enhanced wound healing and immune stimulation. Good studies on animals and early work with humans shows an anti-cancer activity. Can be used in an oral drink flavored as follows. Recipes created by Alfred Hinga, chef. Full therapeutic benefit obtained at 6 cans per day.

Orange Impact:
4 ounces Impact (1/2 can)
8 ounces orange concentrate or 3 whole peeled oranges
1 teaspoon lemon extract (hides fish flavor)
emulsifier to bind water & fat soluble fractions together (1 teaspoon of lecithin), or Thicken Up from Sandoz
  Combine ingredients (except lecithin) and mix in electric blender for one minute, then slowly add lecithin.

Pineapple Impact
4 ounces Impact
8 ounces diced fresh pineapple, plus pineapple extract if desired
1/3 cup honey
1 teaspoon lemon extract
  Follow same directions as above, combining lecithin last and slowly.

Raspberry Impact
4 ounces Impact
8 ounces organic raspberry popsickle or 6 ounces cranberry juice
1/3 cup honey
1 teaspoon lemon extract
1 teaspoon lecithin
  ★ ImmunAid, by Kendall McGaw, is fortified with gamma linolenic acid,

glutamine and protein. May help the cancer patient without the tolerance problems of arginine and fish oil that are found in Impact.

PARENTERAL FORMULAS

Total parenteral nutrition (TPN) should be reserved for clinically malnourished patients and must be administered by a physician. For less severity in cachexia, use oral "shakes" or enteral formulas, or J tube (into jejunum) enteral feedings. The TPN formula must be disease-specific to fight cancer:

- High in protein (at least 100 grams/day); >30% kcal
- Little or no dextrose; 0-40% of kcal
- Balance of calories from fat, preferably monounsaturated oleic acid and medium chain triglycerides (MCT); >30% kcal. Take L-carnitine orally (1-2 grams) to help minimize fatty accumulation in the liver.
- 10-50 grams of buffered ascorbate intravenously, whatever intake is necessary to achieve 50-80 mg/dl serum C concentration
- High dose of broad spectrum vitamin/mineral supplementation, given at 4 times RDA levels.
- 400 mcg selenium
- 4-5 grams L-glutamine taken orally to reduce bacteria crossing the intestinal barrier to create infections in the blood, called bacterial translocation.
- 1-2 grams L-carnitine to augment fat metabolism
- Flow rate (cc/hour) varies according to patient tolerance, beginning at 75 cc and progressing up to 160 cc/hour. Start slowly, build up to 160 cc if possible, then gradually reduce flow before disconnecting.
- Daily blood values need to be monitored and changes made in formula to reflect deviations in pH, blood urea nitrogen or blood ammonia values.

HEALING THE MIND & SPIRIT

- **Ventilate emotions and forgive.** Some people may need professional help for purging deep seated negative emotions of anger, hurt, depression and low self-esteem.
- **Healing the "child within".** A suppressed immune system can stem from the trauma of an abusive or neglected childhood. There are programs to help people recover from these fundamental emotional problems; including PRIMAL THERAPY (Janov), MAKING PEACE WITH YOUR PARENTS (Bloomfield) and HOMECOMING (Bradshaw).

■ **Guided imagery** to assist the immune system in attacking the tumor. Picture your immune factors as sharks, white knights or Rambos zapping cancer cells. See CREATIVE VISUALIZATION (Gawain) or YOU CAN HEAL YOUR LIFE (Hay).

■ **Spend some time daily in play therapy** or right brain fun time, including clay sculpting, artwork, photography, music, singing, kite flying, etc. See THE HEALING JOURNEY (Simonton).

■ **Be here now.** Live for today. "Suck the marrow out of life" said David Thoreau.

■ **Self analysis.** Since few people have spent time introspectively, this exercise is designed to help the individual better understand his or her goals, priorities, fears, limitations, etc. Keep a journal.

■ **Establish a link between yourself and a Higher Power.** This pursuit can be non-denominational and outside of organized religion. Hans Selye, MD, father of the theories of stress, found that humans have a need to rely on a Higher Power. Spiritually based people are happier and healthier than their non-spiritual counterparts. Humans are created with a God-shaped void which needs filling.

■ **Fighting spirit.** Dr. Bernie Siegel found that cancer patients who are assertive and determined to "beat this thing" have a better chance of recovery. It is the uncooperative patient, not the docile patient, who does better in fighting cancer.

■ **Bereavement.** While most cultures around the world accept death as a part of life, Americans have become emotionally constipated about grieving. Grief unexpressed will result in some mental or physical malady. Many people are chronically depressed since they have not expressed the grief of losing a loved one, a job, a home, a phase of life, etc. Find coaching in fulfilling the needs of the grieving process.

■ **Be yourself.** Too many of us in modern society bend to the pressure of others and spend our lives in "quiet desperation" to quote David Thoreau. What would you like to do if you had only 6 months to live? Do it! Dr. Bernie Siegel has found too many cancer patients who enjoyed doing one thing, but entered a completely different profession to please a mate or parents or to make more money—and their health suffered for it. Dr. Siegel asked a young breast cancer patient: "What have you always wanted to do?" She replied, "Be a violinist. I went into law to please my family." She quit law, became a concert violinist, and lost 75% of her income along with her cancer.

A similar story comes from the files of Yosemite National Park. Galen Clark came to Yosemite Park at age 42 in 1856 to die. Coughing up blood from end-stage tuberculosis, Clark first carved his own tombstone, then proceeded to protect and beautify this valley that he loved so much. Death did not come 6 months later, as the doctors had predicted, but rather 54 years later when he was just shy of his 96th birthday. If your life is a lie, then it will probably be shorter and less enjoyable. Make your life a masterpiece painting, and you will probably get more life in your years and more years in your life.

Dr. Michael Partipillo, both a psychologist for cancer patients and a cancer victor himself, says that he views cancer "as a starting point—not the beginning of the end." For more inspirational and educational books on the spiritual aspect of cancer, see the appendix.

BREATHING

Lie on your back on the floor with a book on your stomach. Begin inhaling by trying to push the book up with your stomach muscles. Once you have fully oxygenated the lower lungs with diaphragm breathing, then finish inhaling by expanding your chest fully. Hold your breath for a count of 5, then slowly exhale and give a final "puff" as you breathe out that last air. This deep breathing method will help to fully oxygenate your tissue, even if you cannot do any exercise.

EXERCISE

Whatever you can do will be helpful. Our hospital has an indoor track where we take patients to walk laps accompanied by their IV chemo poles. Exercise elevates immune functions, stabilizes blood sugar levels, oxygenates tissue and improves mental functions.

DETOXIFICATION

Stop taking in toxins by drinking purified water and getting organic produce or thoroughly washing your produce. If the air in your area is questionable, then you may need to seal up your house and install a special air filter system—or move to a cleaner area.

Help the body to purge accumulated poisons by:
- drinking enough water that your urine is light in color and odor
- eating enough fiber and plant purgatives to maintain regularity and discharge poisons through the colon. Enemas may help some cancer patients.
- soak for 20 minutes in a hot tub each day, then cleanse the skin with a natural sponge and soap.

SPINAL ALIGNMENT

All organs and glands are very dependent on nerve stimulation. All nerves throughout the body radiate from the spine. Yet, due to sedentary lives, poor posture, the constant pull of gravity, and lack of muscle development to keep spinal vertebra in alignment, many people suffer indirect illness as a consequence of back problems. Doctors of chiropractic (DC) or osteopathy (DO) have been trained to restore spinal alignment, which can oftentimes boost immune functions.

PATIENT PROFILE

L.J., male 54 years old. For 18 months, LJ had experienced pain in his tailbone region and bright red blood in his stools. In December of 1991, he underwent surgery to remove cancer of the rectum, with considerable metastases (2 of 11 lymph nodes positive and prostate and seminal vesicle involvement). In April of 1992 he was admitted to our facility with a 23 pound weight loss. Began fractionated chemo regimen, parenteral nutrition and supplement program, which dramatically improved his quality of life and energy. As of July 1993, LJ looks and feels better than most people on the street and is actively involved with his career, family and church group.

PARTING COMMENTS

By reading this far, you have already empowered yourself to make a difference in your cancer outcome. You are the pro-active and assertive cancer victor. You have been through some or all of the phases that come with the disease: anger, denial, rejection, isolation, withdrawal and more. While the bulk of this book is spent providing nutritional facts to change the biochemistry of your body, my final parting comments are directed more at your soul. Because cancer is a disease of the mind, body and spirit.

I believe that cancer is far more than an individual physical disease that can be expunged from the body with strong drugs, surgery or radiation. Cancer is also a symptom of modern society that is organically unsound; that needs metabolic healing. In every era, we try to identify the outside enemy. But we have met the enemy–and it is us. Today, we wage full scale chemical warfare on ourselves with potent agricultural and industrial carcinogens, while stripping our once benevolent food supply of any vestige of nutritional value. We are subjected to intolerable stress from work and dissolving family structures, thousands of murders per year on TV and movies, and an endless procession of gut-wrenching stories on the nightly news.

This book is written for you, the cancer patient and soon-to-be victor. But it goes one step further. Since you are reading this section, we can safely assume that you have a mission on earth that is not yet accomplished. Once you beat your own personal cancer, you may find a strong sense of purpose in spreading what you have learned or even addressing the "cancers" in society.

From my cancer patients I have learned of the incredible tenacity of the human body and spirit; of the immeasurable dignity and generosity that is waiting to be expressed by all of us; of the undying passion and commitment shown by a dedicated mate when a loved one is failing; and above all–of the preciousness of life. In our increasingly callous world, it is easy to drift away from the true pleasures in life: love, enthusiasm, laughter, freedom, meaningful work, skills developed, helping one another and savoring the beauty in this emerald paradise planet. For many people, cancer has become the ultimate "truth serum" in helping to establish real priorities.

Nourish your body, mind and spirit. Take every opportunity to say: "I love you". Give away smiles with wreckless abandon. Practice random acts of kindness and beauty. Savor each day as though it may be your last, because the same holds true for all of us. You have the opportunity to be born again with a renewed vigor and purpose in life.

My prayer for you is the same thought that began this book; that you will soon be able to say: "Cancer is the best thing that ever happened to me." Since you have cancer, you might as well turn this ultimate challenge into the ultimate victory: to make your life and that of others into a masterpiece painting.

Chapter 10

For the Technically-Oriented Reader

This chapter is provided for the person who enjoys knowing more of the intimate details on how nutrition interrupts the cancer process. This section is to be considered more exemplary rather than comprehensive. If I included all the data in this field, then this book would be unwieldy. These references provide a scientific foothold upon which to recommend nutrition therapy in conjunction with traditional oncology care. For more information, see:

Non-Technical
- CANCER THERAPY, by Ralph Moss, PhD
- CANCER AND ITS NUTRITIONAL THERAPIES, by Richard Passwater, PhD
- BEATING THE ODDS, by Albert Marchetti, MD
- WHAT YOUR DOCTOR WON'T TELL YOU, by Jane Heimlich
- VITAMINS AGAINST CANCER, by Kedar Prasad, PhD
- HOW TO FIGHT CANCER AND WIN, by William Fischer

Technical
- ADJUVANT NUTRITION IN CANCER TREATMENT, by Patrick Quillin, PhD,RD
- VITAMINS AND CANCER by Frank Meyskens, MD
- VITAMINS AND MINERALS IN THE PREVENTION AND TREATMENT OF CANCER by Maryce Jacobs, PhD
- MODULATION AND MEDIATION OF CANCER BY VITAMINS, by Frank Meyskens, MD
- ESSENTIAL NUTRIENTS IN CARCINOGENESIS, by Lionel Poirier

PURPOSE OF USING ADJUVANT NUTRITION IN CANCER TREATMENT

1. Preventing malnutrition. Cancer is a serious wasting disease, elevating basal metabolism, altering bio-energetics, and oftentimes inducing anorexia. The net effect is that 40% or more of cancer patients actually die from malnutrition, not from the cancer.[1] The American College of Physicians issued a position paper in 1989 stating:"...the evidence suggests that parenteral nutritional support [in cancer treatment] was associated with net harm, and no conditions could be defined in which such treatment appeared to be of benefit."[2] This "meta-analysis" of the literature specifically excluded cancer patients who were malnourished. Nutrition support is meant to relieve malnutrition, not cure cancer. Extensive chemotherapy or radiation therapy are, in themselves, sufficient stressors to induce catabolic malnutrition.[3] Additionally, standard Intensive Care Unit parenteral formulas may be inappropriate for cancer patients since high glucose solutions may feed tumor growth.

2. Bolstering immune functions. From textbooks[4] to extensive reviews of the literature[5], it has been clearly demonstrated that a strong link exists between nutrient intake and the quality and quantity of human immune factors. Researchers provided 30 milligrams of beta carotene (or 50,000 iu, which is 10 times the Recommended Dietary Allowance of vitamin A), to healthy older adult volunteers with a dose dependent increase in natural killer cell activity (NK) and interleukin-2 receptors.[6] Similar results have been found with vitamin E, B-6, C, and zinc.

3. Nutrients as biological response modifiers.

■ **Immune modulation**

cleave immune complexes: i.e. proteolytic enzymes

improve quantity: via precursors for immune cytotoxic activity, nitric oxide from arginine for enhanced chemotaxis; increase NK, TNF, total lymphocytes via beta carotene, vitamin A, C, E, B-6 etc.

improve quality: via increase in tumor recognition using enzymes or emulsified vitamin A

reduce antigens: via oligoantigenic diet

thymotropic: via arginine supplements and thymus gland extract

immune sparing: antioxidants that lower turnover in cell mediated immunity or an increase in circulation of immune factors, i.e. vitamin E protects lymphocytes from oxidative damage in chemotaxis

■ **Alter genetic expression**

down regulate oncogene: i.e. soybean protease inhibitors alter c-myc oncogene

genetic repair: increase DNA polymerase activity and decrease in
base pair fragility via zinc & folate
inhibit episome production: via vitamin D
directly affect gene receptors: i.e. vit. A

■ **Alter cell membrane dynamics**

K to Na ratio: may alter membrane permeability & thus flow of oxygen &
nutrients into & out of cell (an anaerobic environment is more conducive to
tumor cell mitosis)
dietary fat intake: affects lipid bi-layer content in cell membrane, thus membrane
dynamics & oxygenation
prostaglandin metabolism: macronutrients influence hormones which influence
prostaglandin branch points, which can affect aggregation and adhesiveness of
cell membranes, thus metastatic potential of tumor

■ **Influence detoxification**

urinary output: fluid intake & diuretics (e.g. coffee & alcohol)
fecal excretion: fluid and fiber intake coupled with nutrients that encourage
peristalsis
cytochrome P450
endogenous biosynthesis of detoxification enzymes: catalase, SOD, GSH through
selenium and vitamin E
immune stimulation: encourages detox
low temperature saunas encourage excretion of toxins via skin pores
respiratory quotient indicates efficiency of oxidative respiration, which can be
retarded by heavy metal toxicity

■ **Alter acid/base balance**

all foods influence pH. Tumor cells thrive in acidosis.
alkalizing diet (high in most plant food items) encourages detox of heavy metals

■ **Cell/cell communication**

gap cell junctions for ionic communication between cells and nucleus, i.e.
vitamin A may be able to revert abnormal DNA back to normal DNA
(prodifferentiation or cytodifferentiation) and cell content via gap cell junction

■ **Prostaglandin synthesis**

affected by macronutrient intake and serum insulin levels
immune modulation: PGE-1 vs PGE-2, via eicosapentaenoic acid or gamma
linolenic acid
membrane aggregability and metastasis are heavily influenced by prostaglandin
metabolism
estrogen binders: PGE-1 increases endogenous biosynthesis of circulating
estrogen receptors, PGE-1 probably also helps with androgen-driven prostatic
cancer

- **Affect steroid hormone activity**

fat from diet and body influence estrogen output

phytoestrogens in diet (i.e. soybeans): may retard hormone-driven cancer lignans (from plant food) can provide estrogen binders or analogs to educe estrogen activation of tumors

- **Alter polyamine synthesis**

polyamines can accelerate cancer growth, while B-6 creates polyamine complexes and accelerates their excretion

- **Bioenergetics**

selective starve tumors by:

depriving anaerobic and fermenting tumors of their preferential substrate, glucose altering mitochondrial membranes of tumor, such as with Vitamin C

employ nutrients that encourage aerobic metabolism: CoQ, chromium, niacin, riboflavin, polyunsaturated fats, exercise

- **Pro & antioxidants**

therapeutic levels of antioxidants: protect healthy tissue from free radical destruction of chemotherapy & radiation therapy.(i.e. vitamin E, C, beta-carotene, selenium)

certain form and dose of pro-oxidants (i.e. non-heme iron): can accelerate tissue destruction and is sequestered by tumor & pathogens

- **Anti-proliferative agents**

selective toxins for anti-neoplastic activity: i.e. garlic and other minor dietary constituents in plant food

homeostatic mechanism for down regulation of growth: possible role for selenium

anti-angiogenesis factor (hyaluronic acid or other proteins in cartilage, ie. shark cartilage and bovine tracchea)

- **Influence cell differentiation**

retinoids, vitamin D, enzymes

THE PROTECTIVE ACTION OF VITAMINS AGAINST CANCER INCLUDES:[7]

- preventing the formation of carcinogens
- increasing detoxification
- inhibiting transformed cell replication
- controlling expression of malignancy
- controlling differentiation processes
- enhancing cell to cell communication

A SAMPLING OF CANCER ANTAGONISTS FOUND IN VARIOUS FOODS
(WITH ACTIVE INGREDIENT IN PARENTHESES):[8]

- **inhibitors of covalent DNA binding**

broccoli & cabbage (phenethyl isothiocyanate)

fruits, nuts, berries, seeds, and vegetables (ellagic acid)

fruits & vegetables (flavonoids in polyphenolic acid)

- **inhibitors of tumor promotion**

orange & yellow fruits & vegetables (retinol)

nuts & wheat germ (vitamin E)

fruits & vegetables (vitamin C)

green, orange, & yellow fruits and vegetables (beta-carotene)

garlic & onions (organosulfur compounds, reduce the formation of organosoluble metabolites and increase the formation of water soluble metabolites which are easier to excrete)

curry/tumeric (curcumin)

chili peppers (capsaicin, a vanillyl alkaloid)

- **inducing biotransformation**

cabbage, brussel sprouts, spinach, cauliflower and broccoli (indole-3-carbinol)

seafood & garlic (selenium)

- **reducing the absorption of carcinogens**

fruits, vegetables, grains & nuts (fiber)

fruits & vegetables (riboflavin chlorophyllin)

NUTRIENTS CAN REVERSE PRE-MALIGNANT LESIONS

- Vitamin C and beta-carotene are effective at reversing cervical dysplasia and oral leukoplakia in humans.[9]

- Vitamin A derivatives (retinoids) reverse bronchial metaplasia in humans.[10]

- Combination of folate and vitamin B-12 reversed bronchial metaplasia in humans.[11]

- Injections of vitamin E, beta-carotene, canthaxanthin (a carotenoid) and algae extract dramatically bolstered levels of tumor necrosis factor alpha and reversed hamster buccal pouch tumors.[12]

■ 58 adults with familial adenomatous polyps (near 100%   progression to cancer if untreated) were entered into a randomized study providing high dose vitamin C with E and high fiber, or placebo plus low fiber diet. The high fiber group experienced a limited degree of polyp regression.[13]

NUTRIENTS CAN INHIBIT CARCINOGENESIS

■ Beta-carotene, vitamin A, C, E reduce the risk of cancer by radiation and chemical carcinogen exposure. Vitamins A, D, and E inhibit the expression of oncogenes.[14]

■ Calcium supplements (2000 mg/day) provided a marked suppression of rectal proliferation in experimental but not placebo patients. Calcium seems to markedly inhibit the early stages of colon cancer in genetically vulnerable individuals.[15]

■ Taking vitamin supplements was protective against colo-rectal cancer in a large Australian study.[16]

■ The former medical director of Sloan Kettering cancer hospital in New York (Robert Good, MD, DSc) has found that many nutrients modulate immune functions and can protect against cancer.[17]

■ An extensive book by a former National Cancer Institute oncologist, Dr. Charles Simone, shows the potency of nutrients to prevent cancer.[18]

■ Professors at Harvard University have published considerable evidence in the prestigious *New England Journal of Medicine* showing that 90% of all cancer is environmentally caused and therefore preventable. They cite our 500% higher incidence of breast cancer as being related to diet. They highlight fat, selenium, vitamin A, C, E, and fiber and prime proven nutrition cancer preventers.[19]

COMMON MALNUTRITION IN CANCER PATIENTS (AND INTERVENTION WITH TOTAL PARENTERAL NUTRITION, TPN)

A theory has persisted for decades that one could starve the tumor out of the host. Unfortunately, the tumor is quite resistant to starvation. Most studies find more harm to the host than the tumor in either selective or blanket nutrient deficiencies.[23] Protein restriction does not affect the composition or growth rate of the tumor, but does restrict host growth rate.[24] Folate deprivation allowed the tumor to grow anyway.[25] In starved animals, the tumors grew more rapidly than in fed animals, indicating the parasitic tenacity of tumors in the host.[26] In animal studies, starving the host led to continued tumor growth and wasting of host tissue.[27] Overall, the research shows that starvation provokes host wasting while tumor growth continues unabated.[28] Pure malnutrition (cachexia) is responsible for at least 22% and up to 67% of all cancer deaths. While the average "healthy" American is sub-clinically malnourished, the average cancer patient is clinically malnourished. Malnutrition is extremely common in the cancer patient.

Of the 139 lung cancer patients studied, most tested deficient in vitamin C or scorbutic (clinical vitamin C deficiency).[29]

Another study of cancer patients found that 46% tested scorbutic while 76% were below acceptable levels for serum ascorbate.[30]

Experts now recommend the value of nutritional supplements, especially in patients who require prolonged TPN support.[31]

Interleukin-2 therapy induced malnutrition in up to 90% of 20 patients tested. The authors recommend prophylactic nutritional supplements to stem the immune suppression from this iatrogenic malnutrition.[32]

Recommended Dietary Allowances (RDA) are not designed for cancer patients. Supplements of vitamins, minerals, and other nutrients can benefit the cancer patients.[33]

Progressive weight loss is common in cancer patients and is a major source of morbidity and mortality.[34]

Wasting of tissue occurs in hypermetabolic states, most commonly for injury patients and end-stage cancer.[35]

Chemo and radiation therapy are sufficient stressors in themselves to induce malnutrition.[36]

Up to 80% of all cancer patients have reduced levels of serum albumin (a leading indicator of protein/calorie malnutrition).[37]

There is some evidence that tumors are not as flexible in using substrates other than glucose for fuel, hence a low carbohydrate TPN formula may have antineoplastic value.[38]   A recently published position paper from the American College of Physicians basically stated that TPN had no effect on the outcome of cancer patients.[39] Unfortunately, this article selected non-malnourished patients. TPN treats malnutrition, not cancer.[40]

Weight loss drastically increases the mortality rate for most types of cancer, while also lowering the response to chemotherapy.[41]

TPN improves tolerance to chemotherapeutic agents and immune responses.[42] Of 28 children with advanced malignant disease, 18 received TPN for 28 days with resultant improvements in weight gain, increased serum albumin, and transferrin with major immunological benefits. In comparing cancer patients on TPN versus those trying to nourish themselves by oral intake of food, TPN provided major improvements in calorie, protein, and nutrient intake but did not encourage tumor growth.

27 malnourished cancer patients were provide TPN and had a mortality rate of 11%, while the non-TPN group had a 100% mortality rate.[43]

Pre-operative TPN in patients undergoing surgery for GI cancer provided general reduction in the incidence of wound infection, pneumonia, major complications, and mortality.[44]

In one study by Mullen, the patients who were the most malnourished experienced a 33% mortality and 46% morbidity rate, while those least malnourished had a 3% mortality rate with an 8% morbidity rate.

There is evidence that a finely tuned TPN formula can do more than just nourish the patient with broad spectrum nutrient coverage. TPN formulas fortified with arginine have been shown to stimulate the immune system, accelerate wound repair, and promote tumor reduction. Modified diets with low tyrosine (2.4 mg/kg body wt) and low phenylalanine (3.5 mg/kg body wt) were able to elevate natural killer cell activity in 6 of 9 subjects tested.[45]

In 21 adults on TPN, high amino acid solution (designed for pediatric ICU) with 30% branched chain amino acids was able to provide better nitrogen balance than the conventional 8.5% amino acid TPN formula.[46]

In 20 adult hospitalized patients on TPN, the mean daily needs (based on urine and serum ascorbate levels) for vitamin C were 975 mg with the range being 350-2250 mg.[47]

49 patients with small cell bronchogenic carcinoma received chemotherapy with (21 patients) or without (28 patients) TPN. Complete remission was achieved in 85% of the TPN group versus 59% of the non-TPN group.[48]

In an extensive study of 3,047 cancer patients through the Eastern Cooperative Oncology Group, weight loss was an accurate predictor of poor prognosis.[49]

REGULATE BLOOD SUGAR TO SLOW CANCER GROWTH

■ There is a long-standing well-accepted link between elevated insulin levels and risk of cancer.[50]

■ Cancer cells demonstrate a 3 to 5 fold increase in glucose uptake compared to healthy cells.[51]

■ Cancer thrives on glucose while also initiating gluconeogenesis and insulin resistance.[52] Lipid based parenteral solutions for cancer patients slow cancer growth.

■ Modest ingestion of glucose (75 gm) caused a measurable decline in cell-mediated immunity in 7 healthy human volunteers. Mechanism of action is probably via elevated insulin, which competes with mitogens for binding sites on lymphocytes.[53]

■ In animal studies, progressive increase in sucrose in the diet leads to a dose-dependent decline in antibody production.[54]

■ Healthy human volunteers ingested 100 gram portions (average US daily intake) of simple carbohydrates from glucose, fructose, sucrose (white sugar), honey, and orange juice. While simple sugars signficantly impaired the capacity of neutrophils to engulf bacteria, starch ingestion did not have this effect.[55]

■ In a study comparing 50 colorectal cancer patients to healthy matched controls, the cancer patients ate considerably more sugar and fat than the healthy people.[56]

■ An epidemiological study of 21 countries suggests that high sugar intake is a major risk factor toward breast cancer.[57]

■ Animals were fed isocaloric diets of carbohydrates. The group eating more sugar developed significantly more mammary tumors than the starch-fed group.[58]

RISKS OF NUTRITION THERAPY

In an extensive review of the literature, Dr. Adrienne Bendich found the following data on nutrient toxicity[59]:

■ B-6 can be used at up to 500 mg (250 times RDA) for up to 6 years with safety.

■ Niacin (as nicotinic acid) has been recommended by the National Institute of Health for lowering cholesterol at doses of 3000-6000 mg/day (150-300 times RDA). Time release niacin is more suspect of causing toxicity as liver damage.

■ Vitamin C was tested in eight published studies using double blind placebo controlled design. At 10,000 mg/day for years, vitamin C produced no side effects.

■ High doses of vitamin A (500,000 iu daily) can have acute reversible effects. Teratogenecity is the most likely complication of high dose vitamin A intake.

■ Vitamin E intake at up to 3000 mg/day for prolonged periods has been shown safe.

■ Beta-carotene has been administered for extended periods in humans at doses up to 180 mg (300,000 iu) with no side effects or elevated serum vitamin A levels.

In a separate review of the literature on nutrient toxicity by John Hathcock, PhD, a Food and Drug Administration toxicologist, the following data was reported[60]:

■ Vitamin A toxicity may start as low as 25,000 iu/day (5 times RDA) in people with impaired liver function via drugs, hepatitis, or protein malnutrition. Otherwise, toxicity for A begins at several hundred thousand iu/day.

■ Beta-carotene given at 180 mg/day (300,000 iu or 60 times RDA) for extended periods produced no toxicity, but mild carotenemia (orange pigmentation of skin).

■ Vitamin E at 300 iu/day (10 times RDA) can trigger nausea, fatigue, and headaches in sensitive individuals. Otherwise, few side effects are seen at up to 3,200 iu/day.

■ B-6 may induce a reversible sensory neuropathy at doses of as low as 300 mg/day in some sensitive individuals. Toxic threshold usually begins at 2000 mg for most individuals.

■ Vitamin C may induce mild and transient gastro-intestinal distress in some sensitive individuals at doses of 1000 mg (16 times RDA). Otherwise, toxicity is very rare at even high doses of vitamin C intake.

■ Zinc supplements at 300 mg (20 times RDA) have been found to impair immune functions and serum lipid profile.

■ Iron intake at 100 mg/day (6 times RDA) will cause iron storage disease in 80% of population. The "window of efficacy" on iron is probably more narrow than with other nutrients.

■ Copper can be toxic, though dose is probably related to the ratio with other trace minerals.

■ Selenium can be toxic at 1-5 mg/kg body weight intake. This would equate to 65 mg/day for the average adult, which is 812 times the RDA of 80 mcg. Some sensitive individuals may develop toxicity at 1000 mcg/day.

■ Manganese can be toxic, though little specific information can be provided for humans.

ADJUVANT NUTRITION IMPROVES THE EFFECTIVENESS AND/OR REDUCES THE TOXICITY FROM MEDICAL ONCOLOGY

Vitamin C enhanced the chemotherapeutic action of levodopa methylester and increased survival time in B16 melanoma-bearing mice.[61]

Niacin supplementation in animals reduced the cardiotoxicity of the drug without inhibiting the effectiveness of the drug.[62]

Low serum levels of vitamin A and E were indicative of human cancer patients who responded poorly to chemotherapy.[63]

50 previously untreated cancer patients randomly received radiation therapy with or without 5 grams/day of vitamin C supplements. After 1 month, 87% of the vitamin C treated group showed a complete response (disappearance of all known disease) compared to 55% of the control.[64]

Vitamin C and K separately showed anti-tumor activity against human cancer cells in vitro, but became synergistically effective at 2% the regular dosage when used together.[65]

Vitamin C had no effect on the anti-tumor activity of adriamycin but did prolong the life of the animals treated with adriamycin.[66]

B-6 deficient mice exhibited enhanced tumor susceptibility and increased tumor size.[67]

22 patients with precancerous conditions, 19 patients with malignant oral lesions and 13 healthy controls were evaluated with respect to serum selenium levels and response to selenium therapy (300 mcg/day). Using selenium as sole therapy, there was a 38.8% objective response rate in treated patients.[68]

Human prostatic cancer cells in vitro were markedly inhibited when vitamin E was added to the adriamycin.[69]

Vitamin E enhanced the growth inhibitory effect of vincristine on mouse melanoma cells.[70]

Vitamin E therapy (1600 iu/day) begun 5-7 days prior to therapy prevented 69% of adriamycin patients from experiencing baldness.[71] Other studies have not always reached the same conclusion but have not followed this protocol. It appears important to begin vitamin E therapy at least 7 days prior to chemotherapy.

Calcium and vitamin D improved the efficacy of thioTEPA and other anti-neoplastic drugs against Hodgkin's disease and lung cancer.[72]

Selenium supplements (200 mcg/day) in 23 patients with ovarian cancer or metastatic endometrial cancer showed less host tissue damage than the untreated group.[73]

A derivative of ascorbic acid (sodium benzylideneascorbate, SBA) was given in daily dose of 200 mg/m2 to 55 patients with inoperable carcinoma. 8 patients achieved a complete response, 21 achieved partial response, 25 remained stable, and 1 showed progression of disease. The activity of this medication was increased with concurrent tamoxifen use.[74]

While tamoxifen is the commonly used drug to inhibit estrogen-dependent tumor growth, vitamin C has clearly demonstrated the ability to inhibit estrogen-dependent tumor growth in hamsters.[75]

Vitamin E and selenium helped reduce the lipid peroxidation-induced cardiotoxicity from adriamycin in animal models without inhibiting effectiveness of therapy.[76]

Potassium bromate can cause nephrotoxicity via renal oxidative DNA damage. In rat model, pre and post treatment with cysteine and glutathione (amino acids) and vitamin C protected against oxidative damage in the kidneys.[77]

Niacin (vitamin B-3) as nicotinamide is able to dramatically improve the response of hypoxic radioresistant tumors in animal models. Anaerobic tumors do not respond well to radiation therapy, while niacin seems to improve aerobic metabolism to make solid tumors more vulnerable to radiation therapy.[78]

Vitamin E topically applied (400 mg per lesion, twice daily for 5 days) to oral lesions induced by chemotherapy provided substantial relief in 6 of 9 patients while only 1 of 9 placebo treated patients had any relief from oral mucositis. Vitamin E seemed to best help patients taking cisplatin and 5-fluorouracil. Oral mucositis is often the beginning of anorexia which deteriorates into clinical malnutrition.[79]

In mouse and guinea pig models, vitamin C prolonged the life of animals treated with adriamycin without affecting the anti-tumor activity of this drug. Vitamin C was able to prevent the adriamycin-induced cardiomyopathy as determined by electron microscopy.[80]

While tamoxifen is a drug that binds up circulating estrogen, which can incite tumor growth, studies show that wheat fiber does the same thing while also reducing secondary bile acids and bacterial enzymes associated with colon cancer—without the potential carcinogenic effects of tamoxifen.[81]

NUTRIENTS HAVE A PROFOUND IMPACT ON THE IMMUNE SYSTEM

■ Alexander, JW, et.al., Nutritional immodulation in burn patients, Critical Care Medicine, voll.18, no.2, pg.149, 1990

■ Alexander, JW, Nutrition and Infection, Archives of Surgery, vol.121, p.966, Aug.1986

■ Alexander, JW., Nutrition and infection: new perspectives for an old problem, Archives of Surgery, vol.121, pg.966, 1986

■ Baehner, RL, Autooxidation as a basis for altered function by polymorphonuclear Leukocytes, Blood, vol.50, no.2, p.327, Aug.1977

■ Barone J, et.al., Dietary fat and natural-killer-cell activity, Americian Journal Clinical Nutrition, vol.50, no.4, pg.861, Oct.1989

■ Beisel WR, Single nutrients and immunity, American Journal Clinical Nutrition, vol.35, (Suppl.), pg.417, 1982

■ Beisel, WR, et al., Single-Nutrient effects on immunologic functions, Journal of the American Medical Association, vol.245, no. 1, p.53, Jan.2, 1981

■ Beisel, WR, Single nutrients and immunity, American Journal Clinical Nutrition, vol.35, p.417, Feb. supp, 1982

■ Beisel, WR, The history of nutritional immunology, Journal of Nutritional Immunology, vol.1(1), p.5, 1992

■ Bendich, A., Anti-oxidant vitamins and immune responses, in NUTRITION AND IMMUNOLOGY, p.125, Liss, NY, 1988

■ Bower, RH, Nutrition and immune function, Nutrition in Clinical Practice, vol.5, no.5, pg.189, 1990

■ Bowman, TA, et.al., Vitamin A deficiency decreases natural killer cell activity and interfon production in rats, Journal Nutrition, vol.120, no.10, p.1264, Oct. 1990

■ Carver, JD, et.al., Dietary nucleotide effects upon murine natural killer cell activity and macrophage activation, Journal of Parenteral and Enteral Nutrition, vol.14, no.1, pg.18, Jan.1990

■ Cerra, FB, et.al., Effect of enteral nutrient on in vitro tests of immune function in ICU patients: a preliminary report, Nutrition, vol.6, no.1, pg.84, 1990

■ Cerra, FB, Immune system modulation: nutritional and pharmacologic approaches, Critical Care Medicine, vol.18, no.2, Jan.1990

■ Cerra, FB, Nutrient modulation of inflammatory and immune function, Americian Journal of Surgery, vol.161, p.230, Feb.1991

■ Chandra RK, ed., Comtemporary issues in clinical nutrition, vol.11,

NUTRITIONAL IMMUNOLOGY, New York, Alan R. Liss, Inc., 1988

■ Chandra RK, Nutrition, immunity and outcome; past, present and future, Nutrition Research, vol.8, no.3, pg.225, 1988

■ Chandra, RK, et.al., Effect of two feeding formulas on immune responses and mortality in mice challenged with listeria monoclytogenes, Immunology Letters, vol.27, pg.45, 1991

■ Chandra, RK, Immunodeficiency in Undernutrition and Overnutrition, Nutrition Reviews, vol.39, no.6, pg.225, June 1981

■ Chandra, RK, Nutrition and immunity-basic considerations. Part 1., Contemporary Nutrition, vol.11, no.11, 1986

■ Chang, KJ, et.al., Comparison of the effect of lipoxygenase metabolites of arachidonic acid and eicosapentaenoic acid on human natural killer cell cytotoxicity, Prostaglandins Leukotrienes Essentially Fatty Acids, vol.38, no.2, pg.87, Nov.1989

■ Chang, KJ, et.al., Role of 5-lipoxygenase products of arachidonic acid in cell-to-cell interaction between macrophages and natural killer cells in rat spleen, Journal Leucocyte Biology, vol.50, no.3, pg.273, Sept.1991

■ Chang, KJ, et.al., Effect of oral ingestion of eicosapentaenoic acid-ethyl ester on natural killer cell activity in rat spleen cells, Prostaglandins Leukotrienes Essential Fatty Acids, vol.37, no.1, pg.31, July 1989

■ Chowdhury, BA, et.al., Effect of zinc administration on cadmium-induced suppression of natural killer cell activity in mice, Immunology Letters, vol.22, no.4, pg.287, Oct.1989

■ Christou, N, Perioperative nutritional support: immunologic defects, Journal of Parenteral and Enteral Nutrition, vol.14, no.5, supp., Sept.1990

■ Cifone, MG., et.al., In vivo cadmium treatment alters natural killer activity and large granular lymphocyte number in the rat, Immunopharmacology, vol.18,no.3, pg.149, Nov-Dec.1989

■ Daly, JM, etl.al., Enteral nutrition with supplemental arginine, RNA and Omega-3 fatty acids: a prospective clinical trial, Journal of Parenteral and Enteral Nutrition, vol.15, no.1, pg. 19S, 1991

■ Garre MA, et.al., Current concepts in immune derangement due to undernutrition, Journal of Parenteral and Enteral Nutrition, vol.11, no.3, pg.309, 1987

■ Gershwin ME, et.al., NUTRITION AND IMMUNITY, Orlando, Academic Press, Inc., 1985

■ Ghoneum, M., et.al., Suppression of murine natural killer cell activity by tributyltin: in vivo and in vitro assessment, Environmental Research, vol.52, no.2, p.178, Aug.1990

■ Gottschlich MM, Differential effects of three enteral dietary regimens on selected outcome variables in burn patients, Journal of Parenteral and Enteral

Nutrition, vol.14, no.3, pg.225, 1990

■ Hallquist, NA, et.al., Maternal-iron-deficiency effects on peritoneal macrophage and peritoneal natural-killer-cell cytotoxicity in rat pups, Americian Journal Clinical Nutrition, vol.55, no.3, pg.741, March, 1992

■ Halstead, BW, immune augmentation therapy, Journal International Academy Preventive Medicine, vol.9, no.1, pg.5, 1985

■ Ilback, NG, Effects of methyl mercury exposure on spleen and blood natural killer (NK) cell activity in the mouse., Toxicocology, vol.25, no.1, pg.117, March 1991

■ Immune system modulation: symposium on nutritional and pharmacologic approaches, Critical Care Medicine, vol.18, no.2, (S) pg.85, 1990

■ Kafkewitz, D., et.al., Deficiency is immunosuppressive, American Journal Clinical Nutrition, vol.37, pg.1025, 1983

■ Katz, DP, et.al., Enteral nutrition: potential role in regulating immune function, Current Opinion in Gastroenterology, vol.6, pg.199, 1990

■ Kelly, C. et al, Immunosuppression in the surgical oncology patient, Nutrition and Immunology Digest, vol.1, no.2, 1991

■ Kennes, B, et.al., Effect of vitamin C supplements on cell-mediated immunity in old people, Gerontology, vol.29, no.5, pg.305, 1983

■ Kinney, JM, et.al., NUTRITION AND METABOLISM IN PATIENT CARE,Philadelphia, W.B. Saunders Co., 1988

■ Kulkarni, AD, et.al., Influence of dietary glutamine and IMPACT, on in vivo cell-mediated immune response in mice, Nutrition, vol.6, no.1, pg.66, 1990

■ Levy, JA., Nutrition and the immune system, in Stites DP et al., Basic and Clinical Immunology, 4th Edition, Los Altos, Ca., Lange Medical Publications, pg.297, 1982

■ Lieberman, MD, Effects of nutrient substrates on immune function, Nutrition, vol.6, no.1, pg.88, 1990

■ Meadows GG, et.al., Ethanol induces marked changes in lymphocyte populations and natural killer cell activity in mice, Alcohol Clinical Exp Research, vol.16, vol.3, p.47, June 1992

■ Muzzioli, M., et.al., In vitro restoration by thymulin of NK activity of cells from old mice, International Journal of Immunopharmacol, vol.14, no.1, pg.57, Jan.1992

■ Nair, MP, et.al., Immunoregulation of natural and lymphokine-activated killer cells by selenium, Immunopharmacology, vol.19, no.3, pg.177, May-June, 1990

■ Nutrition and the immune response, Dairy Council Digest, vol.56, no.2, March-April, 1985

■ Nuwayri-Salti, N., et.al., Immunologic and anti-immunosuppressive effects of vitamin A, Pharmacology, vol.30, no.4, pg.181, 1985

■ Palombo, JD, et.al., (Collective Review), Endothelial cell factors and response to injury, Surgery, Gynecology & Obstetrics, Vol.173, p.505, Dec. 1991

■ Petrie, HT, et.al., Selenium and the immune response: 2. Enhancement of murine cytotoxic T-lymphocyte and natural killer cell cytotoxicity in vivo, Journal Leucocyte Biology, vol.45, no.3, pg.215, March 1989

■ Petrie, HT, Selenium and the immune response: Enhancement of murine cytotoxic T-lymphocyte and natural killer cell cytotoxicity in vivo, Journal Leucocyte Biology, vol.45, no.3, p.215, March, 1989

■ Randall, HT, Enteral nutrition: tube feeding in acute and chronic illness, Journal of Parenteral and Enteral Nutrition, vol.8, no.2, pg.113, 1984

■ Reynolds, JV, The influence of protein malnutrition on T cell, natural killer cell, and lymphokine-activated killer cell function, and on biological responsiveness to high-dose interleukin-2, Cellular Immunology, vol.128, no.2, pg.569, July 1990

■ Riley, ML, et.al., Failure of dietary restriction to influence natural killer activity in old rats, Mechanisms of Ageing and Development, vol.50, no.1, pg.81, Oct.1989

■ Roth, JA, et.al., In vivo effect of ascorbic acid on neutrophil function in healthy and dexamethasone-treated cattle, American Journal Veterinary Research, vol.46, no.12, Dec., 1985

■ Schlichter, LC, et.al., Interactive effects of Na and K in killing by human natural killer cells, Experimental Cell Research, vol.184, no.1, pg.99, Sep.1989

■ Schriever, MM, et.al., Natural killer cells, vitamins, and other blood components of vegetarian and omnivorous men, Nutrition Cancer, vol.12, no.3, p.271, 1989

■ Spear, AT, et.al., Iron deficiency alters DMBA-induced tumor burden and natural killer cell cytotoxicity in rats, Journal Nutrition, vol.122, no.1, pg.46, Jan.1992

■ Talbott, MC, et.al., Pyridoxine supplementation: effect on lymphocyte responses in elderly persons, Journal of Clinical Nutrition, vol.46, p. 659, 1987

■ Update on Immunonutrition symposium, Nutrition, vol.6, no.1, pg.1, 1990

■ Vijayaratnam, V., et.al., The effects of malnutrition on lymphoid tissues, Nutrition, vol.3, no.3, pg.213, 1987

■ Wagner, PA, et.al., Zinc nutriture and cell-mediated immunity in the aged, International Journal Vitamin Nutrition Research, vol.53, no.1, pg.94, 1983

■ Wan, JMF, et.al. Symposium on the interaction between nutrition and inflammation, Proceedings of the Nutrition Society, vol.48, p.315, 1989

■ Watson, RR, Immunological enhancement by fat-soluble vitamins, minerals, and trace metals,Cancer Detection and Prevention, vol.9, p.67, 1986

■ Wollschlager, C, et.al., A lipid, arginine and RNA supplemented enteral formula (IMPACT) alters airway colonization in intubated patients, Americian Review of Respiratory Diseases, 141:334A, 1990

■ Yamashita, N. et.al., Effect of eicosapentaenoic and docosahexaenoic acid on natural killer cell activity in human peripheral blood lymphocytes, Clinical Immunology Immunopathology, vol.59, lno.3, pg.335, June 1991

■ Yirmiya, R., et.al., Ethanol increases tumor progression in rats: possible involvement of natural killer cells, Brain Behavior Immun, vol.6, no.1, pg.74, March 1992

Many nutrients taken orally can provide pharmacological changes in immune function in humans. Protein, arginine, glutamine, omega-6 and omega-3 fats, iron, zinc, vitamins E, C, and A have all been proven to modulate immune functions.[82]

Vitamin A deficiency causes reduced lymphocyte response to antigens and mitogens, while beta-carotene supplements stimulate immune responses.[83]

There is extensive literature supporting the importance of vitamin B-6 on the immune system. In one study, B-6 supplements (50 mg/day) provided a measurable improvement in immune functions (T3 and T4 lymphocytes) for 11 healthy well fed older adults.[84]

Various B vitamins have been linked to the proper functioning of antibody response and cellular immunity.

Folate deficiency decreases mitogenesis.

Deficiency of vitamin C impairs phagocyte functions and cellular immunity.

Vitamin E deficiency decreases antibody response to T-dependent antigens, all of which gets worse with the addition of a selenium deficiency. In test animals, normal vitamin E intake was not adequate to optimize immune functions.[85] Modest supplements of vitamin E have been shown to enhance the immune response.

While iron deficiency can blunt immune functions, iron excess can increase the risk for cancer.[86]

Zinc exerts a major influence on the immune system. Lymphocyte function is seriously depressed and lymphoid tissues undergo general atrophy in zinc-deficient individuals. The lymphocytes in zinc-deficient animals quickly lose their killing abilities (cytotoxicity) and engulfing talents (phagocytosis) for tumor cells and bacteria. Natural killer cell and neutrophil activity is also reduced. All of these compromised immune activities elevate the risk for cancer.

Copper plays a key role in the production of superoxide dismutase and cytochrome systems in the mitochondria. Hence, a deficiency of copper is manifested in a depressed immune system, specifically reduced microbicidal activity of granulocytes.

Selenium works in conjunction with vitamin E to shield host cells from lipid peroxidation. Humoral immune response is depressed in selenium deficient animals. Selenium and vitamin E deficiencies lead to increased incidence of enteric lesions. Lymphocyte proliferation is reduced in selenium deficiency. The theory is that selenium and vitamin E help to provide the host immune cells with some type of "bullet proof plating" against the toxins used on foreign cells. Hence, one immune body can live on to destroy many invaders if enough vitamin E and selenium allow for these critical chemical shields.

In magnesium deficiency, all immunoglobulins (except IgE) are reduced, along with the number of antibody forming cells. Magnesium is crucial for lymphocyte growth (involvement in protein metabolism) and transformation in response to mitogens. Prolonged magnesium deficiency in animals leads to the development of lymphomas and leukemia.

Iodine plays an important role in the microbicidal activity of polymorphonuclear leukocytes. Activated neutrophils may use the conversion of iodide to iodine to generate free radicals for killing foreign invaders.

Boron is an interesting trace mineral, since it is now recognized for its role in preventing osteoporosis, yet is still not considered an essential mineral. Boron deficiency in chicks creates immune abnormalities like arthritis.

Toxic trace minerals, like cadmium, arsenic and lead all blunt the immune system.

The quality and quantity of fat in the diet plays a major role in dictating the health of the immune system. A deficiency of the essential fatty acid (linoleic acid) will lead to atrophy of lymphoid tissue and a depressed antibody response. And yet excess intake of polyunsaturated fatty acids will also diminish T-cell immune responsiveness. Since fat directly affects prostaglandin pathways, and prostaglandins (depending on the pathway) can either depress or enhance immune function, fat intake is crucial in encouraging a healthy immune system. Oxidized cholesterol is highly immuno-suppressive. Cholesterol is less likely to oxidize while in the presence of anti-oxidants, like vitamin E, C, and beta-carotene.

Basically, nutrition plays a key role in the effectiveness of the immune system. Primary assessment techniques to find the relative nutrient status of the immune system include:

- Clinical: dietary intake, physical examination
- Anthropometric: skin fold thickness, percent body fat
- Hematologic: hemoglobin and ferritin levels
- Biochemical: serum albumin, serum transferrin, creatinine/height index, zinc status
- Immunologic: lymphocyte count, terminal transferase activity, T-cells
- Miscellaneous: hand grip strength, dark adaptation, taste acuity

A main goal of this nutrition program is to optimize the functioning of the immune system via foods and nutritional supplementation (pills, powder, or TPN). A healthy immune system is better able to join in the battle to rid the body of tumor cells.

Therapeutic Supplements May Help Cancer Patients

Vitamins

■ *Vitamin E.*

Was used (via injections) to reverse oral tumor progress in animals with induced tumors.[89]

Prevents and may even reverse tumor growth in animals with chemically induced tumors.[90]

Was able to prevent expected tumors in lab animals exposed to DMBA.[91]

Increased the effectiveness and specific toxicity of chemotherapy agents on tumors in culture.[92]

Relieves most cystic breast disease, which indicates that E can treat pre-cancerous conditions.[93]

May be anti-neoplastic by virtue of its ability to protect the prostaglandin prostacyclin.[94]

Protects against damage from radiation therapy.[95]

In combination with selenium was able to prevent expected tumors in animals after DMBA injections.

Significantly elevated the microsomal hydroperoxidase activity.[96]

And selenium provided partial protection against cardiotoxicity in adriamycin use on rabbits. Best protection was aforded by high dose vitamin E.[97]

Deficiency accentuated the cardiotoxicity of adriamycin in rats.[98]

Increased (in vitro) the therapeutic benefits of chemotherapy agents on human prostate cancer cells.[99]

Directly stunted the growth of mouse melanoma cells in vitro.[100]

Topical application of DMSO and vitamin E produced a 68% decrease in skin necrosis on mice given adriamycin.[101]

Mice with oral cancer were supplemented with injections of vitamin E, beta-carotene, canthaxanthin, and algae extract. Major improvements in tumor necrosis factor were measured in the supplemented mice, who also experienced varying levels of tumor regression.[102]

Reduced the cardiotoxic effects of daunomycin (similar to adriamycin) in test animals.[103]

And vitamin K3 (menadione) enhanced the anti-metabolic activity of the chemotherapy agents 5FU and leucovorin in vitro.[104]

Sensitized tumor cells, but not healthy cells, to radiation therapy for enhanced effectiveness.[105]

Use in radiation therapy reduces toxic side effects.[106]

Patients with peripheral neuropathy (common as a side effect for certain chemo agents) were found to be clinically low in vitamin E in the region of nerve damage.[107] Nerve numbness in cancer patients may be due to the elevated need for vitamin E during chemotherapy.

Elevates lymphocyte proliferation in animals.[108]

Vitamin E, A, and prenylamine blunted the cardiotoxic effects of adriamycin in rabbits.[109]

Provided measurable protection against the cardiotoxicity of adriamycin in rabbits.[110]

Using 1600 iu/day of vitamin E, hair loss in cancer patients was reduced from the typical 90% to 30% in the treated group.[111]

Toxicity. Human studies show no side effects from vitamin E at levels up to 3200 mg/day (3200 iu/day).[112]

■ *Vitamin K*

The primary function of K is as a coagulating factor in the prothrombin cascade in the blood. A normal diet combined with bacterial fermentation in the distal small bowel appears to provide "adequate" levels of K to prevent hemorrhage.[113]

■ Normal daily intake is difficult to estimate since an undetermined amount of K is produced through bacterial fermentation. However, the National Academy of Sciences estimates that the average American diet contains 300-500 mcg/day. [114]

■ Vitamin K exists in 3 distinct chemical analog forms with the following differences

K-1 (phylloquine or phytonadione, relatively non-toxic, preferred form for non-pharmacological purposes)

K-2 (menaquinone, produced by bacterial fermentation in the gut, does not inhibit DNA synthesis in malignant cells)

K-3 (menadione, synthetic derivation, accumulates in the liver, can be toxic, is most effective as an anti-neoplastic agent).

■ Additionally, over the past thirty years, evidence has been gathering that K has anti-neoplastic properties. [115]

Common deficiencies.

■ K deficiency is common in patients with general malnutrition, intestinal malabsorption, or treatment with anti-biotics.[116]

■ A profound deficiency of vitamin K was found in 34 cancer patients on anti-microbial therapy.[117]

■ Therapeutic doses of vitamin E elevate the need for vitamin K.[118]

■ Therapeutic levels required to reverse hemorrhagic clinical vitamin K deficiency range from 20-50 mg/day of K.

Use in cancer treatment.

■ When vitamin K (as Synkavite, menadione, K-3) was given to human cancer patients IV at a 50-100 mg dosage prior to radiation therapy, 5 year survival increased from 20% of the patients without K to 39% of the matched group given radiation plus vitamin K. [119]

Counterindications.

■ Vitamin K-1 (not K-3) supplements will reduce the effectiveness of anti-coagulants at lengthening prothrombin clotting time. Vitamin K-1 (phytonadione) at 1 mg/day does not present any hazard to patients receiving anti-coagulant therapy.[120] According to Dr. Chlebowski, vitamin K enhances the anti-metastatic effects of anti-coagulants.

■ *Vitamin C.*

In animals with implanted Ehrlich carcinoma and L1210 leukemia, injections of vitamin B-12 (hydroxocobalamin) and vitamin C (dehydroascorbic acid) provided dramatic improvements in survival of the animals. By day 19, all 20 of the control animals were dead, while 50% of the treated mice survived 60 days or more. This nutrient combination has a precedence for limiting tumor growth without affecting the host.[121]

Potentiates the value while reducing the toxicity of chemotherapy in animal studies.[122]

Potentiates the value of radiation therapy.[123]

Using chemotherapy in conjunction with nutritional therapy, supplemental levels of vitamins A (Aquasol A 400,000 iu/day), C (8 gm/day), and E (3200 iu/day) were provided to 20 cancer patients over the course of 12 months with 7 (35%) experiencing complete remission, 8 (40%) partial remission, and 5 (25%) failed. Only one patient experienced any symptoms attributed to the mega-vitamin therapy.[124]

Mice with induced liver cancer were then pre-treated with vitamins C and K3 (menadione) before using various chemotherapy drugs. The nutrients provided considerable protection while enhancing the effectiveness of the treatment.[125] Postulated mechanisms include the attack on catalase-deficient cancer cells by the combination of vitamin C and K3.

Vitamin C, thiamin, and cysteine provided nearly complete protection against free radical acetylaldehyde destruction in animals.[126]

Vitamin C (10 gram/day) provided life extension and improvement of quality of life in 100 terminal cancer patients.[127] Other studies have not had such promising results. Possible explanations for the discrepancy may be that the other studies used patients who had been heavily pre-treated with chemo and radiation therapy and considered unresponsive and terminal.

Vitamin C and E provide measurable protection against the carcinogen PCB in various animals.[128]

2-3 grams daily of ascorbate provided stimulation of lymphocyte transformation to certain mitogens.[129]

After 9-12 months on 3 grams daily of vitamin C supplements, rectal polyps were reduced in the treated group by 74% compared to the untreated group reduction of 31%.[130]

Ascorbic acid supplements in cancer patients provided improvements in minor symptoms, pain control, and quality of life.[131]

Vitamin C supplements provided protection against the cytotoxic effects of methotrexate in mice.[132]

Toxicity. Most patients can tolerate 10-20 grams orally. Other patients will experience mild intestinal distress at these levels. Up to 100 grams has been used in TPN formulas.

■ Bioflavonoids

Quercetin increased the cell kill rate in cancer cells (in vitro) exposed to hyperthermia (heat therapy) with no effect on normal healthy cells.[133]

Quercetin inhibited cancer in animals exposed to two carcinogens.[134]

Quercetin caused inhibition of growth (in vivo) in two squamous cell carcinoma lines.[135]

Several bioflavonoids (including quercetin) were able to inhibit DNA binding from benzopyrenes. [136]

■ Vitamin A

Of 102 people who had bladder cancer, the incidence of recurring tumors was 1.8 times higher in those who consumed the lower amounts of vitamin A.[137]

Nine male patients with metastatic unresectable squamous cell carcinoma of the lung were treated with vitamin A palmitate or 13 cis-retinoic acid (analog of vitamin A) without other medical intervention. 60 weeks later, immune function had improved and progress against the tumor had been made.[138]

Vitamin A in combination with BCG suppressed tumor growth in the lung tumors of animals. Vitamin A alone did not affect tumor growth, but only in conjunction with BCG.[139]

Vitamin A prevented impaired wound healing in post-operative and irradiated rats. Vitamin A provided continuous high level of immune competence throughout the normal immunosuppressive phase.[140]

Vitamin A supplements provided complete or partial remission in patients with benign breast disease.[141]

Toxicity.   300,000 iu/day of retinol palmitate (preformed vitamin A) administered to 138 lung cancer patients for at least 12 months produced occasional dry skin, but no significant side effects.[142] Toxicity may begin at levels of 500,000 iu/day (100 times the RDA) long term intake for adults, and proportionately less in children.[143] Toxicity usually involves consumption of 200,000 iu/day for many days, though individuals with compromised immune function may develop toxicity at 25,000 iu.[144] Toxicity of A can be reduced by higher intake of vitamin E to mitigate lipid peroxide effects.

■ Beta carotene

2500 iu of beta-carotene = 250 retinol equivalents =1.5 mg. Beta-carotene has been shown to protect phagocytic cells from auto-oxidative damage, enhance T and B lymphocyte proliferation, enhance macrophages, interleukin production, and natural killer cell tumoricidal abilities.[145]

Beta-carotene probably has effectiveness against cancer as a chain-breaking anti-oxidant.[146]

Vitamin A intake protected workers who were smokers and/or exposed to toxic chemicals against lung cancer. Beta-carotene provided a more protective edge than animal sources of vitamin A.[147]

Using combined supplements of beta-carotene and canthaxanthin, Italian researchers found that cancer patients who had undergone surgery with radiation therapy had a much higher than anticipated survival rate and level of health.

A review of the literature on vitamin A and beta-carotene shows that beta-carotene has anti-oxidant and immune stimulating properties that are not found in vitamin A. Perhaps these are two distinct nutrients.[148]

Beta-carotene has been shown to protect animals against ultra-violet induced skin tumors and carcinogen treatment by preventing malignant transformation and nuclear damage.[149]

Beta-carotene and algae extracts injected into DMBA-provoked tumors in hamsters caused regression of the tumors.[150]

Toxicity. Toxicity of beta-carotene has never been found, since it is not mutagenic, carcinogenic, embryotoxic, or teratogenic and does not cause hypervitaminosis A.[151]

15 mg daily of oral supplements of beta-carotene (25,000 iu.) provided a 10 fold increase in serum beta-carotene without any skin discoloration.[152]

People have consumed 300,000 iu (180 mg) of beta-carotene daily for 15 years with no adverse side effects. In the few beta-carotene reactions, it is always with excess consumption of food components (like carrot juice), which makes other food components and not the beta-carotene suspect in these mild toxicity reactions. Pure beta-carotene supplements have never produced toxicity in any human studies.

■ B-6 (pyridoxine)

While earlier findings indicated that a B-6 deficiency would slow down tumor growth[153] and increase survival in animals with cancer[154], more recent findings indicate the opposite. Animals fortified with B-6 and then injected with melanoma cells showed a greater resistance to this deadly form of cancer.[155]

B-6 inhibited melanoma cells in vivo.[156]

Vitamin B-6 displays important immune modulating activity of the immune system.[157]

Vitamin B-6 at 25 mg/day for 33 bladder cancer patients provided marked improvement in cancer recurrence over the control group.[158]

Vitamin B-6 kills hepatoma cells (in vitro).[159]

Administered as an ointment on a human melanoma patient four times daily for a two week period resulted in disappearance of the cutaneous papules.[160]

High dose supplements (300 mg/day) provided considerable relief from the toxicity of radiation therapy.[161]

Pyridoxine deficiency produces increased tumor resistance.[162]

Newly diagnosed children with leukemia have suboptimal overall nutrition as well as suboptimal vitamin B-6 status.[163]

B-6 inhibits the growth of human malignant melanoma cell line.[164]

B-6 significantly inhibited melanoma cells lines (in vitro) and may be an effective anti-neoplastic agent.[165]

B-6 (300 mg/day) administered throughout the 8 week radiation therapy course for human endometrial cancer patients improved survival by 15% at 5 years.[166]

Toxicity. Less than 500 mg/day in humans appears to be safe.[167] 300 mg/day provide maximal protection against radiation therapy.

MINERALS

■ Selenium.

High dose supplementation (equivalent to 54 mg/day in humans) resulted in 83-90% reduction in the rate of tumor growth in mice.[168]

In mice fed either a high or low PUFA fat diet, selenium provoked a drop in tumor incidence in both groups. Selenium apparently exerts a cancer-protective role beyond its antioxidant function in lipid metabolism.[169]

Enhanced drug detoxification pathways (conjugative, not by P450) in animals.[170]

Reduces the toxicity of paraquat (an herbicide).[171]

In animal studies could (a) inhibit both the initiation and promotion phases of cancer, (b) continuous intake of selenium was necessary to achieve maximum protection, (c) inhibit the re-appearance of tumors after surgery.[172]

Provided fewer DNA strand breaks and greater repair of broken DNA than unsupplemented or less supplemented hamsters.[173]

Administration of sodium selenite (equivalent to 120 mg for an adult) inhibited the growth of leukemia cells and increased the longevity of test mice.[174]

Mega-doses effectively limited tumor growth in mice with Ehrlich ascites tumors. Although high dose selenium supplementation did not affect the growth of healthy normal animals, it did have a definite retarding effect on rapidly dividing cells.[175] Selenium may be an important anti-proliferative factor to squelch rapidly dividing tumor cells.

Provided considerable protection against the toxic effects of cis-platinum, allowing the lethal dose to kill half the animals (LD50) to increase from 9.3 to 17.5 mg/kg, thus allowing higher and more effective doses of chemotherapeutic agents.[176]

In mice provided measurable improvements in natural killer cytotoxicity in spleen cells (70% improvement over unsupplemented mice), specific T-lymphocyte cytotoxicity, and other immune parameters that could be therapeutic against cancer.[177]

Toxicity. The National Academy of Sciences indicates that long-term daily intake of 5000 micrograms of selenium may result in fingernail changes and hair loss. Extrapolated from animal studies, 7 mg (7000 mcg) in humans may halt tumor progression. Selenite is more toxic than selenium bound to amino acids (i.e. selenomethionine). Ingestion of 1-5 mg/kg body weight of selenite will likely produce toxic side effects (65,000 mcg in the 65 kg adult).

FATTY ACIDS

■ *EPA (eicosapentaenoic acid).*

A diet high in menhaden oil (20% of kcal) promoted major increases in cytochrome P450 in test animals.[178]

For one week pre-operative and 4 weeks after tumor implantation, varying levels of EPA and DHA from fish oil induced significant reduction in the weight and volume of the implanted mammary tumors in test animals.[179]

EPA slowed tumor growth in mice with inoculated human colon cancer.[180]

EPA slowed tumor growth and prolonged survival in mice with transplanted human metastatic breast cancer.[181]

EPA in conjunction with anti-human milk fat globule monoclonal antibodies offered the greatest reduction in tumor size (36% below corn oil or lard diets) in mice innoculated with human breast tumors.[182]

EPA diet significantly lowered the level of estradiol (a putative breast tumor marker) in 25 women at risk for breast cancer.[183]

EPA has protective effects against the development and/or progression of various animal tumor models studied.[184]

EPA produced a significant decrease in the development of both the size and number of preneoplastic lesions in animals in induced tumors.[185]

EPA reduced the size and number of tumors while increasing the tumor latent period in rats fed various types of fat in the diet, then exposed to carcinogens.[186]

EPA-fed rats had significant reduction in the growth of induced tumors.[187]

EPA-fed mice had significant slowing of tumor growth.[188]

EPA slowed tumor growth in transplanted mammary tumors in rats.[189]

EPA inhibited the development of tumors in athymic mice inoculated with human breast cancer. EPA also had a synergistic effect with Iodine 131 labeled monoclonal antibodies in reducing tumorogenesis.[190]

EPA rich diet significantly depressed growth rate of human breast tumors transplanted into animals. Tumors in EPA-fed animals are more responsive to chemotherapy agents (mitomycin C, doxorubicin).[191]

EPA reduced tumor growth in transplanted human colon cancer into mice.[192]

EPA-fed animals had fewer and smaller lesions after induced cancer.[193]

EPA slowed tumor growth in animals even when administered several months after tumor induction.[194]

EPA reduced the weight and volume of tumors in transplanted human prostatic cancer to animals.[195]

EPA retarded the development of human prostatic cancer that was inoculated in animals.[196]

EPA reduced both the frequency and rate of metastasis of transplanted tumors in animals.[197]

EPA improves the response of tumor cells to hyperthermia and chemotherapeutic agents by altering the properties of the tumor cell membrane.[198]

EPA increases the adriamycin kill rate on cultured human leukemia cells.[199]

EPA substantially reduced the invasiveness of cultured human tumor cells (both malignant murine melanoma and fibrosarcoma).[200]

EPA and GLA separately were able to selectively kill cultured human tumor cells.[201]

EPA and GLA enhanced the tumoricidal effects of anticancer agents in vitro.[202]

EPA and GLA were selectively toxic to human breast, lung, and prostate cancer cells in vitro. The fatty acids also enhanced the cytotoxic activity of cytotoxic drugs on tumor cells.[203]

EPA and GLA suppressed the growth of cultured human larynx cancer cells.[204]

DHA (accompanying fatty acid with EPA in fish oil) was able to partially reverse adriamycin-resistant small cell lung carcinoma cells in vitro.[205]

EPA modulates estrogen metabolism for reduced risk in breast cancer.[206]

EPA rich diet can slow tumor growth through modulation of both tumor protein synthesis and breakdown.[207]

EPA may have a beneficial role as adjunctive anti-neoplastic therapy in breast cancer.[208]

EPA provided higher survival (7 of 11 versus 2 of 11 in control group) of guinea pigs injected with endotoxin[209].

EPA provided higher survival (87% versus 63% in control group) for guinea pigs injected with endotoxin.[210]

EPA provided higher survival (83% versus 50% in control group) for guinea pigs injected with endotoxin.[211]

HOW DOES EPA SLOW TUMOR GROWTH?
PROPOSED MECHANISMS:

■ Altering membrane fluidity in healthy and/or tumor cells to change the basic cellular metabolism.

■ By altering membrane fluidity, can change the response of tumor cells to growth factors, hormones, antibodies.

■ Alters prostaglandin output, with more anti-inflammatory and anti-aggregatory eicosanoids.

■ Perhaps by prostaglandin metabolism, reduces the "stickiness" (aggregation) of cancer cells, to retard their metastatic abilities. Amount of EPA necessary for the average adult to have measurable reduction in cell aggregation (stickiness): 2-4 gm/day. Gorlin, R., Archives of Internal Medicine, vol.148, p.2043, Sept.1988

■ Stimulates the immume system.

■ Alters bile acid metabolism (may be important in colon cancer).

■ May be directly toxic to tumor cells, which have altered capacity to use any type of fats. Without proper use of fat soluble antioxidants, tumor cells may find the highly unsaturated fatty acids of EPA to be like an internal "hand grenade".

■ Attenuates shock from lactic acidosis in endotoxin-exposed animals. May buffer the impact of cytotoxic drugs on human cancer patients.

■ Alters hormonal balance for estrogen and testosterone dependent tumors.

COUNTERINDICATIONS FOR THE USE OF EPA

■ Can induce vitamin E deficiency, unless supplements of E are added. Suggested dosage: 400 iu vitamin E per every 2500 mg EPA.

■ Reduces platelet aggregation and slows normal blood clotting. High dose counterindicated for patients anticipating surgery.
Yetiv, JZ, Journal of the American Medical Association, vol.260, p.665, Aug.5, 1988

Toxicity A one gram capsule of fish oil usually provides 240-600 mg of EPA. Intake of 6000 mg of EPA may inhibit blood clotting, hence may be counterindicated in patients due for surgery. A minimum of 1000 mg daily of EPA must be consumed to expect any beneficial effects. EPA to GLA in a ratio of 5:1 may encourage the production of prostaglandin PGE-1 for immune stimulating effects.

■ *GLA (gamma linolenic acid)*
Combined intake with vitamin C was able to double the mean survival time for patients with primary hepatic carcinoma.[212]

Provided subjective and objective improvements in 21 patients with untreatable malignancies.[213]

GLA plus iron supplements dramatically increased the tumor cell kill rate with in vitro studies on human cancers, opening the possibility to a relatively safe and selectively toxic cancer regimen.[214]

Varying combinations of GLA and EPA were able to provide a high cancer cell kill rate in vitro.[215]

Toxicity. A one gram capsule of evening primrose oil provides about 200 mg of GLA. Intake of 600 to 3000 mg of GLA may bring about favorable results in the cancer patient.

AMINO ACIDS

■ *Arginine.*
Animals fed arginine rich diets (5%) had considerably fewer and more benign

tumors when later treated with the carcinogen DMBA.[216]

Arginine added to drinking water in animals was able to inhibit subcutaneous tumor growth.[217]

Arginine added to diet of mice (5% of wt.) produced fewer tumors, slower growing tumors, and twice the mean survival time as compared to untreated mice.[218]

Via animal studies, researchers have speculated on two primary functions of arginine in the body: essential for the synthesis of reparative collagen in wound recovery, decreases some of the negative aspects of metabolic responses to injury.[219]

Arginine supplements in animals stimulated thymus activity which resulted in reduced tumor growth.[220] Arginine also dramatically improves wound healing.

Arginine stimulates lymphocyte immune response in 21 healthy human volunteers.[221]

Arginine supplements in tumor-bearing mice provided enhanced T-cell function, increased response to autologous tumors, retarded tumor growth, and prolonged median survival time.[222]

In mice with neuroblastomas, arginine supplements provided significant tumor retardation in the immunogenic group.[223] Arginine's tumoricidal abilities go beyond its protein sparing abilities or immune stimulation.

Arginine supplements in mice provided significant enhancement of cytotoxic T-lymphocytes, natural killer cell activity, interleukin-2 receptors and general immune improvements.[224]

Toxicity. At therapeutic levels (above 5 grams/day) may activate growth of certain viruses.

■ **Branched chain amino acids** (leucine, isoleucine, valine)
Accelerates protein synthesis and elevates albumin synthesis from 8.5% to 19.7% when used in TPN formula in 10 malnourished cancer patients.[225]

■ **Cysteine** (N-acetylcysteine)
Cysteine enters into various detoxification systems in the body. Can be converted to glutathione, which may become GSH, a potent broad spectrum anti-oxidant enzyme system. May reduce the toxicity of chemotherapeutic agents. N-acetylcysteine neutralizes a toxic by-product (acrolein) of cyclophosphamide therapy, hence preventing harm while allowing the effectiveness.[226]

N-acetylcysteine may neutralize the effectiveness of adriamycin while preventing the cardiotoxicity effects.[227]

N-acetylcysteine reduced the cardiotoxicity of doxorubicin in dogs.[228]

N-acetylcysteine blocked the cardiotoxicity of doxorubicin but did not affect the uptake or metabolism of the drug in the heart or liver.[229]

Acetylcysteine prevented the hemorrhagic cystitis that usually appears from ifosfamide administration.[230]

Topical application of N-acetylcysteine ointment may reduce toxic side effects (skin reactions, hair loss, damage to mucus membranes of the eyes) from radiation therapy.[231]

Cysteine supplements promoted glutathione synthesis, which resulted in protection from the toxic effects of acetaminophen in mice.[232]

Toxicity. Although safe in dosages up to 10 grams/day, the nauseating taste and smell can cause vomiting. Normal dosage is 2-3 grams every 6 hours.

■ *Methionine.*

Methionine supplements reduced the uptake of mercury in test animals.[233] This may help reduce the amount of toxins (chemotherapy) stored in healthy tissue.

OTHER NUTRIENT FACTORS

■ *Green tea.*

Tea catechins (tannins) are potent inhibitors of platelet aggregation in rabbit platelets.[234]

Green tea is a more potent scavenger of free radicals than vitamin C or E.[235]

Green tea contains potent anti-carcinogenic agents.[236]

Green tea was able to inhibit tumor initiation and promotion in animals.[237]

■ *Maitake mushroom*

Oral administration of maitake mushroom extract (Grifola frondosa) completely inhibited tumor growth in animals.[238]

Intraperitoneal injections of Maitake in tumor-induced animals showed an increase in cytostatic activity toward syngeneic tumor cells.[239]

Maitake supplements potentiated host-mediated antitumor activity in mice.[240]

Intraperitoneal injections of Maitake extract into tumor-induced animals showed marked inhibitory activity on the growth of solid form sarcoma.[241]

■ *Plant phytosterols*

Phytosterols in plants reduce the risk for colon cancer through a variety of factors.[242]

■ *Plant carotenoids*

A plant dormancy hormone and vitamin A analog (abscisic acid) showed profound anti-tumor activity in rats.[243]

■ *Cartilage anti-angiogenesis factor*

Inhibits tumor growth by preventing the tumor from developing an expanded circulatory network.[244]

Angiogenesis may be a key marker of tumor progression in 30 patients with malignancies and 19 without.[245]

There is an induction of angiogenesis during the transition from hyperplasia to neoplasia.[246]

A cartilage extract (Catrix) was able to markedly inhibit human tumor cell line growth from 22 different patients with malignancies.[247]

Extract of shark cartilage inhibited tumor growth in vivo.[248]

Infusion of cartilage extract markedly reduced tumor growth in animals.[249]

An isolated fraction of cartilage inhibited tumor neovascularization.[250]

Inhibition of vascularization via a factor in cartilage slows tumor growth.[251]

Cartilage extract inhibits neo-vascularization (growth of new blood vessels).[252]

Catrix (preparation of bovine tracheal cartilage rings) was able to provide improvement in 90% of patients and complete remission in 61% of 31 cancer patients given first injections and then oral supplements (eight 375 mg caps every 8 hrs). There was no evidence of toxicity.[253]

An extract of shark cartilage was used to prevent tumor growth in implanted cornea tumors in rabbits.[254] It could be that the extremely low incidence of tumors in sharks is due to the high presence of this cartilage anti-angiogenesis factor.

Calf scapular cartilage inhibited and reversed tumor growth for implanted tumors in rabbits and mice. No toxic effects were observed.[255]

Toxicity. No toxicity observed.

■ *Glutamine*.

May protect against enteritis resultant from radiation therapy.[256]

■ *Alkylglycerols*.

Highest sources are mother's milk, human bone marrow, and shark oil. Shown to enhance the regression of uterine cancer when administered prior to radiation therapy.[257]

Use of alkylglycerols prior to, during, and after radiation therapy reduced injuries by as much as two thirds.[258]

■ *Coenzyme Q*.

Reduces adverse side effects of chemotherapy with adriamycin, including cardiac output, anginal symptoms, and EKG abnormalities. Hair loss was also reduced.[259]

■ *Cesium*.

Neither an essential nor toxic mineral, cesium therapy is able to slightly alter the pH of the cancer cells to make them more vulnerable to immune attack.[260]

■ *Maharishi-4* (an herbal preparation, ayurvedic food supplement)

Mice who were treated with M-4, then exposed to DMBA had reduced incidence and multiplicity of tumors. Those M-4 treated mice who did get cancer showed tumor regression in 60% of cases within 4 weeks.[261]

■ *Nucleic acids (RNA/DNA)*

In protein depletion, RNA supplements may be mandatory in order to return immune functions to normal.[262]

ASSESSMENT

Fatty acids: serum fatty acid profile (both volumetric and germane ratios) are accurate indicators of metastatic progress.[263] This test provides guidance for adjusting dietary fat intake, test available from Center for Human Functioning (316-682-3100) or Metametrix (800-221-4640).

Allergies: An overloaded immune system is compromised in its ability to destroy tumor cells. The debate continues on which is the best allergy test. ELISA/ACT measures immune delayed type hypersensitivity (Serammune 800-553-5472); Elisa measures IgE and IgG levels (Immuno Labs 800-231-9197).

Immune capability. Natural Killer cells are generally recognized as the most predictive aspect of the tumor killing capacity of the human immune system. Send blood sample to ImmunoSciences Lab (800-950-4686)

General diagnostics. Various tests at International Diagnostics (800-622-2343) or Metametrix

Vitamins (functional assay of enzymatic activity): by Metametrix (800-221-4640), or Pantox (619-272-3885), or Doctor's Data (800-323-2784)

C-strip: litmus paper dipped in fresh urine to indicate ascorbic acid content of blood (at or near saturation level) from Seraphim (800-525-7372)

Minerals: Provocative assay via chelating agent inducing urinary excretion. Volumetric and germane ratio recorded from Doctor's Data (800-323-2784)

Venous pH: Mild variations from normal indicate need for balancing using acid or alkaline diet.

Percent body fat by Futrex (800-545-1950) indicates serious long term lean tissue wasting or obesity that may accelerate tumor growth

Indirect calorimetry (INDC): Measures oxygen consumed and carbon dioxide exhaled to determine exact metabolic needs for calories. Essential test in cachectic TPN patients. Also called Metabolic Cart

Skin patch anergy test: indicates overall responsiveness of immune system

Oxidative stress: breath pentane as measured on gas chromatograph helps guide the balance between pro-oxidants (chemo & radiation) and anti-oxidants (nutrients)

Questionnaire: Quality of life indicators which help to track overall response from therapy.

Computer diet analysis: Helps educate patient on errant dietary habits by comparing patient's dietary intake with accepted standards of nutrient intake.

Digestion: Heidelberg capsule which is swallowed, then transmits the pH of the stomach and intestines to a nearby receiver (Heidelberg 404-449-4888)

Digestion, absorption, intestinal parasites: Send stool sample to appropriate labs.

PATIENT PROFILE

My final patient profile comes from two dear friends who I observed as an outsider many years ago, not as a clinical nutritionist in cancer treatment. Harry and Barbara (not their real names) were an enviable couple with 4 healthy children and a thriving business. Harry was the exuberant ex-Marine who devoured life, smoked, drank a bit, but stayed in good health because of his passion for life. Barbara was his soul mate. She was the ultimate health-oriented individual who did not smoke or drink. She vowed that "If Harry goes, then I'm going with him." In his 50s, Harry developed unresectable and advanced cancer of the prostate. He was told that there was no therapy for him and death was inevitable within a year. Harry attended a retreat of cancer patients who were instructed to re-evaluate their lives. Harry had gone straight from high school, to the military service, to a vigorous career and family rearing. In his moments of quiet inner reflection, he decided that he wanted to be free of his responsibilities and burdens, including his business and wife, Barbara. Harry left Barbara and found a lover. Harry's cancer went away. Within a year, Barbara developed a mysterious brain cancer and died within 6 weeks of diagnosis. Harry had biochemically invoked cancer through his lifestyle, then beat cancer through his mental transformation. Then Barbara, the ultimate non-risk for cancer, died of cancer from a broken spirit. This true story outlines the distinct physical and metaphysical components to cancer. Use both to your advantage.

REFERENCES

1. Grant, JP, Proper use and recognized role of TPN in the cancer patient, Nutrition, vol.6, no.4, p.6S, July/Aug 1990 supplement

2. American College of Physicians, Parenteral Nutrition in Patients receiving cancer chemotherapy, Annals of Internal Medicine, vol.110, no.9, p.734, May 1989

3. Wilmore, DW, Catabolic illness, strategies for enhancing recovery, N. England J. Med., vol.325, no.10, p.695, Sept.1991

4. Bendich, A, and Chandra, RK (eds), MICRONUTRIENTS AND IMMUNE FUNCTIONS; CYTOKINES AND METABOLISM, New York Academy of Sciences, vol.587, 1990; see also Burns, JJ, et al. (eds), THIRD CONFERENCE ON VITAMIN C, New York Academy of Sciences, vol.498, 1987

5. Beisel, WR, Single nutrients and immunity, Amer. J. Clin. Nutr., vol.35, p.417, Feb.supplement 1987

6. Watson, RR, et al., Effect of beta-carotene on lymphocyte subpopulations in elderly humans: evidence for a dose response relationship, Amer. J. Clin. Nutr., vol.53, p.90, 1991

7. Weisburger, JH, American Journal Clinical Nutrition, vol.53, p.226S, 1991

8. Byers, T., et al., Patient Care, vol.11, p.34, 1990

9. Singh, VN, et al., American Journal Clinical Nutrition, vol.53, p.386S, 1991

10. Gouveia, J, et al., Lancet, no.1, p.710, 1982

11. Heimburger, DC, et al., Journal American Medical Association, vol.259, p.1525, 1988

12. Shklar, G., et al., European Journal Cancer Clinical Oncology, vol.24, no.5, p.839, 1988

13. DeCosse, JJ, et al., Journal National Cancer Institute, vol.81, p.1290, 1989

14. Prasad, KN, Journal American College of Nutrition, vol.9, no.1, p.28, 1990

15. Wargovich, MJ, et al., Gastroenterology, vol.103, p.92, July 1992

16. Kune, GA, et al., Nutrition & Cancer, vol.9, p.1, 1987

17. Good, RA, et al., Medical Oncology & Tumor Pharmacotherapy, vol.7, no.2, p.183, 1990

18. Simone, CB, CANCER & NUTRITION, Avery, Garden City, NY, 1992

19. Willett, WC, and MacMahon, B., New England Journal of Medicine, vol.310, p.633, Mar.8, 1984; and again p.697, Mar.15, 1984

20. Sakamoto, A, et al., in MODULATION AND MEDIATION OF CANCER BY VITAMINS, P.330, Karger, Basel Switzerland, 1983

21. Foster, HD, International Journal Biosocial Research, vol.10, no.1, p.17, 1988

22. Hoffer, A., et al., Journal Orthomolecular Medicine, vol.5, no.3, p.143, 1990

23. Axelrod, AE, and Traketelis, AC, Vitamins and Hormones, vol.22, p.591, 1964

24. Lowry, SF, et al., Surgical Forum, vol.28, p.143, 1977

25. Nichol, CA, Cancer Research, vol.29, p.2422, 1969

26. Norton, JA, et al., Cancer, vol.45, p.2934, 1980

27. Goodgame, JT, et al, American Journal Clinical Nutrition, vol.32, p.2277, Nov.1979

28. Goodgame, JT, et al., American Journal of Clinical Nutrition, vol.32, p.2277, 1979

29. Anthony, HM, et al., British Journal of Cancer, vol.46, p.354, 1982

30. Cheraskin, E., Journal of Alternative Medicine, p.18, Feb.1986

31. Hoffman, FA, Cancer, vol.55, 1 sup.1, p.295, Jan.1, 1985

32. Baker, H, et al., Journal American College Nutrition, vol.11, no.5, p.482, 1992

33. Hoffman, FA, Cancer, vol.55, p.295, 1985

34. Daly, JM, et al., Journal Parenteral and Enteral Nutrition, vol.14, no.5, p.244S, Sept.1990

35. Rennie, MJ, et al., Lancet, p.323, Feb.11, 1984

36. Flier, JS, et al., New England Journal Medicine, vol.325, no.10, p.695, Sept.1991

37. Dreizen, S., et al., Postgraduate Medicine, vol.87, no.1, p.163, Jan.1990

38. Dematrakopoulos, GE, and Brennan, MF, Cancer Research, (sup.),vol.42, p.756, Feb.1982

39. Annals of Internal Medicine, vol.110, no.9, p.735, May 1989

40. Kaminsky, M. (ed.), HYPERALIMENTATION: A GUIDE FOR CLINICIANS, Marcel Dekker, NY,

Oct.1985
41. Dewys, WD, et al., American Journal of Medicine, vol.69, p.491, Oct.1980
42. Eys, JV, Cancer, vol.43, p.2030, 1979
43. Harvey, KB, et al., Cancer, vol.43, p.2065, 1979
44. Muller, JM, et al., Lancet, p.68, Jan.9, 1982
45. Norris, JR, et al., American Journal of Clinical Nutrition, vol.51, p.188, 1990
46. Gazzaniga, AB, et al., Archives of Surgery, vol. 123, p.1275, 1988
47. Abrahamian, V., et al., Journal of Parenteral and Enteral Nutrition, vol.7, no.5, p.465, 1983
48. Valdivieso, M., et al., Cancer Treatment Reports, vol.65, sup.5, p.145, 1981
49. Dewys, WD, et al., American Journal of Medicine, vol.69, p.491, Oct. 1980
50. Yam, D, Medical Hypothesis, vol.38, p.111, 1992
51. Demetrakopoulos, GE, et al., Cancer Research, vol.42, p.756S, Feb.1982
52. Rossi-Fanelli, F., et al., Journal Parenteral and Enteral Nutrition, vol.15, p.680, 1991
53. Bernstein, J., et al., American Journal Clinical Nutrition, vol.30, p.613, 1977
54. Nalder, BN, et al., Journal Nutrition, Apr.1972
55. Sanchez, A., et al., American Journal Clinical Nutrition, vol.26, p.180, 1973
56. Bristol, JB, et al., Proceedings American Association of Cancer Research, vol.26, p.206, Mar.1985
57. Horrobin, DF, Medical Hypotheses, vol.11, no.3, p.319, 1983
58. Hoehn, SK, et al., Nutrition & Cancer, vol.1, no.3, p.27, Spring 1979
59. Bendich, A., in BEYOND DEFICIENCY, New York Academy of Sciences, vol.669, p.300, 1992
60. Hathcock, JN, et al., in MICRONUTRIENTS AND IMMUNE FUNCTION, vol.587, p.257, New York Academy of Sciences, 1990
61. Meadows, GG, et al., American Journal of Clinical Nutrition, vol.54, p.1284S, 1991
62. Schmitt-Graff, A, et al., Pathology Research Practice, vol.181, no.2, p.168, 1986
63. Brown, RR, et al., Proceedings American Association Cancer Research, vol.22, p.184, 1981
64. Gupta, S., Progress in Clinical Biological Research, vol.259, p.307, 1988
65. Noto, V., et al., Cancer , vol.63, p.901, 1989
66. Shimpo, K, et al., American Journal Clinical Nutrition, vol.54, p.1298S, 1991
67. Ha, C, et al., Journal Nutrition, vol.114, p.938, 1984
68. Toma, S., et al., Cancer Detection and Prevention, vol.15, no.6, p.491, 1991
69. Ripoll, EA, et al., Journal Urology, vol.136, p.529, 1986
70. Prasad, KN, et al., Proceedings Society Experimental Biological Medicine, vol.164, no.2, p.158, 1980
71. Wood. L., New England Journal Medicine, vol.312, no.16, p.1060, 1985
72. Iakovkeva, SS, Arkh Patol, vol.42, no.9, p.93, 1980
73. Sundstrom, H., et al., Carcinogenesis, vol.10, p.273, 1989
74. Kochi, M., et al., Progress in Cancer Research and Therapy, vol.35, p.338, 1988
75. Leihr, JG, American Journal Clinical Nutrition, vol.54, p.1256S, 1991
76. Coudray, C, et al., Basic Research in Cardiology, vol.87, p.173, 1992
77. Kimie, S, et al., Japanese Journal Cancer Research, vol.83, p.45, Jan.1992
78. Horsman, MR, Radiotherapy & Oncology, vol.22, p.79, 1991
79. Wadleigh, RG, et al., American Journal Medicine, vol.92, p.481, May 1992
80. Shimpo, K., et al., American Journal Clinical Nutrition, vol.54, p.1298S, 1991
81. Baute, L., Journal National Cancer Institute, vol.83, no.22, p.1614, Nov.20, 1991
82. Alexander, JW, et al., Critical Care Medicine, vol.18, p.S159, 1990
83. Rhodes, J., and Oliver, S., Immunology, vol.40, p.467, 1980
84. Talbott, MC, et al., American Journal of Clinical Nutrition, vol.46, p.659, 1987
85. Bendich, A., et al., Journal of Nutrition, vol.116, p.675, 1986
86. Cerutti, PA, Science, vol.227, p.375, 1985
87. Boyd, JN, et al., Food Chemistry and Toxicology, vol.20, p.47, 1982
88. Quillin, P., SAFE EATING, p.129, M.Evans, NY, 1990
89. Shklar, G., et al., Journal of the National Cancer Institute, vol.78, no.5, p.987, May 1987
90. Cook, MG, and McNamara, P., Cancer Research, vol.40, p.1329, Apr.1980
91. Trickler, D., and Shklar, G., Journal of the National Cancer Institute, vol.78, no.1, p.165, Jan.1987

92. Prasad, KN, et al., Proceedings of the Society for Experimental Biology and Medicine, vol.164, p.158, 1980

93. Journal of the American Medical Association, vol.244, no.10, p.1077, Sept.5, 1980

94. Panganamala, RV, and Cornwell, DG, Annals of NY Academy of Sciences, vol.393, p.376, 1982

95. Myers, CE, et al., Annals of NY Academy of Sciences, vol.393, p.419, 1982

96. Horvath, HM, and Ip, C., Cancer Research, vol.43, p.5335, Nov.1983

97. Van Vleet, JF, and Ferrans, VJ, Cancer Treatment Reports, vol.64, p.315, 1980

98. Singal, PK, and Tong, J., Molecular and Cellular Biochemistry, vol.84, p.163, 1988

99. Ripoll, EA, et al., Journal of Urology, vol.136, p.529, 1986

100. Prasad, KN, et al., Cancer Research, vol.42, p.550, Feb.1982

101. Svingen, BA, et al., Cancer Research, vol.41, p.3395, Sept.1981

102. Shklar, G., and Schwartz, J., European Journal of Cancer Clinical Oncology, vol.24, no.5, p.839, 1988

103. Wang, YM, et al., MOLECULAR INTERRELATIONS OF NUTRITION AND CANCER, Arnott, MS (eds.), Raven Press, NY, 1982

104. Waxman, S., and Bruckner, H., European Journal of Cancer and Clinical Oncology, vol.18, no.7, p.685, 1982

105. Kagerud, A., et al., Oncology, vol.20, p.1, 1981

106. Kagerud, A., and Peterson, H., Anticancer Research, vol.1, p.35, 1981

107. Traber, MG, et al., New England Journal of Medicine, vol.317, p.262, 1987

108. Nutrition Reviews, vol.45, no.1, p.27, Jan.1987

109. Milei, J., et al., American Heart Journal, vol.111, p.95, 1986

110. Wang, YM, et al., Cancer Research, vol.40, p.1022, Apr.1980

111. Wood, LA, New England Journal of Medicine, Apr.18, 1985

112. Bendich, A., and Machlin, LJ, American Journal of Clinical Nutrition, vol.48, p.612, 1988

113. Suttie, JW, HANDBOOK OF VITAMINS, Machlin (ed.), Marcel Dekker Publ., NY, p.146, 1991

114. National Academy of Sciences, RECOMMENDED DIETARY ALLOWANCES, National Academy Press, p.69, 1980

115. Chlebowski, RT, et al., Cancer Treatment Reviews, vol.12, p.49, 1985

116. Dreizen, S., Postgraduate Medicine, vol.87, no.1, p.167, Jan.1990

117. Conly, J., et al, American Journal of Clinical Nutrition, vol.50, p.109, 1989

118. March, BE, et al., Journal of Nutrition, vol.103, p.371, 1973

119. Krishnamurthi, S., et al., Radiology, vol.99, p.409, 1971

120. Long, JW, ESSENTIAL GUIDE TO PRESCRIPTION DRUGS, Harper & Row, NY, p.790, 1982

121. Poydock, ME, American Journal Clinical Nutrition, vol.54, p.1261S, 1991

122. Taper, HS, et al., International Journal of Cancer, vol.40, no.4, p.575, Oct.15, 1987

123. Crary, EJ, et al., Medical Hypotheses, vol.13, p.77, 1984

124. Sakamoto, A., et al., in MODULATION AND MEDIATION OF CANCER BY VITAMINS, p.330, Karger, Basel, 1983

125. Taper, HS, et al., International Journal of Cancer, vol.40, p.575, 1987

126. Sprince, H., et al., Agents and Actions, vol.5, no.2, p.164, 1975

127. Cameron, E., and Pauling, L., Proceedings of the National Academy of Sciences USA, vol.75, no.9, p.4538, Sept.1978

128. Kawai-Kobayashi, K., et al., Journal of Nutrition, vol.116, p.98, 1986

129. Anderson, R., et al., American Journal of Clinical Nutrition, vol.33, p.71, 1980

130. Bussey, JR, et al., Cancer, vol.50, p.1434, 1982

131. Tschetter, L., et al., Proceedings of the American Society of Clinical Oncology, vol.2, p.92, 1983

132. Poydock, E., IRCS Medical Science, vol.12, p.813, 1984

133. Kim, JH, et al., Cancer Research, vol.44, p.102, Jan.1984

134. Verma, AK, et al., Cancer Research, vol.48, p.5754, Oct.1988

135. Castillo, MH, et al., American Journal Surgery, vol.158, p.351, Oct.1989

136. LeBon, AM, et al., Chemical Biological Interactions, vol.83, p.65, 1992

137. Michalek, AM, et al., Nutrition and Cancer, vol.9, p.143, 1987

138. Micksche, M., et al., Oncology, vol.34, p.234, 1977
139. Kurata, T., and Micksche, M., International Journal of Cancer Research and Treatment, vol.34, no.5, p.1, 1977
140. Levenson, SM, et al., Annals of Surgery, vol.200, no.4, p.494, Oct.1984
141. Band, PR, et al., Preventive Medicine, vol.13, p.549, 1984
142. Pastorino, E., et al., Oncology, vol.48, p.131, 1991
143. Bendich, A., and Langseth, L., American Journal of Clinical   Nutrition, vol.49, p.358, 1989
144. Bendich, A., American Journal Clinical Nutrition, vol.49, p.358, 1989
145. Bendich, A., Journal of Nutrition, vol.119, p.112, 1989
146. Burton, GW, Journal of Nutrition, vol.119, p.109, 1989
147. Bond, GG, et al., Nutrition and Cancer, vol.9, p.109, 1987
148. Bendich, A., Clinical Nutrition, vol.7, p.113, 1988
149. Krinsky, NI, Journal of Nutrition, vol.119, p.123, 1989
150. Schwartz, J., et al., Journal of Oral Maxillofacial Surgery, vol.45, p.510, 1987
151. Bendich, A., Nutrition and Cancer, vol.11, p.207, 1988
152. Costantino, JP, et al., American Journal of Clinical Nutrition, vol.48, p.1277, 1988
153. Bischoff, F., et al., Archives Pathology, vol.35, p.713, 1943
154. Tryfiates, GP, et al., Anticancer Research, vol.1, p.263, 1981
155. DiSorbo, DM, et al., Nutrition and Cancer, vol.5, no.1, p.10, 1983
156. DiSorbo, DM, et al., Nutrition & Cancer, vol.7, p.43, 1985
157. Gridley, DS, et al., Nutrition Research, vol.8, p.201, 1988
158. Byar, D. et al., Urology, vol.10, no.6, p.556, Dec.1977
159. DiSorbo, DM, et al., Nutrition and Cancer, vol.3, no.4, p.216, 1982
160. DiSorbo, DM, et al., Nutrition and Cancer, vol.7, p.43, 1985
161. Ladner, HA, et al., in VITAMINS AND CANCER, Meyskens, FL, (eds.), p.429, Humana Press, Clifton, NJ, 1986
162. Stone, OJ, Medical Hypotheses, vol.30, p.277, 1989
163. Pais, RC, et al., Cancer, vol.66, p.2421, 1990
164. DiSorbo, DM, et al., Nutrition and Cancer, vol.5, no.1, p.10, 1983
165. Shultz, TD, et al., Anticancer Research, vol.8, p.1313, 1988
166. Ladner, HA, et al., Nutrition, Growth, & Cancer, p.273, Alan Liss, Inc., 1988
167. Cohen, M., and Bendich, A., Toxicology Letters, vol.34, p.129, 1986
168. Watrach, AM, et al., Cancer Letters, vol.25, p.41, 1984
169. Ip, C., and Sinha, D., Carcinogenesis, vol.2, no.5, p.435, 1981
170. Davies, MH, et al., Drug Nutrition Interactions, vol.5, p.169, 1987
171. Nutrition Reviews, vol.42, no.7, p.260, July 1984
172. Ip, C., Cancer Research, vol.41, p.4386, Nov.1981
173. Lawson, T., and Birt, DF, Chemical Biological Interactions, vol.45, p.95, 1983
174. Milner, JA, and Hsu, CY, Cancer Research, vol.41, p.1652, May 1981
175. Greeder, GA, and Milner, JA, Science, vol.209, p.825, Aug.1980
176. Ohkawa, K., et al., British Journal of Cancer, vol.58, p.38, 1988
177. Petrie, HT, et al., Journal of Leukocyte Biology, vol.45, p.215, 1989
178. Dharwadkar, SM, et al., Nutrition and Cancer, vol.10, p.163, 1987
179. Karmali, RA, et al., Journal of the National Cancer Institute, vol.73, p.457, 1984
180. Sakaguchi, M., et al., British Journal of Cancer, vol.62, p.742, Nov.1990
181. Szeluga, DJ, et al., American Journal of Clinical Nutrition, vol.45, p.859, 1987
182. Blank, EW, et al., Journal of Steroid Biochemistry, vol.34, p.149, 1989
183. Karmali, RA, Journal of Internal Medicine (suppl), vol.225, p.197, 1989
184. Karmali, RA, Preventive Medicine, vol.16, p.493, July 1987
185. O'Connor, TP, et al., Journal of the National Cancer Institute, vol.75. p. 959, Nov. 1985
186. Braden, LM, et al., Lipids, vol.21, p.285, 1986
187. Karmali, RA, et al., Journal of the National Cancer Institute, vol.73, p.457, 1984
188. Gabor, H., et al., Journal of the National Cancer Institute, vol.76, p. 1223, 1986

189. Kort, WJ, et al., Carcinogenesis, vol.8, p.611, 1987
190. Pritchard, GA, et al., British Journal of Surgery, vol.76, p.1069, 1989
191. Borgeson, CE, et al., Lipids, vol.24, p. 290, 1989
192. Cannizzo, F., et al., Cancer Research, vol.49, p.3961, 1981
193. Roebuck, BD, et al., Cancer Research, vol.41, p.3961, 1981
194. O'Connor, TP, et al., Journal of the National Cancer Institute, vol.81, p.858, 1989
195. Karmali, RA, et al., Anticancer Research, vol.7, p.1173, 1987
196. Rose, DP, et al., Carcinogenesis, vol.9, p.603, 1988
197. Adams, L., et al., Proceedings of the American Association of Cancer, vol.28, p.159, 1987
198. Burns, CP, et al., Nutrition Reviews, vol.48, p.233, June 1990
199. Guffy, MM, et al., Cancer Research, vol.44, p.1863, 1984
200. Reich, R., et al., Biochemical and Biophysical Research Communication, vol.160, p.559, 1989
201. Begin, ME, et al., Prostaglandins, Leukotriennes, and Medicine, vol.19, p.177, Aug.1985
202. Begin, ME, et al., Anticancer Research, vol.6, p.291, 1986
203. Begin, ME, et al, Journal of the National Cancer Institute, vol.77, p.1053, 1986
204. Booyens, J., et al., IRCS Medical Science, vol. 14, p.396, 1986
205. Zijlstra, JG, et al., International Journal of Cancer, vol.40, p.850, 1987
206. Osborne, MP, et al., Cancer Investigation, vol.6, p.629, 1988
207. Wan, JM, et al., Federation of the American Society for Experimental Biology, vol.A350, p.21, 1988
208. Wan, JM, et al., World Review of Nutrition and Dietetics, vol.66, p.477, 1991
209. Mascioli, EA, et al., Lipids, vol.23, p.623, 1988
210. Mascioli, EA, et al., American Journal of Clinical Nutrition, vol.49, p.277, 1989
211. Pomposelli, JJ, et al., Journal of Parenteral and Enteral Nutrition, vol.13, p.136, 1989
212. van der Merwe, CF, South African Medical Journal, vol.65, p.712, 1984
213. van der Merwe, CF, et al., British Journal of Clinical Practice, vol.41, no.9, p.907, 1987
214. Takeda, S., et al., Anticancer Research, vol.12, p.329, 1992
215. Begin, ME, et al., Journal National Cancer Institute, vol.77, p.1053, 1986
216. Takeda, Y., et al., Cancer Research, vol. 35, p.2390, Sept.1975
217. Pryme, IF, Cancer Letters, vol.5, p.19, 1978
218. Milner, JA, et al., Journal of Nutrition, vol.109, p.489, 1979
219. Seifter, E., et al., Surgery, vol.84, no.2, p.224, 1978
220. Critselis, AN, et al., Federation Proceedings, vol.36, p.1163, 1977
221. Barbul, A., et al., Surgery, vol.90, no.2, p.244, 1981
222. Reynolds, JV, et al., Annals of Surgery, p.202, Feb.1990
223. Reynolds, JV, et al., Journal of Surgical Research, vol.45, p.513, 1988
224. Reynolds, JV, et al., Surgery, vol.104, no.2, p.142, Aug.1988
225. Tayek, JA, et al., Clinical Research, vol.33, no.1, p.72A, 1985
226. Palermo, MS, et al., International Journal of Immunopharmacology, vol.8, no.6, p.651, 1986
227. Schmitt-Graff, A., and Scheulen, ME, Pathology Resident Practice, vol.181, no.2, p.168, 1986
228. Morgan, LR, et al., Seminars in Oncology, vol.10, 1 sup.1, p.56, 1983
229. Doroshow, JH, et al., Journal of Clinical Investigation, vol.68, no.4, p.1053, 1981
230. Watson, RA, Urology, vol.24, no.5, p.465, 1984
231. Kim, JA, et al., Seminars in Oncology, vol.10, 1 sup.1, p.86, 1983
232. Williamson, JM, et al., Proceedings of the National Academy of Sciences, vol.79, p.6246, Oct.1982
233. Meydani, Mohsen, and Mathcock, JN, Drug-Nutrient Interactions, vol.2, p.217, 1984
234. Mitane, Y., et al., Chemical Pharmaceutical Bulletin, vol.38, no.3, p.790, 1990
235. Zhao, B., et al., Cell Biophysics, vol.14, p.175, 1989
236. Wang, ZY, et al., Drug Metabolism & Disposition, vol.16, no.1, p.98, 1988
237. Katiyar, SK, et al., Nutrition and Cancer, vol.18, p.73, 1992
238. Hishida, I., et al., Chemical Pharmaceutical Bulletin, vol.36, no.5, p.1819, 1988
239. Adachi, Y, et al., Journal Pharmacobiodynamics, vol.10, no.11, p.644, Nov.1987
240. Adachi, K, et al., Chemical Pharmacological Bulletin, vol.35, no.1, p.262, Jan.1987
241. Ohno, N, et al., Journal Pharmacobiodynamics, vol.9, no.10, p.861, Oct.1986

242. Rao, AV, et al., Nutrition and Cancer, vol.18, p.43, 1992
243. Shearer, RW, Modulation and Mediation of Cancer by Vitamins, p.89, Karger, Basel, 1983
244. Folkman, J., et al., Nature, vol.339, p.58, 1989; see also Langer, R., et al., Science, vol.193, p.70, 1976
245. Weidner, N., et al., New England Journal of Medicine, vol.324, no.1, p.1, 1991
246. Folkman, J, et al., Nature, vol.339, p.58, May 1989
247. Durie, BG, et al., Journal of Biological Response Modifiers, vol.4, p.590, 1985
248. Oikawa, T., et al., Cancer Letters, vol.51, p.181, 1990
249. Langer, R., et al., Proceedings National Academy Science, vol.77, no.7, p.4331, July 1980
250. Langer, R. et al, Science, p.70, July 1976
251. D'Amore, PA, Seminars in Thrombosis and hemostasis, vol.14, no.1, p.73, 1988
252. Moses, MA, et al., Science, vol.248, p.1408, June 1990
253. Prudden, JF, Journal of Biological Response Modifiers, vol.4, no.6, p.551, 1985
254. Langer, R., and Lee, A., Science, vol.221, p.1185, 1983
255. Langer, R., and Murray, J., Journal of Applied Biochemical Biotechnology, vol.8, no.9, p.1983; see also Langer, R., et al., Proceedings of the National Academy of Science USA, vol.77, p.4331, 1980; see also, Luer, CA, Federation Proceedings, vol.45, p.949, 1986
256. Klimberg, S., presentation to the annual meeting of Society of Surgical Oncology and American Society of Clinical Oncology, San Francisco, 1989
257. Brohult, A., et al., Acta Obstetric Gynecologica Scandinavica, vol.65, no.7, p.779, 1986
258. Brohult, A., et al., Acta Obstetric Gynecologica Scandinavica, vol.58, no.2, p.203, 1979
259. Werbach, M., NUTRITIONAL INFLUENCES ON ILLNESS, Third Line Press, Tarzana, CA 1988
260. Sartori, HE, Pharmacology, Biochemistry, & Behavior, vol.21, sup.1, p.7, 1984
261. Sharma, HM, et al., Pharmacology Biochemistry and Behavior, vol.35, p.767, 1990
262. Pizzini, RP, et al., Surgical Infection Society abstract, p.50, 1989
263. Wood, B, et al., European Journal of Surgical Oncology, vol.11, p.347, 1985; see also Wood, B., et al., British Medical Journal, vol.291, p.163, July 1986

APPENDIX

EDUCATIONAL CENTERS

Some of the following organizations offer information about specific therapies that they promote, as opposed to general information on cancer therapies.

■ *Coping* Magazine, living with cancer, 2019 N. Carothers, Franklin, TN 37064

■ Creative Health Institute, 918 Union City Rd, Union City, MI 49094, (517) 278-6260: Nutrition

■ Health Action, 19 East Mission St., Suite 102, Santa Barbara, CA 93101, (805) 682-3220; Oriental medicine

■ Hippocrates Health Institute, 1443 Palmdale Ct., West Palm Beach, FL 33411, (407) 471-8876: Nutrition

■ International Association for Oxygen Therapy, P.O. Box 1360, Priest River, ID 83856, (208) 448-2504; Oxygen therapy

■ The Kushi Institute, P.O. Box 7, Beckett, MA 01223, (413) 623-5741; Macrobiotics

■ Optimum Health Institute of San Diego, 6970 Central Ave., Lemon Grove, CA 91945, (619) 464-3346; Nutrition

■ Linus Pauling Institute of Science and Medicine, 440 Page Mill Rd., Palo Alto, CA 94306, (415) 327-4064: Orthomolecular

■ Project Cure, 5910 North Central Expressway, Suite 760, Dallas, TX 75206, (214) 891-6111; Legal issues

■ Syracuse Cancer Research Institute, Inc., Presidential Plaza, 600 East Genesee St., Syracuse, NY 13202, (315) 472-6616; Hydrazine sulfate

■ Ann Wigmore Foundation, 196 Commonwealth Ave., Boston, MA 02116, (617)267-9424; Nutrition

SUPPORT GROUPS

The following groups provide counselling, individual therapy, and group support in various settings.

- Bosom buddies, CanCare, 2929 Selwyn Ave., Charlotte, NC 28209, (704) 372-1232
- Cancer Counseling Center of Ohio, 1515 Lake Martin Dr., Kent, OH 44241; (216) 922-1855; Psychosocial
- Cancer Counseling Centre - Hope program, 2574 West Broadway, Vancouver, British Columbia V6K 2G1, Canada, (604) 732-3412; Psychosocial
- Cancer Self-Help Retreats, 2126 Green Hill Rd., Sebastopol, CA 95472, (800) 745-1837; Meditation and other self-help books
- Cancer Support Community, 401 Laurel St., San Francisco, CA 94118, (415) 929-7400; Support
- Cancer Support and Education Center, 1035 Pine St., Menlo Park, CA 94025, (415) 327-6166; Intensive self-help training programs
- Cancer Support Network, 802 East Jefferson, Bloomington, IL 61701, (309) 829-2273
- Candlelighters Foundation, 2025 Eye Street NW, Ste.1011, Washington, DC 20006, (202) 659-5136
- Center for Attitudinal Healing, 19 Main St., Tiburon, CA 94920, (415) 435-5022; Psychosocial
- Challenging Cancer Therapy Group, 18275 Gum Tree Lane, Huntington Beach, CA 92646; Psychosocial
- Challenging Cancer Wellness Workshop, 2205 Main St., Suite 42, Seacliff Village Shopping Center, Huntington Beach, CA 92648, (714) 848-3473: Support workshop, information sharing
- Colorado Outward Bound School, 945 Pennsylvania Ave., Denver, CO 80203, (303) 837-0880; Experientially-based wilderness program
- Commonweal Cancer Help Program, P.O. Box 316, Bolinas, CA 94924, (415) 868-0970; Psychosocial
- The Concern for Dying, 250 West 57th St., New York, NY 10019
- Consciousness Research and Training Project, Inc., NYC, Psychosocial
- Encore, National Board YWCA, 726 Broadway, New York, NY 10003, (212) 614-2700
- Exceptional Cancer Patients, 1302 Chapel St., New Haven, CT, 06511, (203) 865-8392; Support
- Healing Light Center Church, P.O. Box 758, Sierra Madre, CA 91025, (818) 244-8607; Spiritual healing
- Intl. Assoc. for Enterostomal Therapy, 505-A Tustin Ave., Ste.282, Santa

Ana, CA 92705, (714) 972-1725

- Intl. Assoc. of Laryngectomies, 777 Third Ave., New York, NY 10017, (212) 371-2900
- Institute of Behavioral Medicine, 2200 Colorado Ave., Santa Monica, CA 90404, (310) 453-2300; Psychosocial
- Institute of Behavioral Medicine, 610 Anacapa St., Santa Barbara, CA 93101-1615, (805) 963-1661; Psychosocial
- Lawrence LeShan, Ph.D., 263 West End Ave., New York, NY 10023; Psychosocial
- Let's Face It, Box 711, Concord, MA 01742, (508) 371-3186, for people who have facial disfigurements
- Life-Affirming Support Group, 85 Aspinwall Rd., P.O. Box 950, Briarcliff Manor, NY 10510, (914) 941-8926; Support
- Life-Affirming Support Group, 441 West End Ave., Prof. Suite 1B, New York, NY 10024, (212) 496-9136; Support
- Los Angeles Healing Arts Center, 2211 Corinth Ave., Suite 204, Los Angeles, CA 90064, (304) 477-8151; Unconventional therapies
- Make-a-Wish Foundation of America, 1624 East Meadowbrook, Phoenix, AZ, (602) 248-9474
- National Coalition for Cancer Survivorship, 323 8th Street SW, Albuquerque, NM 87102, (505)-764-9956
- The National Hospice Organization, 1901 N Fort Meyer Dr., Ste.307, Arlington, VA 22209, (703) 243-5900
- New Hope Institute, 500 Main St., El Segundo, CA 90245, (310) 640-6605; Psychosocial
- Ronald McDonald Houses, Golin/Harris Communications, Inc., 5000 N Michigan Ave., Chicago, IL 60611, (312) 836-7114
- Sandra McLanahan, M.D.. Route 1, Box 1680, Buckingham, VA 23921, (804) 969-4680; Complementary therapies
- Share, 817 Broadway, 6th Floor, New York, NY 10003, (212) 260-0580
- Simonton Cancer Center, 15601 Sunset Blvd., Pacific Palisades, CA 90272, (310) 459-4434; Psychosocial
- Sunshine Foundation, 4010 Levick St., Philadelphia, PA 19135
- Sunshine Kids, 2902 Ferndale Place, Houston, TX 77098, (713) 524-1264
- The Skin Cancer Fund, Box 561, New York, NY 10156
- United Ostomy Association, 36 Executive Park, Ste.120, Irvine, CA 92714, (714) 660-8624
- Vital Options, 4419 Coldwater Canyon Ave., Studio City, CA 91604, (818) 508-5657
- Wainwright House Cancer Support Programs, 260 Stuyvesant Ave., Rye, NY 10580, (914) 967-6080, Psychosocial

■ Wellness Community National Headquarters, 1235 5th St., Santa Monica, CA 90401, (213) 393-1415 or 800-PRO-HOPE

■ Wellspring Center for Life Enhancement, 3 Otis St., Watertown, MA 02172, (617) 924-8515; Support

INFORMATIONAL SERVICES

Some of the following charge fees for their services, which include providing information on a wide range of unconventional cancer therapies. You should ask at the outset what the total fees are. The value of each service may depend on what you are looking for. Some services run computer searches, and others do in-person or over-the-telephone consultations.

■ The Arlin J. Brown Information Center, Inc., P.O. Box 251, Fort Belvoir, VA 22060, (703) 752-9511

■ Cancer Control Society, 2043 North Berendo St., Los Angeles, CA 90027, (213) 663-7801

■ Cancer Federation, P.O. Box 52109, Riverside, CA 92517, (714) 682-7989

■ CanHelp, 3111 Paradise Bay Rd., Port Ludlow, WA 98365, (206) 437-2291, FAX (206) 437-2272

■ Center for Advancement in Cancer Education, P.O. Box 215, 200 East Lancaster Ave., Wynnewood, PA 19096, (215) 642-4810

■ Foundation for Advancement in Cancer Therapy (FACT), P.O. Box 1242, Old Chelsea Station, New York, NY 10113, (212) 741-2790

■ The Health Resource, 209 Katherine Drive, Conway, AR 72032, (501) 329-5272

■ International Health Information Institute, 14417 Chase St., Suite 432, Panorama City, CA 91402

■ International Holistic Center, Inc., P.O. Box 15103, Phoenix, AZ 85060, (602) 957-3322

■ DATIC Health Resources, Inc. (Diagnostic Aides Therapeutic Information Computerized), Apt. 114, 1075 Bernard Ave., Kelowna, British Columbia V1Y 6P7, Canada, (604) 862-3228 or P.O. Box 218, Chilliwack, British Columbia V5P 6J1, Canada, (604) 792-7175

■ National Health Federation, 212 West Foothill Blvd., P.O. Box 688, Monrovia, CA 91016, (818) 357-2181

■ National Self-Help Clearinghouse, 25 West 43rd St., Room 620, New York, NY 10036

■ Nutrition Education Association, Inc., 3647 Glen Haven, Houston, TX 77025, (713) 665-2946

■ Patient Advocates for Advanced Cancer Treatments, Inc. (PAACT), 1143 Parmelee NW, Grand Rapids, MI 49504, (616) 453-1477

■ People Against Cancer, P.O. Box 10, Otho, IO 50569, (515) 972-4444

■ Planetree Health Resource Center, 2040, Webster St., San Francisco, CA 94115, (415) 923-3680

■ World Research Foundation, 15300 Ventura Blvd., Suite 405, Sherman Oaks, CA 91403, (818) 907-5483

General Resources

■ American Cancer Society, 1599 Clifton Rd., NE, Atlanta, GA 30329, Ph# 404-320-3333 or 800-ACS-2345

■ Assn. of American Cancer Insttiutes, Elm & Carlton Sts., Buffalo, NY 14263, Ph# 716-845-3028/Fax: 716-845-3545

■ Association for Brain Tumor Research, 3725 N. Talman Ave., Chicago, IL 60618, Ph# 312-286-5571

■ Assn. of Community Cancer Centers, 11600 Nebel St., Ste.201, Rockville, MD, 20852, Ph# 301-984-9496

■ Assn. for Research of Childhood Cancer, PO Box 251, Buffalo, NY 14225, Ph# 716-681-4433

■ Breast Cancer Advisory Center, PO Box 224, Kensington, MD 20895, Ph# 301-718-7293, Fax: 301-949-1132

■ Breast Health Program of New York, 28 West 12th Street, New York, NY 10011, Ph# 212-645-0052

■ Cancer Federation, Inc., 21250 Box Springs Rd., No.209, Moreno Valley, CA, 92387, Ph# 714-682-7989

■ Cancer Guidance Institute, 1323 Forbes Ave., Ste.200, Pittsburgh, PA 15219, Ph# 412-261-2211

■ Cancer Information Service, Boy Scout Bldg., R.340, Bethesda, MD 20892, Ph# 301-496-8664 or 800-4-CANCER

■ Corporate Angel Network, Westchester County Airport Bldg. One, White Plains, NY 10604, Ph# 914-328-1313/Fax: 800-328-4226

■ Damon Runyon-Walter Winchell Cancer Research Fund, 131 East 36th St., New York, NY 10016, Ph# 212-532-7000

■ DES Action, USA, Long Island Jewish Medical Center, New Hyde Park, NY 11040, Ph# 516-775-3450

■ Intl. Society for Preventive Oncology, 217 East 85th Street, Ste.303, New York, NY 10028, Ph# 212-534-4991

■ Komen Foundation (Breast Cancer), 6820 LBJ Fwy, Ste.130, Dallas, TX 75240, Ph# 214-980-8841/Fax: 214-980-4971

■ Latin American Cancer Research Project, 525 Twenty Third Street, NW Washington, DC 20037, Ph# 202-861-3200/Fax: 202-223-5971

■ Leukemia Society of America, 733 3rd Avenue, New York, NY 10017, Ph#

212-573-8484/Fax: 212-972-5776

■ Make Today Count, 101 1/2 S. Union St., Alexandria, VA 22314, Ph# 703-548-9674

■ Natl. Alliance of Breast Cancer Orgs., 1180 Ave. of the Americas, 2nd Fl., New York, NY 10036, Ph# 212-719-0154

■ National Cancer Care Foundation, 1180 Avenue of the Americas, New York, NY 10036, Ph# 212-221-3300

■ Natl. Coalition for Cancer Survivorship, 323 8th St. SW, Albuquerque, NM 87102, Ph# 505-764-9956

■ National Leukemia Association, 585 Stewart Ave., Ste.536, Garden City, NY 11530, Ph# 516-222-1944/Fax: 516-222-0457

■ Prostate Health Program of New York, 785 Park Ave., New York, NY 10021, Ph# 212-988-8888

■ R.A. Block Cancer Foundation, H and R Block Bldg., 4410 Main, Kansas City, MO 64111, Ph# 816-932-8453

■ Reach for Recovery, c/o American Cancer Society, 1599 Clifton Road, Atlanta, GA 30329, Ph# 404-320-3333

■ Skin Cancer Foundation, 245 Fifth Avenue, Ste. 2402, New York, NY 10016, Ph#212-725-5176

■ Spirit and Breath Association, 8210 Elmwood Ave., Ste.209, Skokie, IL 60077, Ph# 708-673-1384

■ Y-ME National Organization for Breast Cancer Info. and Support, 18220 Harwood Ave., Homewood, IL 60430, Ph# 800-221-2141, 24-hour hotline: 708-799-8228

INFORMATION AND REFERRALS ON ALTERNATIVE TREATMENTS

■ American Assoc. of Orthomolecular Medicine, 7375 Kingsway, Burnaby, British Columbia, V3N3B5 Canada

■ American College of Advances in Medicine, 231 Verdugo Drive, Suite 204, Laguna Hills, CA 92653, Ph# 714-583-7666

■ Arlin J. Brown Information Center, PO Box 251, Ft. Belvoir, VA 22060, Ph#703-451-8638

■ Cancer Control Society, 2043 N. Berendo St., Los Angeles, CA 90027, Ph# 213-663-7801

■ Comm. for Freedom of Choice in Medicine, 1180 Walnut Av., Chula Vista, CA 92011, Ph# 800-227-4473/Fax: 619-429-8004

■ European Institute for Orthomolecular Sciences, PO Box 420, 3740 A.K., Baarn, Holland

■ Found. for Advancement in Cancer Therapy, Box 1242, Old Chelsea Sta., New York, NY 10113, Fax: 212-741-2790

■ Gerson Institute, PO Box 430, Bonita, CA 91908, Ph# 619-267-1150/Fax: 619-267-6441

■ Intl. Academy of Nutrition and Preventive Medicine, PO Box 18433, Asheville, NC 28814, Ph# 704-258-3243/Fax: 704-251-9206

■ Intl. Assn. of Cancer Victors & Friends, 7740 W. Manchester Ave., No.110, Playa del Rey, CA 90293, Ph#213-822-5032/Fax: 213-822-5132

■ We Can Do!, 1800 Augusta, Ste.150, Houston, TX 77057, Ph# 713-780-1057

PSYCHONEUROIMMUNOLOGY (MENTAL, SPIRITUAL) READING LIST

General

■ Dossey, L., *Meaning & Medicine*, New York, Bantam, 1991

■ Anderson, G., *The Triumphant Patient*, 1992

■ Anderson, G., *The Cancer Conquerer*, Kansas City, Andrews & McMeel, 1988

■ LeShan, L., *Cancer as a Turning Point*

■ Rosenberg, S.A., *The Transformed Cell: Unlocking the Mysteries on Cancer*, New York, Putnam, 1992

■ Dienstfrey, H, *Where the Mind Meets the Body*, New York, Harper, 1991

Imagery

■ Achterberg, J., *Imagery in Healing*

■ Epstein, G., *Healing Visualizations: Creating Health Through Imagery*, New York, Bantam, 1989

Relaxation/Meditation

■ Keating, T., *Open Mind, Open Heart: The Contemplative Dimension of the Gospel*, New York, Amity House, 1986

■ LeShan, L., *How to Meditate*, New York, Bantam, 1974

Forgiveness

■ Casarjian, R., *Forgiveness: A Bold Choice for a Peaceful Heart*, New York, Bantam, 1992

Healing

■ Borysenko, J., *Minding the Body, Mending the Mind*, New York, Bantam, 1987

■ Simonton, O.C., & Henson, R., *The Healing Journey*, New York, Bantam, 1992

■ Moyers, B., *Healing the Mind*, New York, Bantam Doubleday, 1993

Thought, Attitude, and Negativity

■ Benson, H., *Your Maximum Mind: Changing Your Life by Changing the Way You Think*, New York, Random House, 1987

■ Cousins, N., *Head First: The Biology of Hope*, New York, E.P. Dutton, 1989

■ Martorano, J.T. & Kildahl, J., *Beyond Negative Thinking: Reclaiming Your Life Through Optimism*, New York, Avon, 1989

■ Pennebaker, J.W., *Opening Up: The Healing Power of Confiding in Others*, New York, Avon Books, 1990

■ Seligman, M.E.P., *Learned Optimism: How to Change Your Mind and Your Life*, New York, Pocket Books, 1990

Spirituality

■ Borysenko, J., *Fire in the Soul*, New York, Warner, 1993

■ Buhler, R., *New Choices New Boundaries: How to Make Decisions that are Emotionally and Spiritually Nourishing for Yourself and Others*, Nashville, Thomas Nelson, 1991

■ Dossey, L., *Recovering the Soul: A Scientific and Spiritual Search*, New York, Bantam, 1990

Relationships

■ Jampolsky, G.G. & Cirincione, D.V., *Love is the Answer: Creating Positive Relationships*, New York, Bantam, 1990

INDEX

13-cis retinoic acid, 37-38
714X, 22

A

A retinyl palmitate, 184
Abel, Ulrich, 29
Abnormal biochemistry, 1
Abnormal cell growth, 37
Acetylcysteine, 190
Acid/alkaline balancing, 6, 18, 21, 199. SEE ALSO pH.
Action plan against cancer, 179-196: diet, 180-182; food supplements, 182-191; enteral formulas, 191-192; parenteral formulas, 192; healing mind and spirit, 192-194; breathing, 194; exercise, 194; detoxification, 194; spinal alignment, 195; empowerment, 195-196
Adjuvant nutrition (cancer treatment), 198-200: prevention of malnutrition, 198; immune function support, 198; nutrients as biological response modifiers, 198-200
Adriamycin, x, 31
Aerobic capacity, 101
Aerobic-enhancing nutrients, 101-102
Aging, 11
AIDS, 12, 14
ALA, 189
Alfalfa sprouts, 21
Alkylglycerols, 227
Allergenic foods, 118
Allergies, 11, 43, 117-118, 228
Allicin, 72
Allopathic medical system, 34, 48
Aloe vera extract, 181
Alternative therapies, xii-xiii, xv, 12-14, 242-243: costs, 13
Alternative treatment information/referral, 242-243
Alzheimer's disease, xii, 12
Ames, Bruce, 4
Amine groups, 44
Amino acids, 189, 224-226
Amygdalin, 20
Amylase, 17
Anablast, 22
Anaerobic cancer, 1, 5-6, 21
Ancestral heritage diet, xiii, 18, 120
Angina, xii
Angiogenesis, 21
Antibiotics, 4
Antibody response, 44
Antigens, 44
Antimony trisulfide, 19
Antioxidants, 41, 45-46, 53, 87, 113, 186-187, 200: formula, 186-187
Anti-cancer mechanisms, 96-113: primary defense, 96-101; secondary defense, 101-113; tertiary defense, 113-115
Anti-coagulants, 111
Anti-neoplastons, 14
Anti-plastons, 19-20
Anti-proliferation (tumors), 41-42, 200: agents, 200
Appetite reduction, 1, 44
Applesauce, 151
Apple bran muffin, 152
Apple crisp, 174-175
Apricots, 20
Arginine, 44, 190, 224-225
Arsenic, 45
Arthritis, 11-12, 43, 52
Asparagus, 181
Aspirin, 111
Assertiveness, 193
Assessment (nutrition), 57
Asthma, 11
Astragalus, 19, 190
Attitude, xiii, 123-125
Australian tea tree oil, 190
Authorities' viewpoint (nutrition and cancer), 50-51
Autism, 40
Autonomic bodily functions, 14
Auto-immune disease, 43
Avocado dressing, 149

B

Bacteria, 21
Bailar, John, 27
Banana bread, 167-168
Banana nut salad, 165-166
Banana pudding, 155-156
Banana Waldorf, 157
Barberry, 19
Barley stew, 168
Barley, 144, 168: barley stew, 168
B-cells, 44
Be yourself, 193
Bean burrito, 174
Bean taco, 168
Beans, 143, 168, 174: taco, 168; burrito, 174
Bedell, Berkley, 13
Bereavement, 193
Beta carotene, 37, 41-42, 45-46, 49, 51, 53, 113, 184, 219-220
Betel nuts, 37
Beverage choices, 140
Biochemical individuality, 82-86